WOMEN IN PUBLIC 1850-1900

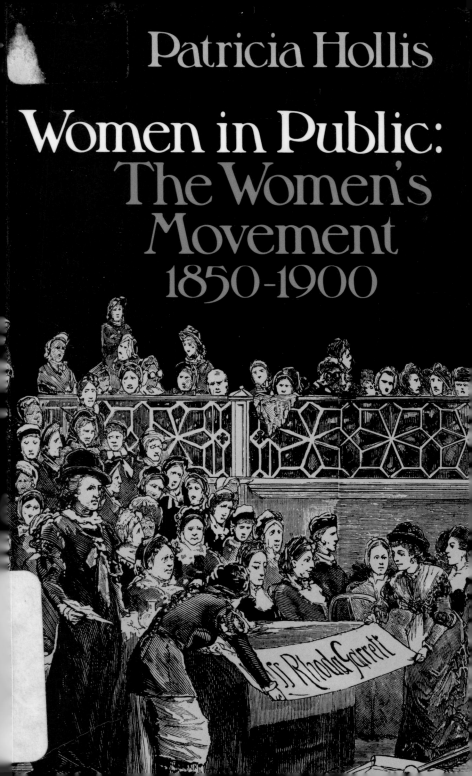

Patricia Hollis

Women in Public:
The Women's Movement 1850-1900

Women in Public
1850–1900

Documents of the Victorian Women's Movement

PATRICIA HOLLIS
Lecturer in English and American Studies, University of East Anglia

London
GEORGE ALLEN & UNWIN
Boston   Sydney

First published in 1979

GEORGE ALLEN & UNWIN LTD
40 Museum Street, London WC1A 1LU

© George Allen & Unwin (Publishers) Ltd, 1979

British Library Cataloguing in Publication Data

Hollis, Patricia
  Women in public, 1850-1900.
  1. Feminism—Great Britain—History
  I. Title
  301.41'2'0941   HQ1593   78-40788

ISBN 0-04-900033-0

Typeset in 10 on 11 point Times by
Trade Linotype Ltd and printed in Great Britain
by Unwin Brothers Ltd, Old Woking, Surrey.

Preface

Despite a scatter of feminist writing in the 1830s and 1840s, the feminist movement in England truly began in the 1850s. It was motivated by three main concerns: the concern with 'surplus women' and their need for work if they were to be self-dependent; a more particular concern with the plight of governesses, which led directly to the movement for women's education; and the increasing awareness of women's status at law, publicised by the case of Caroline Norton, summarised by Barbara Leigh Smith Bodichon's *Brief Summary of the Laws*. Not until the 1860s did the demand for the vote become prominent.

It was in the 1850s that women acquired their public heroine in Florence Nightingale, whose work in the Crimea, to quote Anna Jameson, broke through a 'Chinese wall of prejudice'. The movement's first circle of workers came from that courageous and happy group around Barbara Leigh Smith Bodichon, Emily Davies, Elizabeth Garrett, Maria Rye, Jessie Boucherett; and associated with them Octavia Hill, Helen Taylor, Frances Buss and Dorothea Beale. In 1857 this circle founded their Ladies Institute at Langham Place, in 1858 they published their *English Woman's Journal* (later renamed *Englishwoman's Review*), which was to be the voice of the women's movement until the founding in the 1870s of the *Women's Suffrage Journal* by Lydia Becker and the *Women's Union Journal* by Emma Paterson. Through Isa Craig as assistant secretary, as well as the contributions of Emily Davies and Elizabeth Garrett, they were linked to the Social Science Association, founded in 1857, which did much to 'professionalise' women's public service. And they were to form the first women's suffrage committee when they lined up John Stuart Mill as their parliamentary spokesman in 1867.

Half a century later, by 1900, women had obtained new careers in retailing and commerce, and transformed teaching and nursing as work for women. Women in workshops and factories had acquired a degree of protection, through legislation and combination. Medicine had been opened up as a profession; a network of high schools and women's colleges had been established; and legal changes in custody, property and separation had made major advances towards equity for women at law. The CD campaigns had been an explicitly feminist and highly successful pressure group, by women, for women; and in the fields of politics and public service, women now voted for and served on a wide range of bodies and boroughs. The most significant exception remained the parliamentary vote.

Most prefaces tend to be defensive, and this one is no different. The first defence is of the chronological scope of the book. It attempts to reflect the range of women's public activity from around 1850, when the movement began, to around 1900, when new figures, most notably the Pankhursts in the suffrage campaign, and Mary Macarthur and Margaret Bondfield in the trade union movement, were to take women into a more militant and confident era. Their work and their generation require a book of their own.

The second defence is of women in *public*. Domestic and marital life, women's health and women's childbearing, have been excluded, partly for reasons of space, but also because the material chosen seeks to illustrate the consciousness of women both of their position and of their claims to a 'wider sphere'.

The third defence is of the somewhat arbitrary nature of the divisions in the book, and the location of certain of its contents. To take one example, the CD campaign was crucially about prostitution (Part 7); but is was also about the status of women at law (Part 6), and was as well a most important Victorian pressure group (Part 9). Nursing, to take another example, has been split between hospital nursing (Part 3) and poor law and district nursing (Part 8) when arguably they should have been kept together.

Most sections contain what I believe to be some of the most significant 'statements' of the period—such as John Stuart Mill's House of Commons speech in 1867, or Caroline Norton's description of the wrongs done to her by law; or W. T. Stead on 'The maiden tribute of modern Babylon', or Beatrice Webb on women and the Factory Acts. They also try to suggest some of the changes in attitudes and aspirations over time. Inevitably there are many omissions, and equally as many pieces condensed that deserve to be reprinted in full. I can only plead lack of space. There is not, as yet, any collection of primary material on the women's movement, and very few reprints, comparable to the material available for studying labour movements and industrial conditions in the nineteenth century. Later books by others will rectify my omissions and abbreviations.

Some particular debts. Of the many libraries I have used, two deserve especial thanks. The skilled and courteous staff at the Fawcett Library (newly located in the City of London Polytechnic) helped me find many of the political pamphlets of the 1870s. And the library staff, particularly the patient inter-library loan staff, of the University of East Anglia allowed me to reach more source material than would otherwise have been accessible to an author confined throughout with a broken leg. To Dr B. H. Harrison of Corpus Christi, Oxford I owe the temperance reference (9.1.3). I would also like to acknowledge permission to quote from Margaret Llewelyn Davies, *Life As We Have Known It*, published by the Hogarth Press; Adelaide Anderson, *Women in the Factory*, published by John Murray; E. Moberley Bell, *Octavia Hill*, and Barbara Stephen, *Emily Davies and Girton College*, both published by Constable.

Contents

PART 3   WOMEN AT WORK

PART 8   PUBLIC SERVICE

Part One

Images of Women

Introduction

Behind parliamentary debates on law reform as it affected women; behind pamphlets opposing women's suffrage; behind the articles which doubted whether girls' health could stand the strain of higher education, lay an image or stereotype of Victorian womanhood, which deemed that 'women in public' were unwomanly (1.1.1). Most of the women who became publicly prominent were self-consciously ladylike, as an aid to disarm the opposition (1.1.2). Mary Carpenter, while careless about her clothes, and while bombarding ministers with memoranda, would refuse to chair a meeting and in her early days even to speak at one, as it was not respectable. Many an early public suffrage meeting concluded with resolutions congratulating the 'lady speakers' on their 'heroism' in mounting the platform. In part it was to give her students some privacy that Emily Davies was reluctant to build her college at Cambridge. Though it was an image which most constricted middle-class women (see below, W. R. Greg, 3.1.2), trade union organisers at the end of the century explained their failure to recruit women by describing the orthodox teaching for women as 'submission' whereas trade unionism 'means rebellion' (see below, 3.13.6).

At its simplest, the stereotype drew on three main bodies of ideas. The first was religious in orientation. Woman had been made from and was therefore dependent on man, and she should glory in her God-given weakness (1.2.1). Thoughtful women replied, as had Mary Wollstonecraft in 1792, that women like men had immortal souls and mortal reason, the responsibility for which could not be off-loaded even on to a husband's shoulders (1.2.2). More practically, women like Harriet Martineau pointed out that there were too many 'surplus' women for all to be protected by and dependent on men (see below, Part 2); women must become self-dependent, in an economic as well as in a moral sense. The *Saturday Review* dismissed their arguments (1.2.3). Marriage was a woman's business, and if a woman failed to marry, she had simply failed in business. An exception might be made of female servants, however, since like wives they ministered to men (1.2.4). Mrs Grey and her sister Emily Shirreff, later to found the Girls' Public Day School Trust (see below, 4.5), pointed out that the lot of the single woman, bleak though it was, did not lack advantages compared with the continuous self-abnegation required of married women (1.2.5); and their *Thoughts on Self-Culture* mapped out a mental and moral education for women forced to be self-sufficient. Later writers like Clara Collett, Assistant Commissioner in 1893, emphasised the contribution that could be made by active socially aware single women (see below, 3.12). Engels was only summarising a view held by many women when he stated that marriage was for many women legalised prostitution (1.2.6) and the married state economic bondage.

A second source of the stereotype was socio-political. Society was a community of families and each family, in W. Cooke Taylor's phrase, was 'a sovereign commonwealth'. At the heart of the family, and therefore of social stability, was the patriarchal principal: any challenge to the husband's rights, over his wife or his children, was represented as undermining all that was stable in the social order (see below, 9.2.5). And central to the family was its division of labour, the separate spheres of world and home. Mrs Ellis produced a series of best-selling moral etiquette books (1.3.1) which asserted that where man was an individual, woman was one of a social circle, whose life belonged to others and not to herself; and whose greater sensitivity, selflessness and religious sense made her the moral arbiter of her society, guardian of its moral health. Ruskin's well-known romantic description of the home (1.3.2) pushed the separate spheres metaphor to absurdity, judged Emily Davies (1.3.3), for 'men have no monopoly of working, nor women of weeping'. John Stuart Mill, and Mrs Catherine Booth (co-founder of the Salvation Army) denied that women's 'traditional' characteristics of passivity rather than activity, feeling rather than thinking, being rather than doing, were innate, but were rather the artificial products of the economic and social educational arrangements of a society still appealing to feudal concepts of physical force (1.3.4). Mrs Lynn Linton defended the 'womanly woman' against the 'shrieking sisterhood' who claimed self-determination (1.3.5), and Beatrice Webb noted the prevalence of such views even among 'chaffing' colleagues (1.3.6).

Perhaps the most insidious (and third) source of the stereotype came from the new 'science', that woman's biology was her destiny (1.4). Darwinian arguments were used to show that the greatest differentiation of male and female roles was to be found in the most advanced societies and therefore represented 'progress'. Doctors were enrolled to show the baneful effect that emancipation in general and higher education in particular had on women's menstrual rhythms and therefore on the health of the race as a whole (1.4.2). The novelist Grant Allen judged that the very existence of the race was being threatened by an obsessive attention to the claims of barren spinsters (1.4.3).

It was the unreality of the stereotype, given the number of women forced to be self-dependent, as well as its constrictiveness, that feminists deplored. But a more common note was struck by Mrs Josephine Butler in 1869: 'We need the extension beyond our homes of the home influence.' Just *because* women had distinctive traits and alternative perceptions to offer, they should enter public life. And, as the century progressed, just because government increasingly trespassed on the domestic dimension of health and education, housing and the relief of poverty, so women found their philanthropy politicised and themselves 'in public'.

Suggestions for further reading:
M. Vicinus (ed.), *Suffer and Be Still,* 1973; *The Widening Sphere,* 1977; K. Thomas, 'The double standard', *Journal of the History of Ideas,* 1959; P. Cominas, 'Late Victorian respectability and the social system', *International Review of Social History,* 1963; L. Davidoff, *Best Circles,* 1973.

1.1 Respectability and Public Life

1.1.1 *Impropriety of public life*
It is averred that 'public life' is injurious to women; they are meant for the domestic ... What is meant by it? Is there any woman living who does not go more or less into public ... The work of a medical practitioner is scarcely more public than that of a district visitor ... the business of a chemist and druggist is no more public than a confectioner ... Fathers who would shake their heads at the idea of taking their daughters into their own counting-houses, allow them to stand behind a stall at a bazaar, or to lead off at a charity ball—far more public scenes, and, where indeed, publicity is essential to success.

Emily Davies, *Letters to a Daily Paper,* Newcastle, 1860

1.1.2 *The Image of a Lady*
Many people in the University disapproved strongly of the presence of women students in Cambridge, and probably most people looked upon them with some suspicion. If any inconvenience followed from their being there, or if any individual deviated in the slightest degree from the ordinary standards of society, it would be considered as a complete justification of this attitude ... Miss Clough was keenly alive to these things ... education should be kept quite apart from other questions and causes, and she meant to show that a desire for education, and even the possession of it, did not involve any departure from recognised customs and conventions ...

I remember someone had been complaining that Newnham students went along the streets buttoning their gloves. The Principal gave us a sympathetic address on the subject. 'I know, my dears, that you have a great deal to do, and have not much time; but I don't like people to say such things about you, and so, my dears, I hope you'll get some gloves that don't want buttoning.'

B. A. Clough, *Memoir of Anne Jemima Clough*, 1897, pp. 195, 240

Experience is modifying my notions about the most suitable style of dress for me to wear at the hospital. I feel confident now that one is helped rather than hindered by being as much like a lady as lies in one's power. When my student life begins, I shall try to get very serviceable, rich, whole coloured dresses that will do without trimmings and not require renewing often.

Elizabeth Garrett to Emily Davies, 5 September 1860,
quoted in Barbara Stephen,
Emily Davies and Girton College, 1927, p. 59

It was evident that the audiences came expecting to see curious masculine objects walking on to the platform, and when we appeared, with our quiet black dresses, the whole expression of the faces of the audience would instantly change. I shall never forget the thrill which passed through us when, on one occasion, a Nonconformist minister assured the audience in his speech from the chair, that we were 'quite respectable'—meaning to convey that we were people with some position, and not merely seeking notoriety or earning money by our speaking.

> Lilias Ashworth on her West of England speaking tour
> for the suffrage, 1872, quoted in Helen Blackburn,
> *Women's Suffrage,* 1902, pp. 110-11

1.2   Dependence and self-dependence

1.2.1   *The strength of weakness*

But let it be granted, for argument's sake, that it is substantial power, and no mere shadow of additional influence, which a woman would gain by such a change [the franchise]; and we then ask, will the consequent result be an improvement in their position? We decidedly think that it would not. In all modern civilized communities, and especially in the most refined and cultivated portion of those communities, women are treated by men with peculiar deference, tenderness, and courtesy. Do they owe this treatment to their strength or to their weakness? Undoubtedly to the latter. The deference, the tenderness, the courtesy of man towards the other sex, are founded principally on the feeling that they need his protection, and can never question his power. But let women be made ostensibly powerful; let a sense of competition be introduced; let man be made to feel that he must stand on the defensive—and the spirit of chivalry, so eloquently described by Burke, will speedily cease; and it will be useless to expect a continuance of that feeling, to which women can now appeal with confidence, and which lends the most essential charms to the ordinary intercourse of civilized society. Women, as a class, cannot enjoy, at the same time, the immunities of weakness and the advantages of power.

T. H. Lister, 'Rights and conditions of women',
Edinburgh Review, vol. 73, 1841

Woman's strength lies in her essential weakness. She is at this hour what 'in the beginning' the great Creator designed her to be—namely Man's help; not his rival but his help. Sheltered throughout her earlier years from all polluting influences: accustomed from the first to ministrations of domestic kindness and the sweet charities of home: removed from the stifling atmosphere in which perforce the battle of life has to be fought out by the rougher sex—she is, what she was intended to be, the one great solace of Man's life, his chiefest earthly joy.

J. Burgon, *Sermon,* 1884

1.2.2   *The indignity of dependence*

Woman is taught to believe, that for one half of the human race, the highest end of civilization is to cling upon the other, like a weed upon a wall.

Mrs Hugo Reid, *A Plea for Women,* 1843, p. 200

Our duty in this world is to try and make it what God intends it shall become: we are his tools ... To do God's work in the world is the duty of all, rich and poor, of all nations, of both sexes ... Women must, as children of God, be trained to do some work in the world. Women may not take a man as a God: they must not hold their first duty to be towards any human being ...

Fathers have no right to cast the burden of the support of their daughters on other men. It lowers the dignity of women; and tends to prostitution, whether legal or in the streets. As long as fathers regard the sex of a child as a reason why it should not be taught to gain its own bread, so long must women be degraded. Adult women must not be supported by men, if they are to stand as dignified, rational beings before God ... Women must have work if they are to form equal unions.

Barbara Leigh Smith, *Women and Work*, 1856, pp. 6, 11

From that time [the emergence of a middle class] to this, the need and the supply of female industry have gone on increasing, and latterly at an unparalled rate, while our ideas, our language, and our arrangements have not altered in any corresponding degree. We go on talking as if it were still true that every woman is, or ought to be, supported by father, brother or husband ...

A social organization framed for a community of which half stayed at home, while the other half went out to work, cannot answer the purposes of a society, of which a quarter remain at home, while three-quarters go out to work.

Harriet Martineau,
'Female industry', *Edinburgh Review,* vol. 109, 1859

From babyhood women are given to understand that helplessness is feminine and beautiful ... We women are, no less than men, each of us a distinct existence ... accountable only, in the highest sense to our own souls, and the Maker of them. Is it natural, is it right, even, that we should be expected—and be ready enough too, for it is the easiest way—to hang our consciences, duties, actions, opinions, upon some one else—some individual, or some aggregate of individuals yclept Society?

... We *must* help ourselves by self-dependence ... Marriage ought always to be a question not of necessity, but of choice.

Mrs Craik, *Women's Thoughts about Women*, 1862, pp. 25-6

That women spend the best part of their lives in preparing for an event which may never happen—an event for which the very worst preparation is to hanker after it, while the very best is to be strenuously occupied with something different, is the result, not of God's decision that one form of life should be *happier* than another, but of man's invention that it should be deemed more *womanly*.

> Julia Wedgwood, 'Female suffrage',
> in Josephine Butler (ed.),
> *Woman's Work and Woman's Culture,* 1869

What dignity can there be in the attitude of women in general, and towards men in particular, when marriage is held (and often necessarily so, being the sole means of maintenace) to be the one end of a woman's life, when it is degraded to the level of a feminine profession, when those who are soliciting a place in this profession resemble those flaccid Brazilian creepers which cannot exist without support, and which sprawl out their limp tendrils in every direction to find something—no matter what—to hang upon; when the insipidity or the material necessities of so many women's lives make them ready to accept almost any man who may offer himself? There has been a pretence of admiring this pretty helplessness of women. But let me explain that I am not deprecating the condition of dependence in which God has placed every human being, man or woman,—the sweet interchange of services, the give and take of true affection, the mutual support and aid of friends or lovers, who have each something to give and to receive. That is a wholly different thing from the abject dependence of one entire class of persons on another and a stronger class. In the present case such a dependence is liable to peculiar dangers by its complication with sexual emotions and motives, and with relations which ought, in an advanced and Christian community, to rest upon a free and deliberate choice,—a decision of the judgment and of the heart, and into which the admission of a necessity, moral or material, introduces a degrading element.

I cannot believe that it is every woman's duty to marry, in this age of the world. There is abundance of work to be done which needs men and women detached from domestic ties; our unmarried women will be the greatest blessing to the community when they cease to be soured by disappointment or driven by destitution to despair . . .

> Josephine Butler, Introduction, loc. cit.

1.2.3 *Marriage, a woman's profession*

We say that the greatest of social and political duties is to encourage marriage. The interest of a State is to get as many of its citizens married as possible. The equality of the sexes demonstrates this to be a law of nature. And we add that man, in European communities, has deliberately adopted the view that, as much as possible, women should be relieved from the necessity of self-support. The measure of civilization is the maximum at which this end is attained in any given community or nation. Women labourers are a proof of a barbarous and imperfect civilization. We should be retrograding in the art and science of civilization were more women encouraged to be self-supporters. And the reason of this is plain enough. Wherever women are self-supporters, marriage is, *ipso facto*, discouraged. The factory population is proof of this. In the manufacturing districts women make worse wives and worse helpmates than where they are altogether dependent on the man. And where there are fewer marriages there is more vice ... The prevailing theory is, let as many women as possible be dependent on marriage. Let women be trained to this as the end of her being. And though it is not seldom more roughly expressed, there is the highest social wisdom in it. Distressed governesses and distressed workwomen are social anomalies, but the social fabric is for the greatest happiness of the greatest number. And this is attained by making marriage the rule. In a community where all the women were clerks, telegraph-workers, watchmakers, and book-keepers, the inducements to marriage would be lessened on either side. Men do not like, and would not seek, to mate with an independent factor, who at any time could quit—or who at all times would be tempted to neglect—the tedious duties of training and bringing up children, and keeping the tradesmen's bills, and mending the linen, for the more lucrative returns of the desk or counter. It is not the interest of States, and it is not therefore true social policy, to encourage the existence, as a rule, of women who are other than entirely dependent on man as well for subsistence as for protection and love.

Married life is woman's profession; and to this life her training—that of dependence—is modelled. Of course by not getting a husband, or losing him, she may find that she is without resources. All that can be said of her is, she has failed in business; and no social reform can prevent such failures. The mischance of the distressed governess and the unprovided widow, is that of every insolvent tradesmen. He is to be pitied; but all the Social Congresses in the world will not prevent the possibility of a mischance in the shape of broken-down tradesmen, old maids, or widows. Each and all are frequently left without resources; and each and all always will be left without resources; but it would be just as reasonable to demand that every boy should be taught two or three professions because he may fail in one, as it is to argue that all our social habits should be changed because one woman in fifty—or whatever the statistics are—is a spinster or widow without any resources.

'Queen bees or working bees',
Saturday Review, 12 November 1859

1.2.4 *Service, a woman's career*
Female servants do not constitute any part (or at least only a very small part) *of the problem* [of surplus women] *we are endeavouring to*

solve. They are in no sense redundant; we have not to cudgel our brains to find a niche or an occupation for *them*; they are fully and usefully employed; they discharge a most important and indispensable function in social life; they do not follow an obligatory independent, and therefore for their sex an unnatural, career:—on the contrary, they are attached to others and are connected with other existences, which they embellish, facilitate, and serve. In a word, they fulfil both essentials of woman's being; *they are supported by, and they minister to*, men. We could not possibly do without them. Nature has not provided one too many. If society were in a perfectly healthy state, we should no doubt have to manage with fewer female servants than at present; they would earn higher wages; they would meet with more uniform consideration; and they would, as a rule, remain in service only for a few years, and not for life: but they must always be a numerous class, and scarcely any portion of their sex is more useful or more worthy.

W. R. Greg, 'Why are women redundant?',
National Review, April 1862

1.2.5   *The advantages of single life*

A woman should be reminded . . . that in marrying she gives up many advantages. Her independence is, of course, renounced by the very act that makes her another's. Her habits, pursuits, society, sometimes even friendships, must give way to his, and this readily and cheerfully, as part of the obligations of a wife . . . The husband has less pliancy, and considers it as his undoubted right that his wife should regulate her mode of life upon his wishes. The wife, therefore, must yield or be prepared for perpetual discord . . . Where a woman's affection for her husband is only a tenderer kind of friendship, continual concession may sometimes appear burdensome. She may find it difficult to renounce what would give her great pleasure in compliance to a mere fancy, perhaps to caprice or indolence. She may chafe at her dependence, and the habitual want of consideration in men for women's pursuits and friendships. Above all, she will feel it hard to be forced to check her devotion to her children . . . but if once she allows these feelings to become apparent, her domestic happiness is in jeopardy. These are the things which a girl should be taught to weigh well before she takes so irretrievable a step as marriage, and they may perhaps be set against the less advantageous social position, and the comparative isolation, of the unmarried woman . . . The single woman must repress these affections and renounce the hope of being the object of exclusive love; but on the other hand she retains her independence, and her own friends, from whom marriage would probably have separated her to a great extent; and the feelings and capacities which with the married woman are concentrated within the home, may by her be exercised on a higher scale for the benefit of a larger circle, and bring her all the happiness (perhaps the surest we can enjoy on earth) which results from the active exercise of our faculties towards a worthy object . . .

Perhaps in time even mothers might be found wise enough to prefer their daughters remaining cheerful amiable old maids, to becoming miserable wives . . . If the balance, therefore, be fairly struck, we shall find the average degree of happiness in both conditions more nearly equal than is commonly supposed, with this advantage on the side of the single woman, that her happiness is less dependent on the character and conduct of others, and therefore much more with her own power.

The question is seldom tried fairly on its own merits, owing to the injustice which condemns women to the dependence of poverty, from which they can only escape by marrying. Brought up in comfort . . . they are left without the means of maintaining [themselves]. This error of our social system forces women too often to consider marriage, not as a question of happiness, but of subsistence, and it would be little flattering to the vanity of men, who are apt enough to think women cannot live without them, to know how many a one has shrunk with repugnance from the ties her poverty compels her to form, and represses her warmest feelings, to enable her to bear the trials of a condition she would not have entered into had she been free.

Maria Grey and Emily Shirreff,
Thoughts on Self-Culture, 1872 edn, pp. 181-3

1.2.6 *The domestic enslavement of women*

The position is no better with regard to the juridical equality of man and woman in marriage. The inequality of the two before the law, which is a legacy of previous social conditions, is not the cause but the effect of the economic oppression of women. In the old communistic household, which embraced numerous couples and their children, the administration of the household, entrusted to the women, was just as much a public, a socially necessary industry as the providing of food by the men. This situation changed with the patriarchal family, and even more with the monogamian individual family. The administration of the household lost its public character. It was no longer the concern of society. It became a *private service*. The wife became the first domestic servant, pushed out of participation in social production. Only modern large-scale industry again threw open to her— and only to the proletarian woman at that—the avenue to social production; but in such a way that, when she fulfils her duties in the private service of her family, she remains excluded from public production and cannot earn anything; and when she wishes to take part in public industry and earn her living independently, she is not in a position to fulfil her family duties. What applies to the woman in the factory applies to her in all the professions, right up to medicine and law. The modern individual family is based on the open or disguised domestic enslavement of the woman; and modern society is a mass composed solely of individual families as its molecules. Today, in the great majority of cases, the man has to be the earner, the bread-winner of the family, at least among the propertied classes, and this gives him a dominating position which requires no special legal privileges. In the family, he is the bourgeois; the wife represents the proletariat. In the industrial world, however, the specific character of the economic oppression that weighs down the proletariat stands out in all its sharpness only after all the special legal privileges of the capitalist class have been set aside and the complete juridical equality of both classes is established. The democratic republic does not abolish the antagonism between the two classes; on the contrary, it provides the field on which it is fought out. And, similarly, the peculiar character of man's domination over woman in the modern family, and the necessity, as well as the manner, of establishing real social equality between the two, will be brought out into full relief only when both are completely equal before the law. It will then become evident that the first premise for the emancipation of women is the reintroduction of the entire female sex into public industry; and that this again demands that the quality possessed by the individual family of being the economic unit of society be abolished.

F. Engels,
The Origin of the Family,
Private Property and the State, 1884, pp. 232-3 (1962 edition)

1.3   Separate spheres

1.3.1   *Women's role*

As women, then, the first thing of importance is to be content to be
inferior to men—inferior in mental power, in the same proportion
that you are inferior in bodily strength ... You are not alone; you are
one of a family—of a social circle—of a community—of a nation.
You are a being whose existence will never terminate, who *must* live
for ever, and whose happiness or misery through that endless future
which lies before you, will be influenced by the choice you are now in
the act of making ...

I am perfectly aware that there are intricate questions brought
before our Senate, which it may require a masculine order of intellect
fully to understand. But there are others which may, and ought, to
engage the attention of every female mind, such as the extinction of
slavery, the abolition of war in general, cruelty to animals, the
punishment of death, temperance, and many more, on which neither
to know, nor to feel, is almost equally disgraceful ...

For a man it is absolutely necessary that he should sacrifice the
poetry of his nature for the realities of material and animal existence;
for women there is no excuse—for women, whose whole life from the
cradle to the grave is one of feeling rather than of action; whose
highest duty is so often to suffer and be still; whose deepest
enjoyments are all relative; who has nothing, and is nothing, of
herself; whose experience, if unparticipated, is a total blank; yet
whose world of interest is as wide as the realm of humanity, boundless
as the ocean of life, and enduring as eternity! For woman, who, in her
inexhaustible sympathies, can live only in the existence of another,
and whose very smiles and tears are not exclusively her own. A woman
without poetry is like a landscape without sunshine. We see every
object as distinctly as when the sunshine is upon it; but the beauty of
the whole is wanting ... the spirituality of the scene is gone ...

It is that habitual tendency of feeling or tone of mind which I have
called taste, that decides their choice; and it is thus that our moral
worth or dignity depends upon the exercise of good taste, in the selection we make of the intellectual materials we work within the formation
of character, and the general arrangement of the whole ... It is strictly
in subservience to religion that I would speak of good taste as being of
extreme importance to women, because it serves her purpose in all
those little variations of human life, which are too sudden in their
occurrence, and too minute in themselves, for the operation of
judgment; but which at the same time constitutes so large a sum of

women's experience ... The exercise of good taste will in time become so easy, and habitual, as to operate almost like an instinct ... Not that delicacy which is perpetually in quest of something to be ashamed of, which makes a merit of a blush, and simpers at the false construction its own ingenuity has put upon an innocent remark; this spurious kind of delicacy is as far removed from good taste, as from good feeling, and good sense; but that high-minded delicacy which maintains its pure and undeviating walk alike amongst women, as in the society of men; which shrinks from no necessary duty, and can speak when required with seriousness and kindness at things it would be ashamed indeed to smile or to blush ... that delicacy which can give alms without display and advice without assumption; and which pains not the most humble or susceptible being in creation.

[What in man is ambition, in women is love of distinction.] In women it is a selfish desire to stand apart from the many; to be something, of and by, herself; to enjoy what she does enjoy, and to appropriate the tribute which society offers her, distinct from the sisterhood to which she belongs ... Love is women's all—her wealth, her power, her very being. Man, let him love as he may, has ever an existence, distinct from that of his affections. He has his worldly interests, his public character his ambition, his competition with other men—but woman centres all that in one feeling ... In woman's love is mingled the trusting dependence of a child, for she ever looks up to a man as her protector, and her guide; the frankness, the social feeling and the tenderness of a sister—for is not man her friend? the solicitude, the anxiety, the careful watching of the mother—for would she not suffer to preserve him from harm?

Sara Ellis, The Daughters of England, 1842

1.3.2 *Doing and being*

We are foolish, and without excuse foolish, in speaking of the 'superiority' of one sex to the other, as if they could be compared in similar things. Each has what the other has not: each completes the other, and is completed by the other: they are in nothing alike, and the happiness and perfection of both depends on each asking and receiving from the other what the other only can give . . .

The man's power is active, progressive, defensive. He is eminently the doer, the creator, the discoverer, the defender. His intellect is for speculation and invention; his energy for adventure, for war, and for conquest, wherever war is just, wherever conquest is necessary. But the woman's power is for rule, not for battle—and her intellect is not for invention or creation, but for sweet ordering, arrangement, and decision. She sees the qualities of things, their claims, and their places. Her great function is Praise; she enters into no contest, but infallibly adjudges the crown of contest. By her office, and place, she is protected from all danger and temptation. The man, in his rough work in open world, must encounter all peril and trial;—to him, therefore, must be the failure, the offence, the inevitable error: often he must be wounded, or subdued; often misled; and *always* hardened. But he guards the woman from all this; within his house, as ruled by her, unless she herself has sought it, need enter no danger, no temptation, no cause of error or offence. This is the true nature of home—it is the place of Peace; the shelter, not only from all injury, but from all terror, doubt, and division. In so far as it is not this, it is not home; so far as the anxieties of the outer life penetrate into it, and the inconsistently-minded, unknown, unloved, or hostile society of the outer world is allowed by either husband or wife to cross the threshold, it ceases to be home; it is then only a part of that outer world which you have roofed over, and lighted fire in. But so far as it is a sacred place, a vestal temple, a temple of the hearth watched over by Household Gods, before whose faces none may come but those whom they can receive with love—so far as it is this ... so far it vindicates the name, and fulfils the praise, of Home.

And wherever a true wife comes, this home is always round her. The stars only may be over head; the glowworm in the night-cold grass may be the only fire at her foot; but home is yet wherever she is; and for a noble woman it stretches far round her, better than ceiled with cedar, or painted with vermillion, shedding its quiet light far, for those who else were homeless.

This, then, I believe to be—will you not admit it to be—the woman's true place and power? But do not you see that, to fulfil this, she must—as far as one can use such terms of a human creature—be incapable of error? So far as she rules, all must be right, or nothing is. She must be enduringly, incorruptibly good; instinctively, infallibly wise—wise, not for self-development, but for self-renunciation: wise, not that she may set herself above her husband, but that she may never fall from his side: wise, not with the narrowness of insolent and loveless pride, but with the passionate gentleness of an infinitely variable, because infinitely applicable, modesty of service—the true changefulness of woman . . .

J. Ruskin, 'Of Queens' Gardens', in *Sesame and Lilies,* 1865

1.3.3 *A false division*

The man is intended for the world, woman for the home; man's strength is in the head, woman's in the heart; the man's function is to protect, woman's to soothe and comfort; men must work, and women must weep: everywhere we are to have a sharply marked division, often honestly mistaken for the highest and most real communion. Closely connected with these separatist doctrines is the double moral

code, with its masculine and feminine virtues, and its separate law of
duty and honour for either sex . . .

We make the world even more puzzling than it is by nature, when
we shut our eyes to the facts of daily life; and we know, as a fact, that
women have a part in the world, and that men are by no means ciphers
in the home circle—we know that a man who should be all head would
be as monstrous an anomaly as a woman all heart—that men require
the protection of law, and women are not so uniformly prosperous as
to be independent of comfort and consolation—men have no
monopoly of working, nor women of weeping . . . Are women to be
regarded, and to regard themselves, primarily as children of God,
members of Christ, and heirs of the kingdom of heaven, and,
secondarily, as wives, mothers, daughters, sisters? or are the family
relationships to overshadow the divine and the social, and to be made
the basis of a special moral code, applying to women only?

Emily Davies,
'Ideals', in *The Higher Education of Women,* 1866

1.3.4   *The artificial nature of women*

From the very earliest twilight of human society, every woman (owing
to the value attached to her by men, combined with her inferiority in
muscular strength) was found in a state of bondage to some man.
Laws and systems of polity always begin by recognising the relations
they find already existing between individuals. They convert what was
a mere physical fact into a legal right, give it the sanction of society,
and principally aim at the substitution of public and organised means
of asserting and protecting these rights, instead of the irregular and
lawless conflict of physical strength. Those who had already been
compelled to obedience became in this manner legally bound to it.

All causes, social and natural, combine to make it unlikely that
women should be collectively rebellious to the power of men. They are
so far in a position different from all other subject classes, that their
masters require something more from them than actual service. Men
do not want solely the obedience of women, they want their
sentiments. All men, except the most brutish, desire to have, in the
woman most nearly connected with them, not a forced slave but a
willing one, not a slave merely, but a favourite. They have therefore
put everything in practice to enslave their minds. The masters of all
other slaves rely, for maintaining obedience, on fear; either fear of
themselves, or religious fears. The masters of women wanted more
than simple obedience, and they turned the whole force of education
to effect their purpose. All women are brought up from the very
earliest years in the belief that their ideal of character is the very
opposite to that of men; not self-will, and government by self-control,

but submission, and yielding to the control of others. All the moralities tell them that it is the duty of women, and all the current sentimentalities that it is their nature, to live for others; to make complete abnegation of themselves, and to have no life but in their affections. And by their affections are meant the only ones they are allowed to have—those to the men with whom they are connected, or to the children who constitute an additional and indefeasible tie between them and a man. When we put together three things—first, the natural attraction between opposite sexes; secondly, the wife's entire dependence on the husband, every privilege or pleasure she has being either his gift, or depending entirely on his will; and lastly, that the principal object of human pursuit, consideration, and all objects of social ambition, can in general be sought or obtained by her only through him, it would be a miracle if the object of being attractive to men had not become the polar star of feminine education and formation of character. And, this great means of influence over the minds of women having been acquired, an instinct of selfishness made men avail themselves of it to the utmost as a means of holding women in subjection, by representing to them meekness, submissiveness, and resignation of all individual will into the hands of a man, as an essential part of sexual attractiveness. What is now called the nature of women is an eminently artificial thing—the result of forced repression in some directions, unnatural stimulation in others.

J. S. Mill, *The Subjection of Women*, 1869, ch. 1

In your discourse on Sunday morning, when descanting on the policy of Satan in first attacking the most assailable of our race, your remarks appeared to imply the doctrine of women's intellectual and even moral inferiority to man ... I for one cannot but deeply regret that a man for whom I entertain such a high veneration should appear to hold views so derogatory to my sex, and which I believe to be unscriptural and dishonouring to God ...

That woman is, in consequence of her inadequate education, generally inferior to man intellectually, I admit. But that she is *naturally* so, as your remarks seemed to imply, I see no cause to believe. I think the disparity is as easily accounted for as the difference between women intellectually in this country, and under the degrading slavery of heathen lands. No argument, in my judgement, can be drawn from past experience on this point, because the past has been false in theory and wrong in practice. Never yet, in the history of the world, has woman been placed on an intellectual footing with man. Her training from babyhood, even in this highly favoured land, has hitherto been such as to cramp and paralyse, rather than to develop and strengthen her energies, and calculated to crush and wither her aspirations after mental greatness, rather than to excite and stimulate them.

Catherine Mumford (later Catherine Booth) to her pastor,
Dr David Thomas, 1853, quoted in F. de L. Booth-Tucker,
The Short Life of Catherine Booth, 1893, pp. 45-6

1.3.5 *The Womanly Woman*

She knows that part of her natural mission is to please and be charming, and she knows that dress sets her off, and that men feel more enthusiastically towards her when she is looking fresh and pretty than when she is a dowdy and a fright. And, being womanly, she likes the admiration of men, and thinks their love a better thing than their indifference. If she likes men she loves children, and never shunts them as nuisances, nor frets when forced to have them about her. She knows that she was designed by the needs of the race and the law of nature to be a mother; sent into the world for that purpose mainly; and she knows that rational maternity means more than simply giving life and then leaving it to others to preserve it. She has no newfangled notions about the animal character of motherhood, nor about the degrading character of housekeeping. On the contrary, she thinks a populous and happy nursery one of the greatest blessings of her state; and she puts her pride in the perfect ordering, the exquisite arrangements, the comfort, thoughtfulness and beauty of her house. She is not above her *metier* as a woman; and she does not want to ape the manliness she can never possess.

She has always been taught that, as there are certain manly virtues, so are there certain feminine ones; and that she is the most womanly among women who has those virtues in greatest abundance and in the highest perfection. She has taken it to heart that patience, self-sacrifice, tenderness, quietness, with some others, of which modesty is one, are the virtues more especially feminine; just as courage, justice, fortitude, and the like, belong to men.

Passionate ambition, virile energy, the love of strong excitement, self-assertion, fierceness, an undisciplined temper, are all qualities which detract from her ideal of womanliness, and which make her less beautiful than she was meant to be. Consequently she has cultivated all the meek and tender affections, all the unselfishness and thought for others which have hitherto been the distinctive property of her sex, by the exercise of which they have done their best work and earned their highest place. She thinks it no degradation that she should take pains to please, to soothe, to comfort the man who, all day long, has been doing irksome work that her home may be beautiful and her life at ease. She does not think it incumbent on her, as a woman of spirit, to fly out at an impatient word; to answer back a momentary irritation with defiance; to give back a Roland to his Oliver. Her womanliness inclines her to loving forbearance, to patience under difficulties, to unwearied cheerfulness under such portion of the inevitable burden as may have been laid on her. She does not hold herself predestined by nature to receive only the best of everything, and deem herself affronted where her own especial cross is bound on her shoulders. Rather, she understands that she too must take the rough with the smooth; but that, as her husband's way in life is rougher than hers, his trials are greater, his burden heavier, it is her duty—and her privilege—to help him all she can with her tenderness and her love; and to give back to him at home, if in a different form, some of the care he has expended while abroad to make her path smooth . . .

She holds to love rather than opposition; to reverence, not defiance; who takes more pride in the husband's fame than in her own; who glories in the protection of his name, and in her state as wife; who feels the honour given to her as wife and matron far dearer than any she may earn herself by personal prowess; and who believes in her consecration as a helpmeet for man, not in a rivalry which a few generations will ripen into a coarse and bitter enmity.

Eliza Linton,
'Womanliness', in The Girl of the Period, 1883

rousseau

1.3.6 *Subordination, not competition*

Interesting talk with Professor Marshall, first at dinner at the Creightons, and afterwards at lunch at his own house. It opened with chaff about men and women: he holding that woman was a subordinate being, and that, if she ceased to be subordinate, there would be no object for a man to marry. That marriage was a sacrifice of masculine freedom, and would only be tolerated by male creatures so long as it meant the devotion, body and soul, of the female to the male. Hence the woman must not develop her faculties in a way unpleasant to the man: that strength, courage, independence were not attractive in women; that rivalry in men's pursuits was positively unpleasant. Hence masculine strength and masculine ability in women must be firmly trampled on and boycotted by men. *Contrast* was the essence of the matrimonial relation: feminine weakness contrasted with masculine strength: masculine egotism with feminine self-devotion.

'If you compete with us we shan't marry you', he summed up with a laugh.

I maintained the opposite argument: that there was an ideal of character in which strength, courage, sympathy, self-devotion, persistent purpose were united to a clear and far-seeing intellect; that the ideal was common to the man and to the woman; that these qualities might manifest themselves in different ways in the man's and the woman's life; that what you needed was not different qualities and different defects, but the same virtues working in different directions, and dedicated to the service of the community in different ways.

Beatrice Webb's diaries, 8 March 1889,
quoted in *My Apprenticeship,* 1889, 'Why I became a Socialist'

1.4 Biology her Destiny

1.4.1 *Birth her mission*

The theory about woman which we have called the Physical, is simply this: That the whole meaning and reason of her existence is, that she may form a link in the chain of generations, and fulfil the functions of wife to one man and mother to another. Her moral nature is a sort of superfluity according to this view, and her intellectual powers a positive hindrance. How such things came to be given her is unexplained. Her affections alone are useful, but the simpler ones of the mother-beast and bird would probably be more convenient. In a word, everything which enables a woman to attract conjugal love, and to become the parent of a numerous and healthful progeny, must be reckoned as constituting her proper endowment. Everything which distracts her attention or turns her faculties in other directions than these, must be treated as mischievous, and as detracting from her merits. The woman who has given birth to a son has fulfilled her 'mission'. The celibate woman,—be she holy as St. Theresa, useful as Miss Nightingale, gifted as Miss Cornwallis,—has entirely missed it . . .

To admit that Woman has affections, a moral nature, a religious sentiment, an immortal soul, and yet to treat her for a moment as a mere animal link in the chain of life, is monstrous; I had almost said, blasphemous. If her existence be of no value in itself, then no man's existence is of value; for a moral nature, a religious sentiment, and an immortal soul are the highest things a man can have, and the woman has them as well as he. If the links be valueless then the chain is valueless too; and the history of Humanity is but a long procession of spectres for whose existence no reason can be assigned . . . Believing that the same woman, a million ages hence, will be a glorious spirit before the throne of God, filled with unutterable love, and light, and joy, we cannot satisfactorily trace the beginning of that eternal and seraphic existence to Mr. Smith's want of a wife for a score of years here upon earth; or to the necessity Mr. Jones was under to find somebody to cook his food and repair his clothes. If these ideas be absurd, then it follows that we are not arrogating too much in seeking elsewhere than in the interests of Man the ultimate *raison d'etre* of Woman.

> Frances Power Cobbe, 'The final cause of woman',
> in Josephine Butler (ed.), *Woman's Work and
> Woman's Culture,* 1869

A stolid indifference to the higher interests of life, complete absorption in petty cares, is supposed to produce a placid, equable animal state of existence, favourable to the transmission of a healthy constitution to the next generation. We have persuaded ourselves that Englishmen of the present day are such a nervously excitable race, that the only chance for their descendants is to keep the mothers in a state of coma ... the theory that starving the brain is the best way of keeping it healthy.

> Emily Davies, *Proposed New College for Women,*
> read at the annual meeting of the Social Science Association, 1868

1.4.2   *Sex in mind*

It is quite evident that many of those who are foremost in their zeal for raising the education and social status of woman, have not given proper consideration to the nature of her organization, and to the demands which its special functions make upon its strength.

The energy of a human body being a definite and not inexhaustible quantity, can it bear, without injury, an excessive mental drain as well as the natural physical drain which is so great at that time? ... When Nature spends in one direction, she must economize in another direction. That the development of puberty does draw heavily upon the vital resources of the female constitution, needs not to be pointed out to those who know the nature of the important physiological changes which then take place. At each recurring period there are all the preparations for conception, and nothing is more necessary to the preservation of female health than that these changes should take place regularly and completely. It is true that many of them are destined to be fruitless so far as their essential purpose is concerned, but it would be a great mistake to suppose that on that account they might be omitted or accomplished incompletely, without harm to the general health. They are the expressions of the full physiological activity of the organism.

Women cannot choose but to be women; cannot rebel successfully against the tyranny of their organization, the complete development and function whereof must take place after its kind. This is not the expression of prejudice nor of false sentiment; it is the plain statement of a physiological fact. Surely, then, it is unwise to pass it by; first or last it must have its due weight in the determination of the problem of woman's education and mission: There is sex in mind as distinctly as there is sex in body; and if the mind is to receive the best culture of which its nature is capable, regard must be had to the mental qualities which correlate differences of sex. To aim, by means of education and pursuits in life, to assimilate the female to the male mind, might well be pronounced as unwise and fruitless a labour as it would be to strive to assimilate the female to the male body by means of the same kind of physical training and by the adoption of the same pursuits.

Let me pause here to reflect briefly upon the influence of sex upon mind. In its physiological sense, with which we are concerned here, mind is the sum of those functions of the brain which are commonly known as thought, feeling, and will. Now the brain is one among a number of organs in the commonwealth of the body; though it is the highest organ of the body, the co-ordinating centre to which impressions go and from which responses are sent, the nature and functions of the inferior organs with which it lives in unity, affect essentially its nature as the organ of mental functions.

Each sex must develop after its kind; and if education in its fundamental meaning be the external cause to which evolution is the internal answer, if it be the drawing out of the internal qualities of the individual into their highest perfection by the influence of the most fitting external conditions, there must be a difference in the method of education of the two sexes answering to differences in their physical and mental natures ... They are formed for different functions, and the influence of those functions pervades and affects essentially their entire beings. There is sex in mind and there should be sex in education.

Let us consider, then, what an adapted education must have regard to. In the first place, a proper regard to the physical nature of women means attentions given, in their training, to their peculiar functions and to their foreordained work as mothers and nurses of children. Whatever aspirations of an intellectual kind they may have, they cannot be relieved from the performance of those offices as long as it is thought necessary that mankind should continue on earth. For it would be an ill thing, if it should so happen, that we got the advantages of a quantity of female intellectual work at the price of a puny, enfeebled, and sickly race. In this relation, it must be allowed that women do not and cannot stand on the same level as men.

In the second place, a proper regard to the mental nature of women means attention given to those qualities of mind which correlate the physical differences of her sex. Men are manifestly not so fitted mentally as women to be the educators of children during the early years of their infancy and childhood: it can hardly be doubted that if the nursing of babies were given over to men for a generation or two, they would abandon the task in despair or in disgust, and conclude it to be not worth while that mankind should continue on earth. But 'can a woman forget her sucking child, that she should not have compassion on the son of her womb?' Those can hardly be in earnest who question that woman's sex is represented in mind, and that the mental qualities which spring from it qualify her specially to be the successful nurse and educator of infants and young children.

Furthermore, the female qualities of mind which correlate her sexual character adapt her, as her sex does, to be the helpmate and companion of man . . .

In America the same method of training for the sexes in mixed classes has been largely applied. It is asserted (by doctors) that the number of female graduates of schools and colleges who have been permanently disabled to a greater or less degree by improper methods of study, and by a disregard of the reproductive apparatus and its functions, is so great as to excite the gravest alarm and to demand the serious attention of the community . . . It is a familiar medical observation that many nervous disorders of a minor kind, and even such serious disorders as chorea, epilepsy, insanity, are often connected with irregularities or suppression of these important functions.

Dr. Weir Mitchell writes: 'To-day the American woman is, to speak plainly, physically unfit for her duties as woman, and is, perhaps, of all civilised females, the least qualified to undertake those weightier tasks which tax so heavily the nervous system of man. She is not fairly up to what Nature asks from her as wife and mother. How will she sustain herself under the pressure of those yet more exacting duties which nowadays she is eager to share with man?'

Here then is no uncertain testimony as to the effects of the American system of female education: some women who are without the instinct or desire to nurse their offspring, some who have the desire but not the capacity, and others who have neither the instinct nor the capacity . . . One body and mind [is] capable of sustained and regular hard labour, and another body and mind for one quarter of each month during the best years of life is more or less sick and unfit for hard work . . . It may be a pity for woman that she has been created woman, but, being such, it is as ridiculous to consider herself inferior to man because she is not man, as it would be for man to consider himself inferior to her because he cannot perform her functions. There is one glory of the man, another glory of the woman, and the glory of the one differeth from that of the other.

H. Maudsley, 'Sex in mind and in education',
Fortnightly Review, April 1874

The educational methods followed by boys being admitted to be better than those hitherto applied to girls, it is necessary to show that these better methods would in some way interfere with the special functions of girls. This Dr. Maudsley has not done. He has not attempted to show how the adoption of a common standard of examination for boys and girls, allowing to each a considerable range in the choice of subjects, is likely to interfere more with a girl's health than passing an inferior examination for girls only . . .

What we want to know is ... how much consideration girls and women ought to show to the fact of the periodic and varying functions of their organization ... When we are told that in the labour of life women cannot disregard their special physiological functions without danger to health, it is difficult to understand what is meant, considering that in adult life healthy women do as a rule disregard them almost completely ... For example, do domestic servants ... show by experience that a marked change in the amount of work expected from them must be made at these times unless their health is to be injured? It is well known that they do not. With regard to mental work it is within the experience of many women that that which Dr. Maudsley speaks of as an occasion of weakness, if not of temporary prostration, is either not felt to be such or is even recognized as an aid, the nervous and mental power being in many cases greater at those times than at any other ... [Rather] its absence usually gives rise to a condition of nervous weakness ... It is surely unreasonable to assume that the same function in persons of good health can be a cause of weakness when present, and also when absent. If its performance made women weak and ill, its absence would be a gain, which it is not ...

The case is, we admit, very different during early womanhood ... [when] a temporary sense of weakness is doubtless more common ... But riding, long standing, lifting heavy weights—e.g. young brothers and sisters—dancing, and rapid or fatiguing walks are the chief sources of risk ... The assertion that as a rule girls are unable to go on with an ordinary amount of quiet exercise or mental work during these periods, seems to us to be entirely contradicted by experience ... The time given to education is, however, being prolonged, and the pressure in the early years of womanhood ... is being lightened ...

It must not be overlooked that the difficulties which attend the period of rapid functional development are not confined to women ... Analogous changes take place in the constitution and organization of young men ... who still further tax their strength, e.g. by drinking, smoking, unduly severe physical exercise, and frequently by late hours and dissipation generally ... The difficulties which attend development are not entirely confined to women ...

The cases ... against continuous mental work ... could be outnumbered many times over even in our own limited experience by those in which the break-down of nervous and physical health seems at any rate to be distinctly traceable [not to over-stimulation] ... but to want of adequate mental interest and occupation in the years immediately succeeding school life. Thousands of young women, strong and blooming at eighteen become gradually languid and feeble ... till in a few years they are morbid and self-absorbed, or even hysterical. If they had upon leaving school some solid intellectual work ... the number of such cases would be smaller ... and it would discourage very early marriages ... and the physiological wear and tear consequent upon marriage ...

Elizabeth Garrett Anderson,
'Sex in mind and education: a reply',
Fortnightly Review, July 1874

I am glad you and Mrs. Anderson have talked over that article. Girton suffers largely, I believe, from the determined opposition of medical men, and as for me, I scarcely expect anything else if a medical opinion be asked in the case of any girl. The smallest ailment always proceeds from over-brainwork!!! never from neglected conditions of health, from too many parties, etc., etc.

Frances Buss to Emily Davies, 13 April 1874
quoted in Barbara Stephen,
Emily Davies and Girton College, 1927, p. 292

1.4.3   *The reproduction of the race*
If every woman married, and every woman had four children, population would remain just stationary as nearly half of them die before reaching the age of manhood. If some women shirk their natural duties, then a heavier task must be laid upon the remainder. It is best for the community at large that most women should marry, and should have moderate families, rather than that fewer should marry and have unwieldily large ones; for if families are moderate there will be a greater reserve of health and strength left in the mothers for each birth, the production of children can be spread more slowly over a longer time, and the family resources will be less heavily taxed for their maintenance and education ... Hence I would infer that the goal a wise community should keep in view is rather more marriages and fewer children per marriage, than fewer marriages and more children per marriage.

Now I have the greatest sympathy with the modern woman's demand for emancipation. I am an enthusiast on the Woman Question. Indeed, so far am I from wishing to keep her in subjection to man, that I should like to see her a great deal more emancipated than she herself as yet at all desires. Only her emancipation must not be of a sort that interferes in any way with this prime natural necessity. To the end of all time, it is mathematically demonstrable that most women must become the mothers of at least four children, or else the race must cease to exist. Any supposed solution of the woman-problem, therefore, which fails to look this fact straight in the face, is a false solution. Seeing then, that these necessities are laid by the very nature of our organization upon women, it would appear as though two duties were clearly imposed upon the women themselves, and upon all those men who sympathize in their welfare: First, to see that their training and education should fit them above everything else for this their main function in life; and, second, that in consideration of the special burden they have to bear in connection with reproduction, all the rest of life should be made as light and easy and free for them as possible. We ought frankly to recognise that most women must be wives and mothers: that most women should therefore be trained, physically, morally, socially, and mentally, in the way best fitting them to be wives and mothers; and that all such women have a right to the fullest and most generous support in carrying out their functions as wives and mothers.

What is the ideal that most of these modern women agitators set before them? Is it not clearly the ideal of an unsexed woman? Are they not always talking to us as though it were not the fact that most women must be wives and mothers? Do they not treat any reference to that fact as something ungenerous, ungentlemanly, and almost brutal? Do they not talk about our 'casting their sex in their teeth'?— as though any man ever resented the imputation of manliness. Nay, have we not even, many times lately, heard those women who insist upon the essential womanliness of women described as 'traitors to the cause of their sex'? ... Women ought to glory in their femininity. A woman ought to be ashamed to say she has no desire to become a wife and mother. Many such women there are no doubt—it is to be feared, with our existing training, far too many: but instead of boasting of their sexlessness as a matter of pride, they ought to keep it dark, and to be ashamed of it—as ashamed as a man in a like predicament would be of his impotence . . .

Out of every hundred women, roughly speaking, ninety-six have husbands provided for them by nature, and only four need go into a nunnery or take to teaching the higher mathematics. Instead of subordinating the claims of the unmarried women to the claims of the wives and mothers, the movement has subordinated the claims of the wives and mothers to the claims of the unmarried women. Almost all the Woman's Rights women have constantly spoken, thought, and written as though it were possible and desirable for the mass of women to support themselves, and to remain unmarried for ever. The point of view they all tacitly take is the point of view of the self-supporting spinster. Now, the self-supporting spinster is undoubtedly a fact—a deplorable accident of the passing moment. We ought not to erect into an ideal what is in reality a painful necessity of the present transitional age. We ought always clearly to bear in mind—men and women alike—that to all time the vast majority of women must be wives and mothers; that on those women who become wives and mothers depends the future of the race; and that if either class must be sacrificed to the other, it is the spinsters whose type perishes with them that should be sacrificed to the matrons who carry on the life and qualities of the species.

For this reason a scheme of female education ought to be mainly a scheme for the education of wives and mothers. And if women realised how noble and important a task it is that falls upon mothers, they would ask no other. If they realised how magnificent a nation might be moulded by mothers who devoted themselves faithfully and earnestly to their great privilege, they would be proud to carry out the duties of their maternity. Instead of that the scheme of female education now in vogue is a scheme for the production of literary women, schoolmistresses, hospital nurses, and lecturers on cookery. All these things are good in themselves, to be sure—I have not a word to say against them; but they are not of the centre. They are side-lines off the main stream of feminine life, which must always consist of the maternal element. 'But we can't know beforehand', say the advocates of the mannish training, 'which women are going to be married and which to be spinsters.' Exactly so; and therefore you sacrifice the many to the few, the potential wives to the possible lady-lecturers. You sacrifice the race to a handful of barren experimenters.

As a body we are, I think, prepared to reconsider, and to reconsider fundamentally, without prejudice or preconception, the entire question of the relations between the sexes—which is a great deal more than the women are prepared to do. We are ready to make any modifications in those relations which will satisfy the woman's just aspiration for personal independence, for intellectual and moral development, for physical culture, for political activity, and for a voice in the arrangement of her own affairs, both domestic and national. As a matter of fact, few women will go as far in their desire to emancipate woman as many men will go. It was Ibsen, not Mrs. Ibsen who wrote the *Doll's House*. It was women, not men, who ostracized George Eliot ... But what we must absolutely insist upon is full and free recognition of the fact that, in spite of everything, the race and the nation must go on reproducing themselves. Whatever modifications we make must not interfere with that prime necessity. We will not aid or abet women as a sex in rebelling against maternity, or in quarrelling with the constitution of the solar system. Whether we have wives or not—and that is a minor point about which I, for one, am supremely unprejudiced—we must at least have mothers. And it would be well, if possible, to bring up those mothers as strong, as wise, as free, as sane, as healthy, as earnest, and as efficient as we can make them. If this is barren paradox, I am content to be paradoxical; if this is rank Toryism, I am content for once to be reckoned among the Tories.

G. Allen, 'Plain words on the woman question',
Fortnightly Review, October 1889

Part Two

Surplus Women and Emigration

Introduction

From the late 1840s there was growing concern at the 'surplus' or 'superfluous' women that threatened the image of women as dependent and protected. The sexual imbalance was partly structural and partly social—structural, because for every 1,000 men there were over 1,050 women (the result of higher child mortality among boys; and their loss by war, and by emigration which carried off three times as many men as women—124,000 to 41,000 in 1861); and partly social, since men were marrying later: over a quarter of all men were unmarried at the age of 30. As a result, two-thirds of all women between 20 and 24 were single in 1871, and 30 per cent of those aged between 24 and 35. Taking widows into account, for every three women over 20 who were wives, there were two who were widows or spinsters.

Many women and some men, therefore, demanded work for women who were forced to be self-dependent (see below, Part 3); but some suggested that women might emigrate and thus rectify the population imbalance.

From 1815, the government had provided assisted passages to the colonies. By 1860 some 5 million people had emigrated. Preference was given to single men and young couples; and older people, or families with several children, were rejected. Concerned to keep families together, Mrs Caroline Chisholm organized a Family Colonization Scheme (2.1); and where possible she introduced young friendless girls into the family groups to afford them protection on the journey and in the colony. Maria Rye's plans developed directly out of her work with her Society for Promoting the Employment of Women (2.2); flooded with applicants for law-copying work, she tried to place governesses in Australia and New Zealand. Her Society for Female Emigration assisted 160 women between 1861 and 1872. Emigration was an ambivalent 'solution' for many feminists with its implication that women were parasitic and unnecessary rather than oppressed, an ambivalence not eased by W. R. Greg's provocative pamphlet 'Why are women redundant?' (2.3) whose arguments for emigration were clearly anti-feminist. Frances Power Cobbe's retort was that his choice amounted to transportation or starvation for single women.

It was soon realized, however, that those who most needed to emigrate (the ill-educated unemployed middle-class women) were also the least suitable, and enough of them drifted back to England to suggest that Australia no more than England needed untrained women. So Maria Rye began to take out children (2.4); though within a few years there were worrying reports that the foster children were overworked by their 'parents', and the Local Government Board withdrew its support. The most robust reply to W. R. Greg came from Jessie Boucherett, Maria Rye's friend. She argued (2.5) that still more men should emigrate to vacate jobs for able-bodied but unemployed women.

Suggestions for further reading:
Margaret Kiddle, *Caroline Chisholm*, 1950; A. J. Hammerton, 'Feminism and female emigration 1861-1886', in M. Vicinus (ed.), *The Widening Sphere*, 1977.

2.1 Family Colonisation

In suggesting the Family Loan Society ... to the heads of families I now turn, and call before them young friendless girls and orphans; I have some on my list. I will ask those parents, 'Will you take charge of these young girls? Will you protect them on board ship?' ... That unprotected young women require guardianship on board vessels, I have only to call your attention ... to the case of the foundling orphan girls from Dublin, and bear in mind how they were sacrificed on board ship by merciless and unprincipled men; I invoke then, of all honest men and virtuous women, protection for these poor girls. How have I seen them agitated with fear when asking me what protection they were to have on board ship! Before, however, heads of families are asked to look after such young girls on board ship, and before they are entered into a Group ... every inquiry should be made as to the character of young girls, so that families may without fear introduce them to their children. The getting up and arranging of such a meeting as this—the grouping of the families, and creating that intimacy between them which is so necessary, may be easily arranged by any benevolent gentleman or lady. The Groups when once thus associated, may keep together when they even get to Australia; they may help each other and form what I call bush-partnerships ... This grouping of families, this system of guardianship I have been working it out on a miniature scale during the last two years, by getting emigrant families to meet at my own residence, making them acquainted with each other, and placing under their charge single females proceeding to the Colonies. Indeed, I consider family colonization to be the only safe and respectable system by which female emigration can be carried on. There is something in any other mode that does not harmonize with a woman's feelings.

Caroline Chisholm, *The A.B.C. of Colonization,* 1850

2.2 Emigration of Ladies

Soon after the establishment of the Society for Promoting the Employment of Women, remonstrances were made by no inconsiderable portion of the press against the movement ... [their advice being] 'Teach your *protegées* to emigrate; send them where the men want wives, the mothers want governesses, where the shopkeepers, the schools and the sick will thoroughly appreciate your exertions, and heartily welcome your women' ...

While I am happy to say that the Victoria Press and the Law-Copying Office are both mercantile successes ... my sympathies and my judgement lean every day more and more towards the establishment of some scheme, by which educated women may with safety be introduced into the colonies, and inclines, less and less, to their commencing new trades at home ... My office is besieged every day by applicants for work ... A short time since, 810 women applied for one situation of £15 per annum; still later (only ten days ago), 250 women applied for another vacancy of only £12 a year ... For my own part, I am convinced that this question will never be satisfactorily answered without the aid of emigration.

Maria Rye, *Emigration of Educated Women*, 1861, pp. 3-4

2.3   Redundant women

Deficiency of women over 20 years—United States 250,003
,,   ,,   ,,   Canadian Colonies 45,000
,,   ,,   ,,   ,, Australian Colonies 145,000
                                                              —————
                                                              440,000

Now the *excess* of women over twenty years of age in Great Britain in
1851, was 405,000. It appears, therefore, on the aggregate that more
women are wanted in those new countries which took their rise hence
than the mother country could supply them with. If the redundant
numbers *here* were transported thither, they would scarcely be filled,
and we should be denuded. Further, such an exodus, such a natural
rectification of disproportions, would reduce the unmarried adult
women in England and Wales from 1,000,000 to 660,000, from more
than a million to little over half a million . . .

We must restore by an emigration of women that natural
proportion between the sexes in the old country and in the new ones,
which was disturbed by an emigration of men, and the disturbance of
which has wrought so much mischief in both lands . . .

The first difficulty is chiefly mechanical. It is not easy to convey a
multitude of women across the Atlantic, or to the antipodes by any
ordinary means of transit. To transport the half million from where
they are redundant to where they are wanted, at an average of fifty
passengers in each ship, would require 10,000 vessels, or at least
10,000 voyages. Still, as 350,000 emigrants *have* left our shores in a
single year before now, and as we do not need and do not wish to
expatriate the whole number at once, or with any great rapidity, the
undertaking, though difficult, would seem to be quite possible . . . If
the mind of Australia and the mind of England are both adequately
impressed with the necessity of solving the problem in the natural
way,—if the 250,000 unmatched men in the colonies were determined
to have wives, and a proportionate number of unprotected women in
the mother country were determined to have husbands,—means could
and would be found of bringing the supply and demand together. The
subject has again been brought before the public by two ladies who are
pursuing a most useful career of judicious benevolence, for the service
and to the credit of their sex—Miss Emily Faithful and Miss Maria
Rye. They find plenty of women of all ranks willing and anxious to go
out; but as yet the funds are wanting and the organization is in its
infancy.

The second difficulty is of a different character. There can be no doubt that three or four hundred thousand women who are condemned to celibacy, struggle, and privation here, might, if transferred to the colonies or the United States, find in exchange a life, not indeed of ease, but of usefulness, happiness, domestic affection, reasonable comfort, and ultimate prosperity. But the *class* of women who are redundant here is not exactly the class wanted in the colonies, or specially adapted for colonial life. The women most largely wanted there would be found among the working classes, and in the lower ranks of the middle classes:—the women who are mostly redundant, the 'involuntary celibates' in England, are chiefly to be found in the upper and educated sections of society. Among the agricultural and manufacturing population, who earn their daily bread by daily labour, comparatively few women remain long or permanently single. It is those immediately and those far above them—who have a position to maintain and appearances to keep up, who are too proud to sink, too sensitive to contrive, too refined or too delicate to toil, or too spoiled to purchase love at the expense of luxury—that chiefly recruit the ranks of the old maids. The redundancy, in a word, is not in the emigrating class. This is true, no doubt; but we have two remarks to make in reference thereto. The first is, that a removal of superfluous numbers, in whatever rank, cannot fail gradually and indirectly to afford relief to the whole body corporate,—just as bleeding in the foot will relieve the head or the heart from distressing and perilous congestion. The second is, that we can see no reason, pride apart, why female emigration should not be proportionate from all ranks. Many gentlemen have gone to New Zealand and Australia, and many more to Canada, preferring a life of honourable industry and eventual abundance in a new country to hollow and pretentious penury at home:—why should not a relative number of ladies display similar good sense and sound appreciation of the *realities* of earthly felicity? The class of women, again, who perhaps are more extensively redundant in England than any other, are those *immediately* above the labouring poor, those who swell the ranks of 'distressed needlewomen', those who as milliners' apprentices so frequently fall victims to temptation or to toil, the daughters of unfortunate tradesmen, of poor clerks, or poorer curates. Now these, though neither as hardy nor as well trained for the severe labours of a colonial life as dairymaids, have all been disciplined in the appropriate school of poverty and exertion, and if their superior instruction and refinement added to their difficulties in one way, it would certainly smooth them in another; for of all qualities which education surely and universally confers, that of *adaptability* is the most remarkable.

W. R. Greg,
'Why are women redundant?', *National Review,* April 1862

2.4 Lessons Learned

Women who are only qualified to teach can only be required in societies already civilized. To be successful in a new country, it is as necessary for women as it is for men to be ready and able to set their hands to all things needful to the art of daily living ... It is much to be regretted that industrial schools similar to those which, we believe, already exist for young men, cannot be established in connection with this and other emigration societies, where, for three or four months before her departure for the colonies, a lady might make herself practically acquainted with these manual arts. If the school was in the country, so that some knowledge of kitchen-garden work and the management of a dairy could also be learned, its utility would be greatly increased. Are there no farm-houses still existing of the old-fashioned type, where intending lady emigrants could be boarded and instructed at a moderate rate? ...

A letter from St. Kilda, near Melbourne (1861), says:—'Any quantity of good servants would be gladly received, but they are just the class that people in England would be glad to keep themselves. The number of inefficient women sent out here is very great, and no registry office in London can show its rooms more full of waiting applicants than ours ... It is pitiable to see whole rows of young women who cannot take a bush situation, because they cannot milk or understand any of the duties of a country life.' ...

In 1862 Miss Rye ... set out for New Zealand with her first company of 100 female emigrants, of whom 8 were governesses, 30 factory girls, and the remainder domestic servants ... But the conviction grew on her that the difficulty of adapting grown women to the changed conditions of colonial life rendered it necessary that the greater number of emigrants should be children ...

In 1869 Miss Rye started with her first party of little workhouse girls. A house, near Niagara, in the west of Canada was purchased and furnished, where the children can remain, unless otherwise provided for, or in case of sickness. Since that time she has taken out more than 1,100 children, most of them girls; 502 of these have been taken to Canada within the last eighteen months. A committee of gentlemen in Canada exercise a vigilant watch over the children, who are thus placed out. 'The rule with respect to these children', says the Liverpool *Daily Post*, 'is that they become practically the adopted of those to whom they are sent. You see a rosy-cheeked girl seated at the farmer's table, and she talks about her father's cows, and how many horses "we" have got, and what "we" are going to do to-morrow, and it is not until your host takes you on one side and tells you that "the girl came from Miss Rye's place", that you for a moment fancy her anything but the real child of the good man. It would be easy to fill a column or two, with the advantages accruing to our colony from such a work. The climatic difficulty is overcome, as the children growing up in the heat and cold become thoroughly acclimatised. The greater difficulty arising from the paucity of labour is relieved, as a hardy race of workers are secured to the country.'*

The difficulty of collecting the children during the short visits Miss Rye has since paid to England caused the establishment of the Emigration Home for Destitute Little Girls, at Avenue House, Peckham, S.E. This was opened in July 1872, and little orphan or deserted girls from five to twelve years old are gathered in, and unless claimed by friends which rarely happens, are drafted off to Canada along with the workhouse children which every large city is anxious to place under Miss Rye's care. The rule of the Home is not to take children over fourteen years of age, and it is worthy of observation that the very few instances where the children sent out have not turned out well have occurred among the older girls, whose habits and principles were formed before their admittance. Help by subscriptions, by children's clothes, old and new, and by volunteer workers, who will either undertake to start small branch homes, or to hunt up and bring in stray children to the Home, are much needed to carry on the good work with increased energy.

In conclusion, we have before us the choice of two ways in which female emigration may be satisfactorily managed—either as Miss Rye is doing, by taking away the forlorn and deserted children before they grow up into an idle, ignorant and vicious class of society, and placing them in homes where they are valued, cared for, and trained up in useful and industrious habits, or by establishing industrial schools in this country for adult untrained emigrants, where they can, *before starting*, acquire a knowledge of the hand-work, without which the head-work for which they are already qualified will too often be but a little use to them.

'Emigration', *Englishwoman's Review*, 1874, pp. 96, 102

*490 farmers have had children from the Home at Niagara, 159 tradesmen and 252 in other professions.

2.5 Surplus Men

The reason of the distress among women is, that men have not emigrated as much as they ought to do. In consequence, the wages in almost all trades which are not protected by trades unions, and especially in agricultural labour, have been driven down so far by competition, that in several counties, men cannot maintain their wives and families, and the wives are forced to go out to work to add to the men's earnings; numbers of men have also engaged in women's trades and taken possession of them; thus the women's labour market has been invaded from both sides, and crowds of women have been rendered superfluous . . .

The plan then which I advocate for providing for superfluous women is that of allowing them to engage freely in all occupations suited to their strength . . . thus converting them into useful members of society.

Jessie Boucherett, 'How to provide for superfluous women', in Josephine Butler (ed.), *Woman's Work and Woman's Culture,* 1869

Part Three

Women at Work

Introduction

At the beginning of the nineteenth century, women's waged work was limited and growing less: agriculture, domestic service, textiles, needlework and governessing. By 1861 some two-fifths of working women were in service, and a further two-fifths in textiles and clothing. But in the last quarter of the century, new occupations for women developed. Certain 'domestic' work came to be done outside the home; servants were supplemented by charladies and laundries, by commercially prepared food and clothing. And the mother's traditional care of children and of the sick devolved to professional teachers and professional nurses. A second major trend was the growth of the tertiary sector, retailing and clerical work. A third was the growth of sweating, explored by Mayhew in the 1840s but now on the increase, as marginal employers farmed work out of the factory back into the working-class home (see 3.5.3 below). Finally, the enlarged educational opportunities for women slowly allowed them to enter public service and the professions. Medicine was the first to be opened.

Recognising the problem of 'surplus women' (see above, Part 2) Boyd-Kinnear argued that women's labour was both necessary and desirable (3.1.1) but commentators regularly distinguished between work for ladies which was physiologically damaging, and work for women which was economically desirable (3.1.2; see also Elizabeth Garrett Anderson, 1.4.2 above).

Agriculture was a traditional employer of women, some 144,000 in 1851, falling to 50,000 in 1881 (3.2). The most skilled work was dairy work; field work, which women shared with children, included turnip and potato pulling, fruit and hop picking, hoeing and haymaking, at from 6d to 8d a day. Field work was regarded as unseemly. At its worst, in the depopulated parishes of East Anglia it gave rise to the gang system (3.2.1) with its long treks to work, its brutality and its improprieties. The 1867 Gang Acts prohibited mixed public gangs. Field work in any case unsuited women for their natural labour, domestic service (3.2.2). The Royal Commission of 1867 inquired whether agricultural hours should be regulated but concluded that it was unnecessary since women's work was seasonal and declining.

Domestic service (waged and unwaged) was the yardstick against which other female occupations were measured for their suitability. Private, personal and a 'service', most men thought it a highly attractive occupation for women (3.3.1; see also W. R. Greg, 1.2.4 above). It employed 1½ million women in 1875, mainly rural girls, three-quarters of whom were to become general servants. Barely literate country girls of 14 or 15, clumsy, lonely, untrained and home-sick, were confronted with the hard labour of houses without plumbing, clean heating or mechanical aids (3.3.2). In 1861 Mrs Beeton estimated that a maid-of-all-work could obtain £9 to £14 a year, plus board; upper servants between £15 and £25 a year. Frances Power Cobbe called for a contractual rather than a patriarchal relation between employer and employed (3.3.3) but this was not sufficient to overcome the distaste for domestic service of independent working women (3.3.4).

Needlework, millinery and dressmaking (3.4) was estimated to occupy some 600,000 women in 1861. Even in the better and more fashionable workshops (3.4.1), the hours and conditions of work destroyed girls' health; and in the better paid fields, destroyed men's trades (3.4.2). It was work of last resort, since, in Milne's words, 'all women are milliners ... it is this competition at home that brings down wages' (*The Social and Industrial Position of Women,* 1857, pp. 185-6). Mayhew's investigations for the *Morning Chronicle* in the late 1840s revealed the total destitution of sweated slop workers (3.4.3). Some modest efforts at self help were made to organise female co-operatives (3.4.4), but paying a living wage produced goods too expensive to sell. The invention of the sewing machine brought more clothing into the factories, but its cheapening to around £8, the need to hand finish garments and the impact of factory and workshop regulation, meant a growth in sweating and slop work in the last decades of the century (3.4.5) for which neither combination nor legislation seemed an appropriate remedy.

Factory work, for the first half of the century, meant textiles (3.5) and here women enjoyed unique legal protection. By 1847, some 300,000 women factory workers, along with children, had been granted a ten-hour day, together with inspection of their conditions of work, as a result of the (male) short time movements of the 1830s and 1840s. This in turn both made female labour more expensive and reduced men's hours along with their own. Not that factory conditions were particularly bad, but factories were highly visible and were substantial employers of children, the main concern of the philan-thropists. The textile unions in the 1840s argued that women should be excluded from factories altogether so that (men's) domestic comfort might be improved (3.5.1), thus fuelling later feminist suspicion about the motives of any trade union advocating greater legislative protection for women. Political economists (3.5.2) denied that factory women were demoralised by their labour, at least by the (revealing) tests of pauperism and prostitution. The next fifty years were to see the Factory Acts extended to wider and wider areas of work: to dangerous trades such as lucifer matches and cartridges; in 1867 to workshops where less than fifty people worked, and in 1891 to domestic workshops, though out-work in the home remained beyond control. But as factories were regulated first, even though better conditions prevailed there, and more stringently than in smaller workshops, marginal employers (3.5.3) sought to evade controls by relying first on workshop and then increasingly on domestic outwork. Suspecting, not without justification, the motives of trade union support for greater regulation of women's labour, the feminists did manage to exclude workshops and laundries from the more stringent factory regulations. However, factory production itself continued to grow. And while textile workers usually enjoyed fairly high wages and equal pay, it was estimated in the 1890s that 30 per cent of factory workers now earned less than 8s a week, and only 10 per cent of them earned over 15s a week. And all factory workers needed constant inspection to ensure that their working conditions did not deteriorate (3.5.4). Particularly notorious was the nail and chain making of the Black Country (3.5.5) with its very heavy labour, unhealthy conditions, and very low pay. This was to become one of the first trades to be regulated by trade boards in 1910, after Mary MacArthur organised a triumphant strike of women chainworkers at Cradley Heath, and with it the recognition that the State could ensure a minimum wage. Some of the most effective and energetic guardians of women's labour were the newly appointed women factory inspectors. Established after the Royal Commission on Employment in 1891/2, five strong in 1897, they had become twenty-one by 1914. Adelaide Anderson (3.5.6), chief woman inspector, emphasised their willingness to play detective in London back streets at night and to take large employers to court by day to ensure that women's legal rights were observed.

Laundries, it was estimated, employed 175,000 women by the 1890s, working extremely long hours in hot and humid conditions and with dangerous machinery (3.6). Not until 1907 were they brought within the regulations of workshops.

Retailing was to become an even more substantial employer of women. The small shop with its skilled work (blending its own tea, for example), employing an apprenticed shopman, was to recede before the larger store employing several assistants selling packaged goods. Where the wage bill was significant and the work light and women were customers, as in clothing, food and flowers, there women were employed. The number of shops doubled to half a million; the number of women shop assistants from an estimated 87,000 in 1861 to 250,000 by 1901. Their hours were very long (up to ninety hours a week), their pay low, the standing very wearying, the fines heavy, and the living-in resented. The Early Closing League and Sir John Lubbock tried to reduce their hours; but feminists like Miss Boucherett were convinced that women would be replaced by men (3.7.1). Others would have preferred the equivalent of licensing hours (3.7.2). The career of a shop assistant (3.7.3) shows part of the sequence of jobs taken by one girl between 1887 and 1889. In 1886 the hours of young persons were nominally limited to seventy-four hours a week; not until 1913 was a maximum working week of sixty-four hours established. Despite the efforts of the two great women trade unionists, Margaret Bondfield and Mary MacArthur, the 'genteel' natures of shop assistants made them hard to unionise into self-help (see below, 3.13.6).

Education was always an approved occupation for women. In 1850, some 21,000 governesses enjoyed insecure status and poor pay (3.8.1). The whole higher education movement for women (see below, Part 4) stemmed from the Governesses' Benevolent Association which in 1847 was to open Queen's College to educate women to educate. Elementary education for working-class children recruited a different class of girl, the artisan's daughter, who then went on to obtain better pay and prospects than many governesses. Miss Burdett-Coutts, the wealthy philanthropist, urged that middle-class girls should enter the field (3.8.2) to the dismay of many who gave evidence to the Newcastle Commission on elementary education in 1861 (3.8.3), as they feared women teachers were already holding themselves too aloof from the realities of labouring life. By 1861 women were 80,000 of the country's 110,000 teachers; by 1901, 172,000 out of 230,000, of which perhaps half were fully trained and certificated, and earning around 75 per cent of the male rate. It was one of the few jobs that could be combined with family life (3.8.4), though men teachers made determined efforts to exclude married women from the work. The National Union of Teachers (3.8.5) was one of the first and most effective professional unions, though it recruited few women country members.

Nursing, like teaching, experienced the same discussion over its recruits and their training. But nursing had Florence Nightingale, perhaps the most remarkable of all Victorian women. Of upper middle class background, cousin of Barbara Bodichon, after protracted rows with her family she acquired a nursing training at Kaisersworth, the deaconesses' home in Germany. The Crimean War in 1854, together with her close friendship with Sidney Herbert, Secretary of State at War, allowed her to lead a miscellaneous and unruly band of nurses and religious sisters out to the East where, in the teeth of male medical opposition, she transformed the nursing situation (3.9.1). On her return she was a national heroine and became for the rest of her life the authority consulted by politicians and doctors alike on all matters of health, nurses' training, sanitary reform, poor law medical reform, a statistician and surrogate architect for hospitals and barracks. With the money collected as a memorial to her, she established the Nightingale Training School in 1860, attached to St Thomas's.

Hospitals were for the sick poor: the better off were better and more safely nursed at home. And those sick poor who were chronic, handicapped, incurable or geriatric cases were to be found in the workhouse wards (for workhouse and district nursing, see 8.7 below). Under nurses were essentially domestic servants with a rough practical knowledge (3.9.2) acquired on the job. Florence Nightingale recruited girls of some education and high moral character, either as unpaid lady pupils for a one-year training, or as two-year salaried probationers; they attended lectures and took examinations as well as worked in the wards, under the watchful eye of a lady matron. Her nurses in turn went on to become matrons elsewhere, training girls in their turn. By 1901 there were some 64,000 nurses and midwives, half of them working in private homes, some 10,000 working in mental and 16,000 in general hospitals. About 10,000 would have been fully trained. The untrained were mainly elderly widows. Florence Nightingale made nursing a career fit for ladies. From the late 1880s, the former matron of St Bartholomews', Mrs Fenwick, organised the British Nurses' Association, in an attempt to make nursing a self-regulating profession (3.9.4). Their specific requirement was for registration, from which amateur and incompetent nurses would be excluded. Florence Nightingale lent her immense authority to the opposition, since she believed that nursing required moral qualities not assessable by public examination; and that a register would not distinguish between the bad nurse and the good; only the testimonial of the hospital from which she had received training could do that. Not until 1919 did the qualification of SRN denote the trained nurse, as scrutinised by the General Nursing Council.

Medicine (3.10) was the male profession most attractive to women, with its affinities to nursing, its care of women and children (3.10.1), its status and its rewards. Elizabeth Blackwell was the first woman in the United States to qualify, and her public lectures (3.10.1) directly inspired Elizabeth Garrett to seek training. But the British Medical Register in 1860 excluded anyone from practising as an MD who possessed a foreign medical degree, and as women were excluded from English universities, an English MD was impossible to get. However, by buying private tuition, Elizabeth Garrett qualified for the diploma of the Apothecaries' Society which gave her a licence to practise in 1865 (and went on to acquire her MD from Paris in 1869). But the Apothecaries promptly changed their constitution to exclude all subsequent women. The real battle to open up medicine for women was to be fought by Sophia Jex-Blake who was to meet bitter and violent male hostility (3.10.2). A small group of women students gathered at Edinburgh, and persuaded some professors to teach them, and others to open their classes to them. But when the men students themselves turned on the women (3.10.3) Edinburgh refused to allow them to qualify. In 1876 Russell Gurney, that staunch proponent of women's rights, obtained a parliamentary bill permitting universities to grant women degrees; Dublin then opened to women, where Sophia Jex-Blake qualified in 1877, followed by the University of London. Despite their mutual dislike, she worked with Elizabeth Garrett to found the London School of Medicine and then opened a medical school herself in Edinburgh. Teaching hospitals were persuaded to accept women medical students and within ten years the battle had been won (3.10.4).

The ladies of Langham Place had early appreciated that clerical work was particularly suitable for women. Maria Rye and Jessie Boucherett had by the mid 1860s placed a few women through their Society for Promoting the Employment of Women into appropriate work (3.11.2). With the growth of large commercial firms in the later part of the century, and the associated growth of insurance, banking and communications; and aided by shorthand and typing (both becoming widely used in the 1880s), opportunities for women expanded. The post office was the first, and remained the largest, government department to employ women (3.11.1), and telegraphy proved another suitable field (3.11.3). From 6,000 women in 1881, the census recorded nearly 60,000 women clerks in 1901 in private firms, and 25,000, mainly in the post office, in government employ. Wages varied according to skills, from 10s a week to the £2 a week and upwards paid to educated secretaries. For the most part it was easy, light, respectable work, but with poor pay, little prospects and usually a marriage bar.

Clara Collet, herself one of the Assistant Commissioners in 1893, surveyed the field of women's work at the end of the century (3.12). Single working women, she argued, were not 'surplus' but economically and socially valuable. 'There is no hardship in women working for a living', she wrote; 'the hardship lies in not getting a living when they work for it' (*Educated Working Women*, 1902, p. 23). That was because parents too willingly subsidised their daughters, who in turn refused to organise and unionise.

Until the 1870s, the only women unionists appear to have been those passively enrolled into men's textile unions. Emma Paterson, herself by training a bookbinder, was impressed by American women's unions, and in 1874 founded the Women's Protective and Provident League (3.13.1). Four years later she had some 600 members, half of them bookbinders, the rest in dressmaking unions, all in the Holborn area of London. With the aid of Lady Dilke, the WPPL slowly extended into the provinces, its workers organising women's unions among Leicester hosiery workers, Glasgow tailoresses, jam and pickle makers, shop assistants, cigar makers; and equally slowly its friendly society role gave way to a more explicitly trade union concern with wages. At her death in 1886, Emma Paterson left some thirty small unstable unions with a total membership of around 3,000 (compared to the 30,000 women enrolled in textile unions). In 1889 the WPPL became the Women's Trade Union League; and with the arrival, first of Margaret Bondfield, of the shop workers, and then of Mary MacArthur, her close friend, who was to become secretary of the WTUL in 1903, both of them socialist, the League went on to the attack. By 1906, 167,000 women were trade unionists (of whom 143,000 were in the textile unions); by 1914 that figure had doubled.

Despite Arabella Shore's work, the trade union movement held aloof from the suffrage movement (3.13.2). However, Emma Paterson had obtained affiliation to the TUC in 1875, and in 1877 persuaded the men to recognise that only when women organised to obtain equal conditions with men would they no longer form a cheap labour reserve, always sucking down men's trades into the swamp of sweating (3.13.3). The tailors accordingly changed their annual resolution from 'The Society would use its strength against the increasing employment of women in the tailoring trades' in 1877 to 'That the work of women must be recognized and the time has now arrived when it should be organized and properly remunerated'. But for men and women organisers alike it was a desperately difficult struggle to persuade women to take trade union organisation seriously (3.13.6). One of the most dramatic strikes was that of the match-girls in 1888 (3.13.4). Annie Besant published the dividends of Bryant and May shareholders in contrast to the girls' wages. When the girls refused to repudiate her articles in *Link*, and their leaders were victimised, 1,400 girls came out on strike. Annie Besant, Herbert Burrows and Clementina Black of the WPPL (later the first woman factory inspector) unionised the girls, arranged their strike fund (which came to some £400), and persuaded the London Trades Council to intervene and negotiate with the Company's directors. Within a fortnight, the girls had won.

Women associated with the suffrage movement and other women's causes had long denounced any state intervention to protect women, claiming that this made women into children, pushed them out of the labour market to the benefit of men in work and men's comfort at home, and reduced women to still greater dependence on their husbands (3.14.1). But being single women, and middle-class women as most of them were, they failed to perceive that the working woman's world was the well-being of her family, and not just herself, and that self-help was the weapon of the strong and not of the weak. Beatrice Webb makes it clear (3.14.2) that legislation was not an alternative to combination but a preliminary to it. Women trade unionists were to insist that trades unionism was not enough.

The central problem of women's work remained. In a half-century where male unemployment was estimated to run at around 10 per cent and deteriorating in bad times, for most work there was a labour surplus, a labour reserve, always available to undercut existing rates. Most women worked in women-only jobs, weak, unskilled, unorganised, very badly paid. But whenever they sought to improve their pay and their prospects by entering male fields, they merely added to the labour reserve and pulled down male rates to their own level. Not surprisingly, men fought off the entry of unorganised women into their trades, just as half a century before the Owenite unions had fought off the swamping of artisan trades by the semi-skilled. It was the coming of full employment in the twentieth century that was to transform men's wage rates; women had to wait another half-century for the legislation of the 1970s.

Suggestions for further reading:

E. Richards, 'Women in the British economy since 1700', *History,* 1974; N. McKendrick, 'Home demand and economic growth', in *Historical Perspectives in Honour of J. H. Plumb,* 1974. On agriculture, J. Kitteringham, 'Country girls in nineteenth century England', *History Workshop* I; P. Horn, *The Victorian Country Child,* 1974; F. Thompson, *Lark Rise to Candleford,* 1939. On domestic service, P. Horn, *The Rise and Fall of the Victorian Servant,* 1975. On factory labour, I. Pinchbeck, *Women Workers in the Industrial Revolution,* 1930; M. Hewitt, *Wives and Mothers in Victorian Industry,* 1958; S. Alexander, 'Women's work in London 1820-1850', in J. Mitchell and A. Oakley (eds), *The Rights and Wrongs of Women,* 1977; B. Hutchins and A. Harrison, *History of Factory Legislation,* 1903; J. Schmiechen, 'State reform and the local economy', *Economic History Review,* 1974. On Mayhew's investigations into the slop trade, E. Thompson and E. Yeo, *The Unknown Mayhew,* 1971.

On white-collar work, L. Holcombe, *Victorian Ladies at Work,* 1973; B. Abel-Smith, *A History of the Nursing Profession,* 1960; C. Woodham-Smith, *Florence Nightingale,* 1950; Asher Tropp, *The Schoolteachers,* 1957; J. Manton, *Elizabeth Garrett Anderson,* 1965; M. Todd, *Sophia Jex-Blake,* 1918.

On trade unionism, B. Drake, *Women in trade unions,* 1920; S. Lewenhak, *Women and Trade Unions,* 1977; H. Goldman, *Emma Paterson,* 1974; A. Stafford, *A Match to Fire the Thames,* 1961 (match-girls); N. Soldon, *Women in British Trade Unions 1874-1976,* 1978.

Women's Work (G.B.)

	1851	1901
domestic service, laundry work	1,135,000	2,003,000
agriculture	229,000	86,000
mining, quarrying	11,000	6,000
metal work	36,000	84,000
wood, furniture	8,000	30,000
bricks, cement, pottery, glass	15,000	37,000
chemicals, soap, etc.	4,000	31,000
skins, leather, hair, feathers	5,000	27,000
paper, printing	16,000	111,000
textiles	635,000	795,000
clothing (sewing, gloves, shoes)	491,000	792,000
food, drink, tobacco	53,000	216,000
professional (teachers, nurses, clerks)	106,000	429,000
others	88,000	104,000
total occupied women	2,832,000	4,751,000
total unoccupied women	5,294,000	10,229,000
total occupied work force (male and female)	9,377,000	16,229,000

Women's trade unionism (G.B.)

	1876	1906
textiles	19,000	143,000
clothing	100	5,082
printing	300	977
pottery	—	530
food and tobacco	—	2,447
distributive	—	4,920
clerical	—	5,315
general labour	100	2,674
metal unions	—	484
various	—	996
	19,500	166,425

3.1 Work for Women and ladies

3.1.1 *Women's need to work*

Women must live. To live they must be fed; and to be fed involves the labour of some one ... Many women have fathers, brothers, or husbands, who provide for them. But we also know too well that there are many women who ... have not only to work for themselves, but who have to work for the maintenance of others dependent on them ...

By the progress of science and the new forms of social existence, that position [of self-support] has been taken from women. Machinery spins, weaves, grinds, and even where women can still gain employment in connexion with machine-labour, it is no longer exclusively their own, no longer domestic, but it exposes them to competition and forces them to compete. Other avocations, such as baking and brewing, once the toil of separate households, are now carried on upon a large scale in manufactories, and men have wholly displaced women from them. Meantime emigration, the source of infinite benefit and the relief from infinite suffering, carries off far more men than women; and while it increases the proportion of women left at home, it diminishes the number of the households in which women can find work. The higher standard of comfort now prevalent disinclines men to marry so early as they used in olden times, and the spread of luxury in an equal degree withholds women of the upper ranks from marriage till suitable establishments are offered to them. But every such restraint of marriage diminishes the field open to women of the humbler classes in domestic service. Gradually also some of the coarser and rougher trades in which women have heretofore worked along with men are, either by direct legislation (as in mines, etc.) or by the influence of public opinion, closed against them ... Thus from every rank and every class of women there rises up the cry that work is wanted and that no work is to be had ...

Whatever needs delicacy, taste, accuracy, what can be done indoors, by the fireside, or in suitable workshops, and what does not need a great deal of manual strength, can, as we all know be done as well by women as by men. Then why should women not do it? Because some of the men will need to resort to other employments? Then let them. There are employments in which, besides skill, strength is needed, and in which they will have no rivalry. What folly in them to reject such employments in order that they may do a woman's work, and drive a woman out of work! ... both male and female work will in fact, when dealt with alike, form one fund, which will be apportioned, according to the irresistible laws of political economy, in such a way as to equalize the rate of wages in proportion to skill, trouble, and risk . . .

J. Boyd-Kinnear, 'The social position of women',
in Josephine Butler (ed.),
Woman's Work and Woman's Culture, 1869

3.1.2 *Work for women but not for ladies*

1. Those wild schemers . . . who would throw open the professions to women, and teach them to become lawyers and physicians and professors, know little of life and less of physiology. The brain and the frame of woman are formed with admirable suitability to their appropriate work, for which subtlety and sensitiveness, not strength and tenacity of fibre are required. The cerebral organization of the female is far more delicate than that of man; the continuity and severity of application needed to acquire real *mastery* in any profession, or over any science, are denied to women, and can never with impunity be attempted by them; mind and health would almost invariably break down under the task . . .

2. We are not at all disposed to echo the cry of those who object to women and girls engaging in this or that industrial career, on the ground that they thus reduce the wages and usurp the employment of the other sex. Against female compositors, tailors, telegraph-workers, and factory-hands this objection has been especially urged. We apprehend that it is founded on an obvious economical misconception. It is an objection to the principle of *competition* in the abstract . . . It is clearly a waste of strength, a superfluous extravagance, an economic blunder, to employ a powerful and costly machine to do work which can be as well done by a feebler and a cheaper one. Women and girls are less costly operatives than men: what they can do with equal efficiency, it is therefore wasteful and foolish (*economically considered*) to set a man to do . . . If only men had been employed in cotton mills, calicoes would have cost three times as much per yard as at present; the population of England would have been smaller by some millions; our ships and commerce would have been proportionally restricted; and distant countries would have been far more inadequately clothed than they actually are. If there be any objection to the employment of women and children in manufacturing or other analogous sorts of labour, it must be based exclusively upon social or moral considerations . . . The employment of married women in factory labour is undoubtedly an evil; but it is so because they continue it after they are mothers, when it does not pay,—and because it disables them from making their husbands' homes comfortable, and from laying out their earnings with economy and skill.

W. R. Greg,
'Why are women redundant?', *National Review,* April 1862

It is said that the exclusion of women from political life, and from every form of intellectual activity, implies on the part of men a deep reverence for the female sex. Women are too good and too pure to be mixed up with the struggles of this wicked world. This view of the matter is most hypocritical. While women may not be doctors they may be nurses; while they may not engage in legal practice, they may scrub legal offices. It would be grossly unbecoming in them to drive to a polling-booth and quietly record their votes; but it is quite right and proper, if their means be scanty, to trudge through slush, and under rain or snow, as visiting governesses. It is not through respect, but through contempt, that women are debarred from every pursuit bestowing wealth and honour—for if men could, they would prevent women from obtaining artistic or literary employment—and are confined exclusively to those callings which are so laborious and so ill-paid that men scorn to engage in them.

N. J. Gossam, *A Plea for the Ladies*, 1875, p. 14

3.2   Agriculture

3.2.1   *Agricultural gangs*
The extensive employment of women and children in rural labour had
its rise in two causes; first, in the extensive reclamation of waste lands;
and secondly in the destruction of cottages and the consequent
removal of the people which inhabited them, rendering labour
difficult to procure, and imposing upon the farmer the necessity of
obtaining it through the instrumentality of a middle man, who made it
his business to supply it at a cheap rate, gaining his living by
organizing bands of women, young persons, and children, of whom
he became the temporary master. And the 'gangs' so constituted have
in some districts displaced the labour of men, and the system is
favoured by the farmers for its economy no less than for its
convenience . . .

The employment of women in gangs has a very decided influence in
increasing the rate of infant mortality . . . Girls quickly become
depraved . . . It seems almost an impossibility that a girl who has
worked for a single season in a gang can become a modest and
respectable woman . . . The effect of gangs on the married women
employed in them is destructive of all the domestic virtues. Absent
from their homes from seven in the morning until late in the evening,
they return jaded and dispirited and unwilling to make any further
exertions. The husband finds the cottage untidy, the evening meal
unprepared, the children querulous and disobedient, his wife dirty and
ill-tempered, and his home so thoroughly uncomfortable that he not
unnaturally takes refuge in the public house.

That which seems most to lower the moral tone of the elder girls
employed in gangs is the feeling of independence which takes
possession of them as soon as they can find remunerative occupation
in the field. They feel at once that they are emancipated from all
parental control, and no longer bound to submit themselves to their
teachers or their spiritual pastors and masters. Gregarious employment, too, almost inevitably induces boldness of deportment and
impudence of manner . . . The behaviour and language of women and
girls in gangs is such that a respectable man, of whatever age, if he
meets them, cannot venture to speak to, scarcely even to look at them,
without the risk of being shocked.

'Agricultural gangs',
Quarterly Review, vol. 123, 1867, pp. 173-90

3.2.2   *Women as agricultural labourers*
Watling, Sarah of Tivetshall St. Margaret's, labourer's wife. Husband

works for Mr. Spelman; has eight children alive; three at home, a girl of 11½, a girl of eight, and a boy of five. Her daughter of 11½ accompanies her to work in the field. Lives in a cottage with three chambers; thinks that, with a family, you must have that number of chambers to live respectably. Her five eldest children can read, and can write a letter home. They had a little schooling at a private school, and then improved themselves at home. As soon as they could earn, was glad to take them into the fields; could not have brought up her family without. Wouldn't like to take a girl into the fields before 10 or 11. Has one girl now in service, who worked with her for two or three years in the fields; couldn't have got her clothes to go out in unless she had. Wouldn't have one of her girls join a gang. If a girl works in the fields, she should work under her mother's eye. Thinks that a girl of 17 or 18 is best in service. Has had a sober husband, and so has been able to keep out of debt.

Royal Commission on the Employment of Children,
Young Persons and Women in Agriculture, 1867, vol. I, p. 197

It is universally admitted that such employment [upon the farm] is to a great extent demoralizing. Not only does it almost unsex a woman, in dress, gait, manners, character, making her rough, coarse, clumsy, masculine; but it generates a further very pregnant social mischief, by unfitting or indisposing her for a woman's proper duties at home. Some of the work on which women are frequently employed, such as serving the threshing machine, weeding high wet corn, drawing turnips or mangolds, is work to which, on physical grounds, they never ought to be put at all. Exposure to wet or cold, from which no farm labour can claim exemption, is likely, owing to the greater susceptibility of the female constitution, to be specially injurious to them. The farmers, almost to a man, complain of the difficulty of getting dairymaids and other domestic servants; and almost to a man again, express the opinion that the proper place for a young single girl is in a household, and not upon the land. It is admitted that the inter-mixture of the sexes is one great cause of demoralization; yet such is the nature of farm work that it would be very difficult even by the best contrived arrangement—it would be almost impossible by legislation—to secure effective separation . . .

In the case of young girls it is admitted further, that farm labour indisposes them for domestic service, both by unfitting them for it and also be generating in them a spirit of independence and a dislike of control . . . [However] not a fifth part of the number of women is employed upon the farms in Gloucester, Essex and Sussex that was employed upon them twenty-five years ago. Many forms of labour—driving carts, for instance,—which they undertook without reluctance then, nothing probably would persuade them to undertake now. The more extensive introduction of machinery is likely to supersede much female, and indeed much juvenile, labour ... From all that I have been able to learn, I do not believe that there is any necessity to limit the hours of work in the case of women and girls ...

Rev. J. Fraser, on Norfolk, Essex, Sussex,
loc. cit., vol. I (Asst. Cmmssr.), pp. 16-17

[Most girls go into service.] Those who continue as young women to work in the fields are very few; and there is generally something against them, either they are deformed or deaf and dumb, or they are girls whom service has not suited; some have had what is called 'a misfortune' in the country districts ...

With married women the case is very different. They do not work out as much as formerly ... most of them only come out for hay-making, harvest, and to work among the turnips and mangolds, which last always seem to be considered the principal women's work ... In some cases the employer will stipulate that she is to come out at such times ... Little or no profit accrues to herself. Her wages are only 8d a day for out-door work and against that she has to set the wear and tear of clothes, the need of more food to support her, the payment to persons employed to make clothes, which she would make herself if at home, and the damage done to house and furniture by children left at home to take care of themselves ... With unmarried women there can be little doubt that working with men and boys, hearing bad language, and seeing sights among the beasts that they had better not see, cannot be for their good ... whereas the work of married women, usually in the fields, is either shared only by other women or by their husbands ...

In some parishes it is only the more old-fashioned, who have been accustomed to work, that keep it on now. The farmers naturally, do not approve of the change; it is an extensive source of cheap labour that is gradually being drawn away from them. But with the spread of education and general improvement the labouring class are beginning to see that the woman's place is by her own fireside.

Mr R. F. Boyle on Somersetshire,
loc. cit., vol. II (Asst. Cmmssr.), pp. 123-4

3.3 Domestic Service

3.3.1 *The charms of domestic service*
The situation of a domestic servant ... is attended with considerable comfort. With abundant work it combines a wonderful degree of liberty, discipline, health, physical comfort, good example, regularity, room for advancement, encouragement to acquire saving habits. The most numerous class of depositors in the Savings Banks is that of domestic servants. The situation frequently involves much responsibility, and calls forth the best features of character. Kind attachment in return for honest service is not uncommon with the master or mistress; and an honest pride in the relation springs up on both sides and lasts throughout life.

J. D. Milne, *The Industrial and Social Position of Women*, 1857
(1870 edn), p. 199

3.3.2 *The Maid-of-all-Work*
The general servant, or maid-of-all-work, is perhaps the only one of her class deserving of commiseration: her life is a solitary one, and in some places, her work is never done. She is also subject to rougher treatment than either the house or kitchen-maid, especially in her earlier career: she starts in life, probably a girl of thirteen, with some small tradesman's wife as her mistress, just a step above her in the social scale ... by the time she has become a tolerable servant, she is probably engaged in some respectable tradesman's house, where she has to rise with the lark, for she has to do in her own person all the work which in larger establishments is performed by cook, kitchen-maid, and housemaid, and occasionally the part of a footman's duty, which consists in carrying messages.

The general servant's duties commence by opening the shutters ... she should then brush up her kitchen-range, light the fire, clear away the ashes, clean the hearth, and polish with a leather the bright parts of the range, doing all as rapidly and as vigorously as possible, that no more time is wasted than is necessary. After putting on the kettle, she should then proceed to the dining-room or parlour to get it in order for breakfast. She should first roll up the rug, take up the fender, shake and fold up the table-cloth, then sweep the room, carrying the dirt towards the fireplace; a coarse cloth should then be laid down over the carpet and she should proceed to clean the grate, having all her utensils close to her. When the grate is finished, the ashes cleared away, the hearth cleaned, and the fender put back in its place, she must dust the furniture, not omitting the legs of the tables and chairs . . . After the rug is put down, the table-cloth arranged, and everything in order, she should lay the cloth for breakfast, and then shut the dining-room door.

The hall must now be swept, the mats shaken, the door-step cleaned, and any brass knockers or handles polished up with the leather. If the family breakfast very early, the tidying of the hall must be deferred till after that meal. After cleaning the boots that are absolutely required, the servant should now wash her hands and face, put on a clean white apron, and be ready for her mistress when she comes downstairs . . .

She will now carry the urn into the dining-room, where her mistress will make the tea or coffee and cooks, if required, the bacon, kidneys, fish, etc.;—if cold meat is to be served, she must always send it to table on a clean dish, and nicely garnished with tufts of parsley, if this is obtainable.

After she has had her own breakfast, and whilst the family are finishing theirs, she should go upstairs into the bedrooms, open all the windows, strip the clothes off the beds, and leave them to air whilst she is clearing away the breakfast things. She should then take up the crumbs in a dustpan from under the table, put the chairs in their places, and sweep up the hearth.

The breakfast things washed up, the kitchen be tidied, so that it may be neat when her mistress comes in to give the orders for the day; after receiving these orders, the servant should go upstairs again, with a jug of boiling water, the slop-pail, and two cloths. After emptying the slops, and scalding the vessels with the boiling water, and wiping them thoroughly dry, she should wipe the top of the wash-table and arrange it all in order. She then proceeds to make the beds, in which occupation she is generally assisted by the mistress, or, if she have any daughters, by one of them. Before commencing to make the bed, the servant should put on a large bed-apron, kept for this purpose only, which should be made very wide, to button round the waist and meet behind, while it should be made as long as the dress. By adopting this plan, the blacks and dirt on servants' dresses (which at all times it is impossible to help) will not rub off on to the bed-sheets, mattresses, and bed furniture. When the beds are made, the rooms should be dusted, the stairs lightly swept down, hall furniture, closets, etc. dusted. The lady of the house, when there is but one servant kept, frequently takes charge of the drawing-room herself, that is to say, dusting it; the servant sweeping, cleaning windows, looking-glasses, grates, and rough work of that sort. If there are many ornaments and knick-knacks about the room, it is certainly better for the mistress to dust these herself, as a maid-of-all-work's hands are not always in a condition to handle delicate ornaments.

Now the servant goes to her kitchen to see about the cooking of the dinner. She should put on a coarse apron with a bib to do her dirty work in, which may be easily replaced by a white one if required. Half an hour before dinner is ready, she should lay the cloth. After taking in the dinner, when everyone is seated, she removes the covers, hands the plates round and pours out the beer; and should be careful to hand everything on the left side of the person she is waiting on ... When she sees every one helped, she should leave the room to make her preparations for the next course ...

When the dinner things are cleared away, the servant should sweep up the crumbs in the dining-room, sweep the hearth, and lightly dust the furniture, then sit down to her own dinner.

After this, she washes up and puts away the dinner things, sweeps the kitchen, dusts and tidies it, and put on the kettle for tea. She should now, before dressing herself for the afternoon, clean her knives, boots, and shoes, and do any other dirty work in the scullery that may be necessary. When the servant is dressed, she takes in the tea, and after tea turns down the beds, sees that the water-jugs and bottles are full, closes the windows and draws down the blinds ... [In addition] On Monday she should thoroughly clean the drawing-room; on Tuesday, two of the bedrooms; on Wednesday, two more; on Thursday, the other bedroom and stairs; on Friday morning she should sweep the dining-room very thoroughly, clean the hall, and in the afternoon her kitchen tins and bright utensils ... The regular work must, of course, be performed in the usual manner.

Before retiring to bed, she will do well to clean up glasses, plates, etc. which have been used for the evening meal, and prepare for her morning work by placing her wood near the fire, on the hob to dry, taking care that there is no danger of it igniting, before she leaves the kitchen for the night. Before retiring, she will have to lock and bolt the doors, unless the master undertakes this office himself.

If the washing, or even a portion of it, is done at home, it will be impossible for the maid-of-all-work to do her household duties thoroughly during the time it is about, unless she have some assistance. Usually, if all the washing is done at home, the mistress hires some one to assist at the wash-tub ...

A bustling and active girl will always find time to do a little needle-work for herself, if she lives with consistent and reasonable people. In the summer evenings she should manage to sit down for two or three hours, and for a short time in the afternoon in leisure days. A general servant's duties are so multifarious, that unless she be quick and active, she will not be able to accomplish this. To discharge these various duties properly is a difficult task, and sometimes a thankless office; but it must be remembered that a good maid-of-all-work will make a good servant in any capacity, and may be safely taken not only

ithout fear of failure, but with every probability of giving
atisfaction to her employer.

Mrs Beeton, *Household Management*, 1861, p. 1001 f

.3.3 *Household service*

'o weave our clothes in the loom ... is honourable; but to give a
elping hand ... to don such attire,—this is a disgrace. To make
arpets is a credit; to sweep them a shame ... Domestic service is
ecoming less really respectable, *because* it is less respected. The better
lass of persons who formerly engaged in it, knowing it to be honest
nd believing it to be honourable ... are ceasing to undertake it, since
hey habitually find it spoken of with disdain; while the humbler class
ho still engage in it do so with a sense of dislike ...

The manhood in a man and the womanhood in a woman suffers,
hey think, by the duties and conditions of household paid labour ...
because] it frequently involves hourly and momentary obedience to
he directions of the employer ... [Yet] in numberless cases employ-
nents not reckoned in any way menial involve the same kind of
ontract, namely, that of agreeing for a certain price, to perform work
f a certain kind under continual direction ... [such as] the army, all
ailors, labourers, shopmen and hundreds more ... Men and women
re *not* degraded by being servants ...

What *ought* the relations of masters and servants in these days to
e? ... All forms of labour are now beginning to be matters of free
ontract ... Therefore employers must strive to eradicate from their
ninds the whole patriarchal idea of service ... A servant is not now or
enceforth a retainer, a dependent, a menial who, in receiving from
is master food and wages, becomes his temporary property—some-
vhat between a child and a slave—to be ordered in all things
oncerning or not concerning, the master's service. He is simply a man
vho instead of contracting to build a wall ... contracts to do certain
ndoor work, for whose performance it is generally desirable that he
hould eat and sleep under the employer's roof. No obedience beyond
he contract can be required of him; nor, on the other hand (and this is
ery needful to mark) has the servant any claims against the master
eyond *his* stipulated contract of food and wages. The old idea of a
claim to care in sickness, pension in old age, and general interest in the
ervant's welfare, must be relinquished, along with the idea that the
contract is anything besides a contract ... Contracts reduced to the
ninimum of interference with the servant's liberty, accurately stated,
nd strictly respected, would, we believe introduce a new spirit along
vith the new relation between masters and servants ... Servants might
earn to feel that honesty and honour alike demanded of them to
erform on their sides punctually the contract faithfully kept by the

master ... Masters ought not to have the monopoly of fidelity to engagements.

Frances Power Cobbe,
'Household service', *Fraser's Magazine*, 1868, pp. 121-34

3.3.4   *Distaste for service*

There are many reasons for the great disinclination which girls have for domestic service, but it would take too long to go fully into these. In all but large, rich households, where there is much idleness and waste, domestic service is incessant hard work at all hours of the day and sometimes of the night also. It is at the best but a kind of slavery, and when a girl has a home it is only a human feeling, and one that we should respect, if she prefers to undertake work in trades, because she can return at night and on Sundays to the home circle. At a meeting last year of factory women at Bristol who were earning only 5s. or 6s. per week, I urged upon them the advisability of going out to service rather than submit to such low wages, but without an exception the advice was rejected by all ... One feasible suggestion of an improvement is a system of superior charwomen, under which servants could go home at night. They would then know when their work for the day was over, and their industry could be organised and thus placed more on a footing with other trades. Heads of households might then have to wait upon themselves a little more than they now do but much of the service now regarded as necessary is really only to gratify pride and to keep up appearances. At any rate, girls of the working class and their parents are just as much entitled to freedom of choice as any other persons are and we must try not to 'bump' people, especially women, into what we think are their places.

Emma Paterson, 'The organization of women's industry',
Women's Union Journal, April 1879

.4 Needlework

4.1 *The fashionable shop*

iss -------, manager:

he common hours of business are from 8 a.m. to 11 p.m. in the
inter; in the summer from 6 or 6.30 a.m. till twelve at night. During
e fashionable season, that is, from April till the latter end of July, it
equently happens that the ordinary hours are greatly exceeded. If
ere is a drawing-room, or grand fete, or mourning to be made, it
ften happens that the work goes on for twenty hours out of twenty-
ur: occasionally all night . . . has herself worked twenty hours out of
venty-four for three months together; at this time she was suffering
om illness; and the medical attendant remonstrated against the
eatment she received. He wished witness to remain in bed at least one
ay longer, which the employer objected to, required her to get up,
nd dismissed the surgeon. The meals are always taken as quickly as
ossible, no fixed time being allowed in any house that witness knows.
he general result of the long hours and sedentary occupation is
eriously to impair, and very frequently to destroy, the health of the
oung woman. Has seen young persons faint immediately after the
ork was over, the stimulus or excitement which had sustained them
aving ceased. The digestion [and the eyesight] especially suffers, and
lso the lungs; pain in the side is very common . . . It commonly
appens that young persons who come from the country healthy and
vell, become so ill that they are obliged to leave the business . . . Her
wn health is so much impaired, that she has spit blood during the last
ix years.

Royal Commission on the Employment of Children, 1843,
Appdx, XIV, p. 206

.4.2 *Tailoring: a male trade*

A journeyman tailor, concerning the employment of women in his
rade:—

'When I first began working at this branch, there were but very few
emales employed in it: a few white waistcoats were given out to them,
inder the idea that women would make them cleaner than men—and
o indeed they can. But since the last five years the sweaters have
mployed females upon cloth, silk and satin waistcoats as well, and
before that time the idea of a woman making a cloth waistcoat would
have been scouted. But since the increase of the puffing and the
sweating system, masters and sweaters have sought everywhere for
such hands as would do the work below the regular ones. Hence the
wife has been made to compete with the husband, and the daughter

with the wife: they all learn the waistcoat business, and must all get a living. If the man will not reduce the price of his labour to that of the female, why he must remain unemployed; and if the full-grown woman will not take the work at the same price as the young girl, why she must remain without any ... Before the year 1844 I could live comfortably, and keep my wife and children (I had five in family) by my own labour ... Now she has been compelled to resort to her needle, as well as myself, for her living.'

H. Mayhew,
London Labour and the London Poor, 1861, Vol. II, pp. 314-15

3.4.3   *Slop shirt making*

I was left a widow with two young children, and far advanced in pregnancy with another ... I got work at slop-shirts ... Perhaps I could earn 9d. a day by hard work, when I get 3d. each shirt; but sometimes I only get 2½d., and I have been obliged to do them for 1½d. each, and with my child sickly, could only earn 4d., or at most 6d., a day. At other times I hadn't work. On the average I calculate that I have earnt 9d. a day when the prices were better.

1s. 9d. a week went for rent; and as to a living, I don't call it that ... I was obliged to live on potatoes and salt; and for nine weeks together I lived on potatoes, and never knew what it was to have a half-quartern loaf—for the loaf was 9d. then ...

H. Mayhew,
'The slopworkers and needlewomen', *Morning Chronicle*,
23 November 1849

At the meeting there were 62 females present ... Of these, 30 were married, 23 were widows, 9 were single ... The earnings of last week were—21 below 1s.; 7 below 1s. 6d.; 6 below 2s.; 5 below 2s. 6d.; 10 below 3s.; 1 below 3s. 6d.; 1 below 4s.; 2 below 5s.;—below 6s., none; and the inquiry as to whether there were any who earned 7s. present was thought so absurd, that it was received with shouts of laughter ... They must sit up till twelve or one at night, to make from 6d. to 9d. a day clear ... They were several months in the year without work ... Four of them had goods pledged to the extent of £4, two to the value of £3, eleven of £2, thirteen of £1, seven of 10s., four of 5s., and fourteen had goods in pawn under 5s. value; thirteen widows and single women had parted with their beds, and twenty-six had parted with their under-clothing ... Of the husbands of married women, nineteen earned under 10s.; six earned under 5s.; three under 4s.; one under 2s.; three under 1s.; while six had earned nothing whatever ... Ten had been forced to go into the workhouse; nineteen had been

ced to pawn their work; thirty-one had been without food for a
ole day through ... seven had been obliged to go without food for
o days through ...

loc. cit.

.4 The need for self-help

e *Home Retail Trade.* Women who worked under the system agreed
at the 'sweaters' were not intentionally cruel, or unjust; that they
re themselves victims of an oppressive system ... At stated hours
e people who wish for work present themselves, and a bargain is
uck between them and the 'giver out'. It is the duty of the latter to
t the work done for as little as possible. Often when some poor
etch, whose whole family are depending on her work for bread, has
most concluded a bargain, she is undersold by a well-dressed woman
girl, who takes out work at a lower price ... The woman who has
en careless is 'drilled'—I use the trade term—i.e. when she applies
r work again she is told to wait, and has to wait sometimes all day
ng—it may be in the bitter cold, and may be is told to come the next
y, and told again to wait—and so on for days together. I have
own a woman who was supporting a bed-ridden mother, to be
rilled' for five bitter cold days. She would have starved if she had
t just joined our association.

Is it not evident that were the well-to-do gentlemen at the head of
ese firms to know the frightful cruelties that are daily practised in
eir names, that they would not allow them to continue; but they are
parated by a chasm from those whose toil enriches them.

It is in the hope of showing that by a system of co-operative
orkshops (none of them so large as for the manager to be ignorant of
e individuality of each worker) these evils may be remedied, that I
ve begun the Working Women's Co-operative Association. Each of
y workers receives a wage according to her skill, thus recognising her
st market value; each will receive an equal share in the profits, thus
cognising that one who does even unskilled labour conscientiously
serves to have her conscientiousness recognised equally with that of
e who is more skilled. We soon find out who is conscientious in
ork and no one who tries to baulk is kept on our books for long. We
ve worked for six months—during the last three we have paid our
penses, and we have about half the money we started with in the
ank, besides all our 'plant', stock, etc. We have executed 260 private
ders in that time for underclothing, shirts, baby-linen, cricketing
its, etc. and we have even made a riding-habit and a ball-dress.
lmost all our work has given satisfaction, and I have been enabled to
crease our establishment from three to seventeen women. What we
ant is more publicity and more orders—if we can procure these I

believe our success is certain, and not only the success of this particular Association, but the success of a system which shall in years to come render such cruelties as are now practised under the name of 'Trade' ugly remembrances of the past.

Sarah Heckford,
Working Women's Co-operative Association,
8 High Street, Shadwell, London, E.
Women's Union Journal, May 1885

3.4.5 Shirt making in Manchester
Evidence of home workers visited—Manchester

Index number	Persons working	Kind of work	Ordinary prices	Amount earned in a day	Average earnings per week in an ordinary week (gross, unless otherwise stated)	Cost of sewings to be deducted from gross earnings	Cost of sewing machine	Hours per day	
524	Married woman	Shirt machining	7d. and 8d. a dozen 'run ups'	Would take 3½ to 4 hours to do one dozen of 7d. work.	About 4s. when well	1d. in 10d. 1d. a week for oil	—	Very irregular; seven young children to look after.	Husband a joiner, away from home; sent her money weekly. She only began to take out work a year ago. Never worked in a warehouse. Used to make pinafores and blouses, but they were only wanted for a season. Paid 6s. a week for a four-roomed back-to-back house.

Index number	Persons working	Kind of work	Ordinary prices	Amount earned in a day	Average earnings per week in an ordinary week (gross, unless otherwise stated)	Cost of sewings to be deducted from gross earnings	Cost of sewing machine	Hours per day	
541	Young single woman	Shirt machining for two employers	7d., 8d., 9d., 10d. a dozen 'run ups' 1s. 4d. a dozen	On 1s. 4d. work could earn 2s. in 10 hours. On 7d. work 1s. 9d. in 10 hours.	9s. or 10s. Once earned 16s. working for a retail draper.	3½d. in every 4s.	2s. 6d. a fortnight	Generally 10 hours a day. Sometimes worked from 8.30 till 10 or 11 to earn 14s.	Was hardly ever slack at the place where she got her cheap work. Used to work in a shirt factory. Was working in a bedroom in a very poor house; said she boarded at this house and slept in the next room with another girl; her landlady and husband slept in the room she was working in. Her father and mother lived in Manchester. She paid 6s. a week for board and lodging; if at home would probably have to give up all her money.

Elderly widow and grandchild aged 14	Shirt machining and finishing	1s. a dozen = 8d. for machining, 4d. for finishing (five buttons and holes). 1s. 4d. a dozen = 1s. 1d. machining, 3d. finishing (two buttons and holes, one tack). 5d. a dozen finishing (eight buttons, six holes)	'If she worked from 7 a.m. to 11 p.m. could make 1½ dozen of the 1s. 4d. work.' Her grandchild would earn 'about 4d. in a day'.	Rarely earned 4s. The most she ever earned 'working day and night' was 8s. 6d.	1d. in 1s.	—	Probably only a few hours a day. Statements inconsistent, but not intentionally incorrect. Professed to work uninterruptedly from morning till night, and perhaps believed she did.

Only began shirt-making five years ago when her daughter was left in difficulties, and she did not like to be idle. Daughter worked at a cotton mill, and would never let her work when she was at home in the evening or on Saturday afternoons. Would rather work than not. Was very talkative, and did not look at all hard worked.

Index number	Persons working	Kind of work	Ordinary prices	Amount earned in a day	Average earnings per week in an ordinary week (gross, unless otherwise stated)	Cost of sewings to be deducted from gross earnings	Cost of sewing machine	Hours per day	
546	Young widow and step-mother, also a widow	Shirt machin-ing	8d. a dozen	Working from 5.30 a.m. to 6.30 p.m. did two dozen of 8d. work together.	About 7s. together	1½d. in 1s.	One machine their own; 2s. 6d. a fortnight for the other.	Long hours if they had the work; often had not.	Said she was a widow with two children, and lived with her step-mother, not much older than herself. Paid 3s. 9d. a week for two rooms in tenement buildings, leaving about 3s. 3d. a week for the four. The sitting-room was very clean and fairly comfortable, but it was a long time before she would admit that she had other sources of income, although her reticence was probably due to shyness. When well, she and her step-mother did what work they could for neighbours, and neighbours helped them very much. Had been very ill with rheumatism, simply through want of food.

577	Young married woman	Shirt machining	10d. a dozen	Earns 2s. 6d. working from 8 a.m. till 11 p.m., but looks after her baby, three weeks old, and her husband's meals.	7. 6d. to 10s.	3½d. in 6s.	Paid for	Went for work three times a week, and never worked the day she did so; might average 10 hours on other days.	Was told that this woman's husband was very lazy; she, however, said nothing on that point. Had never worked anywhere but at home. Paid 3s. 9d. a week for a two-roomed house; lived at a considerable distance from the warehouse, and her husband went to his work at Withington by train.	Her mother-in-law in the country had sent her a great deal during her illness, and was also paying for the sewing-machine. They had only done shirt-making for 18 months, and were very slow.

Index number	Persons working	Kind of work	Ordinary prices	Amount earned in a day	Average earnings per week in an ordinary week (gross, unless otherwise stated)	Cost of sewings to be deducted from gross earnings	Cost of sewing machine	Hours per day	
513	Middle aged single woman	Duck jackets	2s. 7d. a dozen	Would make eight, working from 8 to 8.	Sometimes 9s. or 10s.; sometimes not half so much.	½d. in 1s. Employer only charged 3½d. for two reels; 5d. at a shop.	2s. 6d. a fort-night	—	Was working in a room where an old man was repairing trousers. Said she lodged in the room behind, and paid 1s. 6d. a week for it. Had done this work for quite 16 years. Had been a patient at the hospital on and off for three years. Was in the hospital for 14 weeks, and her machine would have been taken, but the nurse paid 10s. to have it kept for her.

523	Married woman	Duck and serge jackets, button-holed in factory	Lined jackets 5s. 3d. and 5s. 6d. a dozen. Plain 4s. a dozen	2s. 10d. in about 10 hours.	14s. 6d.	1d. or 1½d. in 1s.	Paying 2s. 6d. a week in order to be quick about it, £5 still due.	8.30 to 7 or 8, but looks after her four children. Only house work on Saturday.	Said she was 'as good as unmarried'. Children were very clean and neatly dressed. Had worked in the factory 20 years ago as a braider. Her little boy took her work to the warehouse, and was rarely kept waiting.

Royal Commission on the Employment of Labour, 1893

3.5   Factory Work

3.5.1   *The propriety of female factory work*
The deputation [urged] the gradual withdrawal of all females from factories ... The females employed in factories are generally the offspring of parents who have been similarly situated. They get little if any education worthy the name previous to entering the mills, and as soon as they enter them ... are surrounded by influences of the most vitiating and debasing nature. They grow up in total ignorance of all the true duties of woman. Home, its cares, and its employments, is woman's true sphere; but these poor things are totally unfitted for attending to the one, or participating in the other. They neither learn, in the great majority of cases, to make a shirt, darn a stocking, cook a dinner or clean a house. In short, both in mind and manners, they are altogether unfitted for the occupancy of a domestic position, as is evidenced by the fact, that the wealthy and middle classes very rarely engage any of this class as servants. Yet those who are thus considered unfit even to fill the office of menial to the rich, are the only parties among whom, ordinarily, the male factory labourer has a chance of obtaining a wife. They are married early. Many are mothers before twenty. Thriftlessness and waste even of their small incomes, and consequent domestic discomfort and unhappiness, generally succeed. Through these means is engendered a vast amount of immorality and misery; and while such are its results as respects private life, the operation of the system is not less injurious in a national point of view. It throws the burden of supporting the family on the wife and the children and compels the adult male, upon whose shoulders the duty ought rightfully to fall, to be reluctantly idle. It is an inversion of the order of nature and of Providence—a return to a state of barbarism, in which the woman does the work, while the man looks idly on. The consequence of throwing loose such a mass of partially informed men in such circumstances, cannot fail to be fraught with danger to the state. Disaffection and discontent must be engendered among parties so situated.

Deputation to Sir Robert Peel,
The Ten Hours' Factory Question, a Report addressed to the
Short Time Committees of the West Riding of Yorkshire, 1842

The females not only perform the labour, but occupy the places of men; they are forming various clubs and associations, and gradually acquiring all those privileges which are held to be the proper portion of the male sex. These female clubs are thus described:—'Fifty or sixty females, married and single, form themselves into clubs, ostensibly for protection; but, in fact, they meet together to drink, sing and smoke; they use, it is stated, the lowest, most brutal and most disgusting language imaginable' ... What is the ground on which the woman says she will pay no attention to her domestic duties, nor give the obedience which is owing to her husband? because on her devolves the labour which ought to fall to his share, and she throws out the taunt, 'If I have the labour, I will also have the amusement'.

Lord Shaftesbury's Speech on the Ten Hours' Factory Bill,
House of Commons, Hansard, 15 March 1844

3.5.2 *Factory work defended*

Factory work is supposed to be degrading in the extreme ... [yet] First, by the census of 1851 ... while 1 out of 165 women was an inmate of the workhouse, the proportion of inmates from women engaged in textile manufactures was far less than the average ... Second, by arranging the counties of England according to the proportion ... of paupers, the manufacturing districts occupy a *middle* place in the scale; Third, by the census of 1851 and 1861, the proportion of women in prison belonging to occupations of textile manufacture, was less than the proportion of women in prison who had been in domestic service; and Fourth ... we believe it to be a fact, that the proportion of domestic servants becoming inmates of Magdalen asylums, is larger than the proportion of factory women becoming inmates there ...

Another common remark about factory women is that they have no opportunity of learning household economy; that they have no idea of domestic comfort, or of the management of children; that thus, as wives, they drive their husbands to the gin shop and, as mothers, rear their children in squalor and in the road to vice ... In colliery districts, mining districts, seaport towns without fisheries, and hamlets for agricultural labourers where women have little employment, one finds more squalor, ignorance, and dissipation than in manufacturing towns where employment for women is abundant.

J. D. Milne, The Industrial and Social Position of Women,
1857 (1870 edn, pp. 210-12)

3.5.3 *Factories, workshops and domestic outwork*
Factories and workshops

Qu. 788. Is it your opinion that as a general rule the distinction between factories and workshops should cease?—[Mr Redgrave:] I do think so.

Qu. 789. And in fact that the law affecting factories should be the rule?—Yes.

There are very great grievances urged on the part of owners of factories which come in competition with workshops ... The owner of a workshop is placed in a much better position by the less stringent restrictions which are placed upon him ... The power of distributing the time of labour as they please between the hours of 5 a.m. and 9 p.m. [cf. the 6 a.m. to 6 p.m. of factories], the absence of fixed hours for meals and other privileges give an advantage in the labour market to those who possess them ... Manufacturers will sometimes purposely keep down the number of their work people to 48 or 49 in order to escape the Factory Acts ... The larger establishments farm out work among the smaller, where it is done under less favourable conditions, both sanitary and educational.

Report, paras 17-19

Extension of the Factory Acts. Qu. 5732. It would meet your [male chainworkers,] views if the whole of the labour of women and children was put under the Factory Act?—Yes.
Qu. 6459. The hours of work of those women in the small workshops should be restricted to the hours of work in factories ...
Qu. 8423. We [the operative bleachers and dyers of Bolton] contend that young women employed in the bleach works have more laborious and exhaustive work than they have in factories as a whole ... A hooker in the hooking room is continually in motion all day; she is stooping every minute, and we calculate that she hooks 250 of 40 yards a day ... Then also many of our rooms are very badly ventilated [with temperatures of 90° to 100°].
Qu. 8424. ... From the nature of the process, the unhealthy temperature of the rooms, and the fatiguing character of the work, there is no reason why the hours should not be shortened as in textile factories ...

The women's reply. Qu. 10,132. We were told that hook work is very hard?—[Miss Wilson and Mrs Barrington:] It is not so ... I do not think that it is hard work, it is very nice work.
Qu. 10,134. You do not think that they [the women] want them [their hours] shortened by Act of Parliament any more?—No, I do not think so. We work very short hours indeed.
Qu. 13,190-13,215. [Miss Wilson:] ... The kinds of labour that have hitherto been the subject of legislative interference have really been amongst the lightest and least laborious and amongst the best paid that women are able to follow. Women of the working classes must work, and must work hard, and the only question seems to me to be whether they are allowed to work where they can make conditions and where they can work for wages, or be compelled to work hard where they cannot make conditions, for instance, in domestic labour ... If

he factory population are the only class of workers who are content
o apply to Parliament for protection for them, it is proof that they
are to an extent demoralized ... Under this Act, it is women's
freedom that pays the price of the benefit which both men and women
share ... This is some of the least severe and laborious work, and that
hampering the conditions of it and making it less profitable to employ
women tends to drive them to unprotected occupations which are
more laborious. There are an immense number of maids of all work,
who have no limitation of hours whatever, and no limitation of work,
and whose lives are infinitely harder than those of any workers in any
factory in the country, and it tends to drive women out of the factory
into maidships of all work ... A friend of mine traced some of the
women who were driven from the Lancashire mines, to see what
became of them, and she found them working in the Liverpool docks
as porters, loading and unloading ships ... far more severe [work] ...
Where women take unsuitable work, we may be pretty sure that there
is nothing else open to them, and that the true remedy is not to force
them out of it, but to endeavour to increase the facilities for their
doing something else.

Workshops and domestic outwork. Dressmaking, tailoring, boot and
shoe making, seaming, glovemaking, and a host of other workshop
employments can all be carried on in the homes of the work people ...
under conditions of labour far more injurious to the working people
than if carried on in the workshops, and the undoubted effect of any
further unnecessary restrictions on the hours of women's labour in the
workshops would be to drive the work out of the workshop into the
dwelling house ... It is practically admitted ... that interference in
dwelling houses cannot be carried out.

Report, pp. cxi, cxii

Qu. 2,810. [Mrs Paterson and Mrs Heatherly:] ... If the people are
prevented from working at the workshop they take home the work to
do, and if you stop the working in the workshop you only make the
work get done under more unwholesome conditions.

Royal Commission on Factories and Workshops,
1876, Vol. 29 (the Report) and Vol. 30 (Evidence)

.5.4 *The textile trades*

am of the opinion that the condition of mill life in Yorkshire for
women and children could be much improved by a more thorough
inspection of factories ... The difference of wages for men and
women where both are engaged in the same employment appears to be
a matter for trade organization, but the due ventilation of the workrooms, the safety of machinery, and the necessary sanitary arrange-

ments, could be enforced by law, i.e. if it were possible for the inspection to be efficiently carried out . . .

Unlike Yorkshire all weavers in Lancashire are paid alike, and men and women do the same work. Many women in Lancashire earn, as weavers, about 24s. a week all the year through, whereas in Yorkshire 18s. a week is an exceptional wage for woman weavers, and is seldom maintained for any length of time . . . I found no general preference given to women over men except in Wigan, where the organization is weak and the wages are so low that few men are ready to accept them without protest . . .

As in Yorkshire, serious complaints are made by the operatives of injury to their health arising from badly constructed and neglected sanitary accommodation; from insufficient provision for comfortable meals; from bad ventilation; and from shuttle accidents. Added to these causes of ill-health, the weavers complain of the injurious effects of excessive steaming and sizing, both of which are prevalent in the following districts: Burnley, Blackburn, Darwen, Todmorden, Wigan and Bury.

The cardroom operatives throughout Lancashire complain of the light fibrous dust which is generated by the carding process.

The ring and throstle spinners state that they suffer from the excessively high temperature of the spinning rooms, which in some mills reaches 100°F. [The steam jets mean] the floors are in a very wet and dangerous condition . . . Rheumatism is very common among the weavers working in these mills.

May Abraham, *Royal Commission on the Employment of Labour*, 1893, pp. 113, 116-18

3.5.5   *Nail and chain making*

Qu. 5,734. You propose to place a restriction on the size of chains made by women?—[Deputation of chainmakers:] Yes, I think it would be desirable, for heavy chains is certainly not fit work for women to perform . . . That is my sole motive.

Qu. 5,739. Not because it tends to reduce the men's wages?—No. I think that they are not fit for them to do. It is not altogether the labour, but in summer time we all have to stand very near the fire, and we have to strip, females as well as males . . . and of course that has a tendency towards immorality . . . The larger the chain, the bigger the fire must be.

Royal Commission on Factories and Workshops, 1876, Vol. 30

Mr. Juggins [South Staffordshire] moved: 'That it be an instruction to the parliamentary committee to introduce such amendments to the Factory and Workshop Acts as shall prevent the employment of females in the making of chains, nails and bolts . . .' He maintained that the employment was a most improper one for women. They were engaged for 60 hours a week, and earned not more than 3s. to 3s. 6d. a week, while they were required to work almost in a nude state, and mixed up with men, in order to earn those miserable wages . . .

Miss Black opposed the resolution. . . . That women did suffer the physical evils of which he complained was no doubt true. But there was not one injury which Mr. Juggins had instanced that could not be capped by a worse story of the sufferings of women employed in trades which no one dreamed of forbidding, such as needlework and match-box making. But men never proposed to interfere with these trades. Why? There was no need to ask. Men did not work at these trades and suffered nothing from the competition of women. The real point to be complained of was the low rate of payment earned by the women; and the way to prevent the employment of women in any trade they were unfit for was for men to join in helping them to combine in order that they might receive the same wages for the same work. If employers had to pay women the same prices as men there would be no temptation to them to employ women to do what they were less fit to do than men. But the women were not represented here to speak for themselves and she protested against the attempt of one class of workers—especially a class whose interests were concerned— to impose restrictions upon another class of workers. Not all the horrors described by Mr. Juggins could give them the right to pass such a vote.

'The Trades Union Congress',
Women's Union Journal, 15 October 1887

Mr. and Mrs. Cole, man and wife, work together at spike nails . . . both use the oliver. They expressed a strong opinion that 'women should be prevented by law from doing men's work' . . . With few exceptions, the homes I saw belonging to women who work either in factories or in home workshops are very nearly desolate . . . There is no home life at all . . . The children are either 'minded' by little girls at 2s. a week, or else they are perched on the warm heap of fuel or dangled in an egg box from the shop ceiling . . . all in the stifling vicinity of the forge . . .

As to women and young people not being allowed to work, the chief result would be to drive them out of the factories into home workshops where they can dodge the inspector. The factories give better pay for better work during shorter hours.

Eliza Orme, Senior Assistant Commissioner,
Royal Commission on the Employment of Labour, 1893, p. 572

One may come across sheds with five or six women, each working at her anvil . . . One woman had forged 728 heavy links in the three days, and for this had received 2s. 2d. She had paid 7½d. for firing, and 1s. for the nurse. Her net earnings for the 36 hours were 6½d. ... The work of chain-making consists in heating the iron rods ... bending the red-hot piece, cutting in on the hardy, twisting the link, inserting it into the last link of the chain, and welding or closing it, with repeated blows of the hand hammer and the Oliver worked by a treadle ... The Oliver is a sledge hammer ...

R. Sherard, *The White Slaves of England*, 1897, pp. 226-7

3.5.6   *Evidence of the factory inspectorate*
What were the characteristic features in the earlier days that the Inspectors saw? First, a mute sense of industrial inferiority, outside the great textile industries ... Secondly, an absence in the great majority of factories of any woman in a position of authority. Thirdly, in spite of protective laws, a working day and week in which the standard hours worked by women frequently exceeded those for which men, in certain great trades, had by means of trades unions secured recognition from employers. Fourthly, a frequent lack of suitable or even decent and sufficient sanitary accommodation, of cleanliness of a domestic nature, and of other hygenic requirements, sometimes injuriously affecting conduct and morals. Fifthly, not only low average and individual wages, but on the part of piece-workers an intolerable uncertainty as to what their rates really were; and, for all a liability to arbitrary deductions for fines and alleged damages to work, which often brought earnings below subsistence level ...

Deductions. In a safety-pin factory in the West of England where only good work was paid for and some waste unavoidable ... a married woman bringing in 84 gross of good pins out of 100 gross booked to her, was charged 2s. for 21 pounds short in the metal, and instead of receiving 1s. 11½d. for the 84 gross pins, admittedly well capped, received her pay envelope empty—with a note on it that she owed ½d. Here the firm, aroused by the miserable conditions brought to light by the Inspector, voluntarily returned all deductions exceeding 5% ...

Industrial Diseases. Asbestos sifting, mixing, and carding ... The sharp, jagged edge of the insoluble mineral dust has undoubtedly occasioned much illness and death, from respiratory diseases ...

Silk waste carding and spinning gave rise to woeful complaints of dust from the women, from 1898 onwards ... they were coughing up not silk but silkworms ...

Dust from rag and refuse sorting, fur pulling, in hatters furriers' factories and horsehair factories, in starch rooms of confectionary works, hemp-rope works, sack mending, cotton waste works, india-rubber works, eiderdown and kapok filling factories, clay pipe scouring, embossed paper-lace making. Lead poisoning: the most injurious lead processes—e.g. colour dusting, ware-cleaning—fell to women. They found among these a high degree of childlessness, still births and miscarriages; that thirty-six only had living children averaging three each ... 'A.B., aged twenty-nine, married seven years, had worked in lead ten years, had three miscarriages, five still born children, and one child alive who died in convulsions when a few weeks old' (Chief Inspector's Report, 1897). The glazing of bricks with lead in the glaze, later shown to be unnecessary, was found by Miss Squire in 1898 to be causing fits among the girls who were scraping the edges of the bricks. These attacks had been thoughtlessly attributed to hysteria until brought under medical observation.

Adelaide Anderson, *Women in the Factory, 1893-1921*, 1922, pp. 24-5, 70, 106-7, 116, 120

3.5.7 *The work of the women inspectors*

I may confess that my own first feelings were chiefly of consternation on learning that I had, a few weeks after entering the Department, personally to prosecute an occupier for illegal employment of girls— never having previously entered a police court ... Without warning an Inspector would find herself when in a police court arguing her case not merely with an experienced solicitor acting for the defendant but sometimes with a well known Q.C. Our armour on such occasions was a thorough acquaintance with the facts and circumstances, and with the scope of the Acts which we were trying to enforce ... Taking only the years from 1898 to 1914, the Women Inspectors brought 4,962 cases into court ... and secured convictions in 4,715 cases ...

For peripatetic Inspectors the difficulty was a real one; the fitting in of visits of special inquiry, general routine visits of inspection, visits on extremely varied kinds of complaints, with the successful prosecution of prolonged legal activities in widely scattered places. Yet I know of no case where action failed through omission by an Inspector to serve a notice or complete any legal formality or to be at the necessary spot at the prescribed time. There was a flame burning within that seemed to consume obstacles by the way, and rendered innocuous even very adverse climactic and other conditions. Long cross country drives in Ireland (undertaken simply at times to carry out a formal act) would sometimes last all day in an open car in pouring rain, or a day in a tiny stuffed police court might have to be preceded by a drive beginning before daylight on a stormy winter morning to fetch intimidated witnesses for the case. In Lancashire a start might have to be made at 4.30 a.m. from a hotel ... to reach a distant country mill, unobserved, by a new route, in order to detect time-cribbing before 6 a.m.

loc. cit., pp. 204, 211

3.6   Laundry Work

Regulation of hours

A laundry manager, . . . 'With regard to my views on the Factory Act as applied to laundries, I am clearly of opinion that it would not be beneficial to the women employed . . . There are many domestic reasons that prevent women beginning work at a punctual and stated hour, and in consequence they are glad to work on later to make up for lost time in the morning and again at the dinner hour . . . Again, some women, good hands . . . only work when their husbands are out of employ; these hands are anxious to make as much time, piece-work as they can; it is the only way of feeding the little ones when the husband is unemployed. Others merely come to work to add a little to the money earned by the man, just enough, as they say, to pay the rent . . . Then again with hotel visitors' time, many families arrive at the Grand, Metropole, Victoria, in fact all hotels, who have all their linen used up on the continent and are going further on at once. This linen can only remain three or four hours in the laundry, and has to be done whatever time it may be, and people cannot carry with them sufficient linen to prevent this. It is a peculiar trade, dependent upon the habits and caprice of individuals . . .

Witness 139, laundress, Acton, said that if hours were limited she would lose 6d. on Fridays. She wanted more work not less. She lived apart from her husband, and had two children to support; she had not been able to earn enough by needlework at home, and therefore had gone out to work. Her landlady looked after her baby; she paid her 1s. a week to do so, and 2s. 6d. rent. She generally earned 12s. 6d. a week . . .

Witness 141, laundress, Acton, had been married nine months . . . She did not want a limitation of hours. The women wanted the money they made by overtime. Nothing would induce the men to work in many cases, and their wives were obliged to go out. If the women did not want to work they could settle their own hours; and no one could make them work if they did not want to.

Witness 116, laundress, a widow with one child to support, objected to working such late hours. She would rather have less money than work too long hours. She found all the good shops closed, and had to pay double or buy worse things at the small shops which remained open late. She had brought up seven children without any help for some years . . . The eldest left service because the work was too hard.

Witness 146, laundress, a single woman, said she would rather have shorter hours even with less money. When I pointed out that in her present situation she did not work any longer than was allowed by the

Factory Act, the laundresses present were much excited, and declared
they wanted no Factory Act but an Eight Hours' Bill. They saw no
reason why they should work at the laundry and slave at home, while
their husbands only did eight hours a day.

Clara Collet,
Royal Commission on the Employment of Labour, 1893,
pp. 19-22

Compulsory maternity leave, 1898. A laundry visited on a complaint
of infringement . . . yielded only the information that the woman was
at home, the regulation well known, and 'as soon as it was permissible
she would return to work'. The Inspector, wishing to make sure of all
the facts, 'went straightway to see the woman in her home, and found
her in the act of doing heavy washing for the laundry in question'. The
employer was only legally responsible for knowingly employing the
woman in his laundry within four weeks of childbirth, accordingly he
had 'sent the work to be done in the home. The laundry was clean and
the surroundings . . . in point of fatigue-saving appliances incom-
parably superior to those in which the woman was found. Her
husband was a labourer, she had four living children, and the entire
family inhabited two rooms; the woman was washing over a tub raised
on two stools in one of the rooms . . . she dragged it into the yard to
empty when needful.'

Adelaide Anderson, *Women in the Factory, 1893-1921*,
1922, p. 153

3.7 Shops

3.7.1 *The Shop Hours Regulation Bill*

When the profit to the employer on the labour of each worker he employs does not exceed the difference between the wages of a man and of a woman, there is no possibility of men being substituted for women . . .

Shopkeepers employ few workers . . . Thus the profit on each worker employed is larger than that of the manufacturer . . . The difference in wages between a salesman and saleswoman is from two to three shillings a day, but the profit on the goods sold by each seller in the course of the day far exceeds two or three shillings . . . It cannot in such a case make much difference to the shopkeeper whether he pays his assistants at the rate of three shillings a day or of six.

. . . In the cheap shops in the East and South of London, large numbers of women are employed, and it is in these poor localities that the sales are chiefly effected in the evening. The servant-girl goes out in the evening, after the late dinner or supper of her master and mistress, to make her purchases; the charwoman goes after her day's work is done, and she has put her children to bed and given her husband his supper; the man, woman, or girl employed in a factory or at a handicraft goes out after taking supper and making a change of clothes. At nine o'clock the shops are still busy, busier indeed than in the middle of the day.

It is easy to perceive what the effect of the Shop Hours Bill would be on a shopkeeper who supplies the poor, if he employed women. His shop would be closed at the busiest moment, and he would see his customers going perforce to his rival opposite who employed men. He would of course dismiss his women next week and engage men.

Jessie Boucherett, 'Sir John Lubbock's Bill',
Englishwoman's Review, October 1873

3.7.2 *Early Closing*

I have been startled to discover that it is not the intervention of the law as to the labour of women and young persons akin to the Factory and Workshop Acts that is looked for by either employers or employed; but what they expect and hope for is a law akin to the Licensing Act, which shall compel a positive closing of the shop at a stated hour . . . The employed ask for a positive closing because men want to be relieved, as well as women from their present slavery [of up to 85 hours' labour a week], and the employers ask it on the ground of also

wishing to be free at earlier hours and of competition in various shapes staring them in the face.   Evidence of Mr Beadon to the
Royal Commission on Factories and Workshops, 1876, vol. 29, para. 36

3.7.3 *Shop Assistants' views*

The shop assistants in the poorer neighbourhoods, besides working longer hours and lifting heavy weights usually raised by men in better class shops, are more frequently obliged to work in badly ventilated rooms; the windows are frequently blocked with articles, and so little light admitted from any source, that in some cases gas will be found burning at any time in the day. Seats were only provided in four of the thirty-three shops of which information has been obtained. Witness 75, dealing in light goods also, employs women in all departments, and considered that men could not be obtained to do the same work as women, except at a considerably higher rate; he estimated that where a woman would be paid £25 a year a man would require about £40 or £45. In his shop it would be impossible to replace women by men, many of the articles being such as women would only buy from women. Witnesses were not inclined to think that a limitation of hours affecting women only would place women at a disadvantage with regard to men. I received a general impression that the men were much more actively discontented with their long hours than the women, and, that were a limitation of the hours of the latter by legislation possible, the men would of their own initiative be inclined to secure equally short hours for themselves. This statement, however, only applies to the drapery business; in places where only men are employed, with the exception of a few women as cashiers, a limitation of hours affecting women only might easily have the effect of driving women out of employment, unless a very decided difference in the rate of payment prevails.

On combination. These social differences all stand in the way of trade association. It is not the custom to discuss wages and salaries together, and shop assistants are especially reluctant to mention their salaries in the presence of others. The larger associations of workers who manage homes and clubs for working girls on a religious basis, and do most excellent work, succeed in influencing a larger number of these girls than any other organisations in London, and in the majority of cases their attitude is hostile to trade unionism or any movement which seems to them to stir up antagonism between the girls and their employers. They aim at teaching the girls to conscientiously perform their duties to those in authority over them, and look with disfavour on agitation which seems to them to have only material and intellectual progress as an end.

Royal Commission on the Employment of Labour, 1893, p. 4, 14

3.7.4 The career of a shop-girl

No. of firm	Locality	Date of employment	Hours of opening	Hours of closing	Minimum total hours, including meals	Dinner	Tea	Rest	Arrangements on Sundays	Salary	Seats	Food and accommodation	Time in firm	Effect on health
10	Commercial Road, E.	1887 or 1888	8.30	9.30 or 10. Sat. 11.30 or 12. Th. 5.	75½	½ hour	20 minutes	20 minutes	Not compelled to go out. No breakfast table laid. May go to the kitchen, and take a cup of tea with the servants if you like.	£20	No	Food not sufficient. Linen in bedrooms not changed for months.	1 month	Most injurious
11	Harrow Road	I think 1888	8.30	9.30 or 10. Sat. 12. Th. 5.	76	½ hour	20 minutes	None	Remain in if you like. Comfortable.	£20	No	Very fair	1 month	Prostration

12	Earl's Court	1888 and 1889	9.0	8.30 or 9. Sat. 10. Th. 5.	67	1 hour	½ hour (outdoor)	—	Had nice lodgings.	£10 (outdoor)	No	—	11 months	Completely prostrated and overworked
13	Brompton Road	1889	8.30	9 or 9.30. Sat. 10.	76	½ hour	20 minutes	None	Remain in if you like. Good sitting room.	£20	No	Excellent	3 weeks	Prostration
14	King's Road, Chelsea	1889 or 1890	8.30	9, 9.30 or 10. Sat. 11. Th. 5.	73	½	20 minutes	None	They wished assistants to go out.	£25	No	Not sufficient nourishment. Accommodation good.	About 3 months	Complete prostration
15	Near Baker Street	I think 1890	8.30	9.0. Sat. 10.	76	Could take my own time; managing in absence of employer.			Remain in or go out.	£25	Yes	Left to our own discretion. Good accommodation.	3 weeks	Hours too long
16	Whitechapel Road	1890	8.30	9.30 or 10. Sat. 11.30 or 12. Th. 5.	75½	½ hour	20 minutes	None	Compelled to go out without breakfast, and remain out all day.	£25	No	Food inferior. Accommodation disgraceful.	2 weeks	Complete prostration

loc. cit.

3.8 Teaching

3.8.1 *Governesses*
It is the only profession open to educated women of average ability . . .
It is a platform on which middle and upper classes meet, the one
struggling up, the other drifting down.

'The position of a teacher',
English Woman's Journal, March 1858

What is the position of a governess? she has none. While engaged in a
family . . . she is infinitely less considered than the servants; she has
no companionship whatsoever; very frequently, not a syllable is
addressed to her from week's end to week's end by the members of the
family as if she were in disgrace. Of course! after a whole day's
arduous teaching, the mind at full stretch, what relaxation can a
governess want? The servants have their hall and their social
pleasures; the governess is condemned to solitude . . . though her
habits and manners are to *form* the habits and manners of the young,
they are unfit for those already formed . . . Let those parents who
qualify a daughter for the *genteel* office of governess, reflect a
moment *how* she is looked upon by her superiors and inferiors. Just
let a remote idea be entertained of marriage between a son and the
governess . . . the anger, the scorn, the vituperation lavished upon the
artful creature . . .

Now as servants generally take their cue from the heads, the
governess often has to endure innumerable insults from *them* . . . A
remarkably vulgar wet-nurse told a rather superior governess that
some of the servants had asked, 'Why should there be any difference
between *her* and us?' . . .

There is not one thing which ladies so begrudge as paying for their
children's education . . . Very lately a young lady was required for five
children; French, English, music, drawing, and to look after their
wardrobes: salary twenty guineas . . . At thirty-five or thirty-six she is
cast aside like a blunt tool, young enough to see long years of penury
ahead, yet too old to learn a fresh employment . . . Servants are often
pensioned off . . . not so the governess . . .

Once more we earnestly entreat parents not to doom their daughters
to the wretched life of governesses. Give them a trade. Do not be led
away by insane ideas of silly pride.

'The governess question',
English Woman's Journal, November 1860

3.8.2 *Elementary teaching, a middle-class career?*

From among that large and respectable portion of the middle class upon whose means the burden of education for their children presses heavily, few, comparatively, cause their children to be trained as National Schoolmistresses. The Government plan for educating and providing Mistresses for Elementary Schools appears generally over-looked, more especially by the friends and guardians of young persons left orphans ... Not only is the remuneration larger, and the social position better, than that which many occupations confer, but there is also in the Teacher's office a wide field for the exercise of ability for a good purpose, to promote which many young persons labour at the expense of much self-denial ...

The average emoluments from all professional sources for School-mistresses are £71 per annum in the metropolitan district, and about £59 12s. in the country. In more than half the cases houses are provided rent-free; and it will be seen that in certain cases retiring pensions are allowed by Government ...

The preparation necessary for admission into Training Schools is usually obtained by placing a girl of not more than fourteen in an Elementary School, where she may be apprenticed as a pupil teacher. The apprenticeship lasts five years, during which time the pupil receives from the Government an annual payment, beginning with £10, and increasing every year to £20; and after that she may, if competent, obtain a Queen's Scholarship, which entitles her to a free exhibition to a Training School for two years ... Parents not desiring to place their children as Pupil teachers, or older persons desiring to qualify themselves as Teachers in schools can compete [for the scholarships]. The cost of training a female ... is between £37 and £40 per annum. This sum in the case of Queen's scholars, is wholly, and in all other cases to the extent of one-half, defrayed out of public or private grants, applicable only to the preparation of Mistresses for Elemen-tary Day Schools; so that no person can enter a Training School except for this purpose.

Angela Burdett-Coutts,
letter to the *English Journal of Education,* April 1858

Excellent as the training colleges are, we doubt the wisdom of encouraging young ladies to seek entrance into them ... They would marry the Clergyman or the Squire or their sons in nearly every parish they went to ... The only obstacle to this now is the low birth of the present order of College trained schoolmistresses: and this Miss Burdett-Coutts' plan would remove. It would obviously be a great abuse to use public money to educate the future wives of men of fortune ... Moreover her plan would deprive the girls of industrious poor parents of a post of usefulness ... It is for the same homes and stations that they are intended to train their scholars; and they will do this all the more effectually because it is work in which their own lives have practically experienced them.

English Journal of Education, April 1858

3.8.3 *Female teachers*

The education of trained masters and mistresses is very superficial. It is in fact a cram, fitting them to get through their examination, and very seldom giving solidity to the mind. They are very often much set up, full of airs, and have no moral influence over their scholars or pupil-teachers. I think this is not so much the fault of the training colleges, as it is of the materials they have to work upon. Pupil teachers being taken generally from the very lowest class of society, they are destitute of that mass of information which children of respectable parents imbibe without knowing it, and which forms a solid foundation to build upon when they do receive regular instruction. Trained teachers are very often dissatisfied with their social position; they look down upon their parents and relatives, and wish to get into society above them . . .

It appears to me very desirable that young people of a higher grade should be encouraged to enter on the work of popular education. If you want a nursery governess, on inquiry you are distressed by innumerable applications from well-educated girls, extremely well connected, and anxious to engage for a salary that would not content a lady's maid. Very many would gladly take the charge of schools . . .

Evidence to the Newcastle Commission, 1861
evidence of Eliza Partridge, Vol. 5, p. 333

It has been thought that if the pecuniary advantages held out by the Privy Council were more generally understood, they would draw into the service a higher class of female than those which now offer themselves. I believe this will never to any great extent be realized . . . The rough coarse work of these schools, the publicity, and the low associations, must render the office of teacher extremely repulsive to those who have been brought up as ladies . . .

Evidence of Mr Foster, loc. cit., Vol. 2, pp. 364-5

Ordinarily, the female apprentice teacher is the daughter of a handicraftsman, or a labourer, of a domestic servant, or a farm servant. Her parents earn from 30s. a week down to 12s. She is not unfrequently one of several children, sometimes the only girl, or the only girl above infancy. It is a great wrong to her family if [through her school work] she is prevented from taking her fair share of the usual household work of the home, and a greater injury to herself if she be excused from this . . . Otherwise, if she fail to become a Queen's

cholar; or if she marry an elementary schoolmaster, or a small
hopkeeper, or a small yeoman, she will be anything but a good house-
vife; or if she become a certified schoolmistress she will not be the
person whom sensible thoughtful parents of humble life will care to
ntrust with the formation of the character of their girls ... If they
attach the notion of indignity to the scrubbing brush ... they will bring
up a race of girls of humble life who prefer scribbling to scrubbing, or
eading Walter Scott, Byron, Harrison Ainsworth ... to reading their
Bible or the cookery-book. I have seen this effect produced.

Evidence of the Rev. G. Proctor, Devonport, loc. cit., Vol. 3, pp. 134-6

3.8.4 *Married teachers—female inspectors*

Married women teachers are unjust to the families of the teachers
hemselves ... their children are neglected ... It is an injustice to the
school ... [for] she has not the same incentive to work as one who is
single, for she has her husband to fall back upon ... It is an injustice
to other teachers. Young women, fresh from college, or wishing to
change their situations, complain of this unfair competition ...

Benedict, 'Married women as teachers in our schools',
The Schoolmaster, 3 January 1874

Is there not generally a widowed mother, a younger sister who cares
for the children? After the first few years of infancy, children are
away from home during the same hours as the mother ... 'Benedict'
asserts that the school will suffer ... yet he admits that the number of
appointments given to married women is increasing. Why? Surely not
because managers find them inefficient. Is it not because they have
been mothers themselves? ... 'Benedict' is right upon one point.
Having a husband to fall back upon does make a woman more
independent of managers, School Boards, and all other task masters.
Therefore marriage tends to raise the status of the teacher.

Kitty, *The Schoolmaster,* 10 January 1874

A correspondent of the *Spectator* has been pleading for the opening
up of school inspection as a line of life for ladies. In reply, a School
Board mistress has urged the following plea:—'I imagine that your
correspondent is not a woman, as I feel sure that most of my sex will
agree with me, that if we would have true and impartial justice, we
must seek it—not among ourselves. The woman's nature is too small
for the work of judging, it is too exacting towards its own sex, it is too
much turned on details to the exclusion of generalities, and it is too
concentrated on parts, to be able to grasp a clear view of the whole ...
Domestic economy, in most of its branches, would perhaps be better
understood by a woman, but by no one would the efficiency or value
of practical cookery be so well appreciated as by a man ... As to

counsel and advice, the inspectors we have at present ... are always ready [to help] ... without the persistent interfering and overbearing manner generally assumed by women in power over their less elevated sisters. And another point in favour of the stronger sex for our judges—the varied experience of the world (seldom falling to the lot of women) which prompts them to look on every subject with more clearness, generosity and impartiality.' Miss Frances Power Cobbe remarks: 'My friend Mary Carpenter said to me, "Depend upon it there was never yet a man whom the matron or mistress of an institution could not entirely bamboozle respecting every department under her control"' ... Has that anything to do with her preference? ...

The Schoolmaster, 17 August 1878

3.8.5   *The National Union of Teachers*

The weak point of the National Union of Teachers is the multitude of women teachers unattached to it by membership. For no other class of teachers does so much remain to be done; none need help so much, yet none seek it so little. The women who are members are among the principal sources of the Union's strength; the women who are not members are the Union's greatest danger ... The village school-mistress in particular needs the Union's aid ... Special leaflets have been drawn up dealing with women, class and rural teachers ...

National Union of Teachers, *Annual Report for 1897*

3.9 Nursing

3.9.1 *Florence Nightingale*

Lea Hurst, 7 July

What is my business in this world and what have I done this last fortnight? I have read the *Daughter at Home* to Father and two chapters of Mackintosh; a volume of *Sybil* to Mama. Learnt seven tunes by heart. Written various letters. Ridden with Papa. Paid eight visits. Done company. And that is all.

> Florence Nightingale's diary, 1846, quoted in E. Cook,
> *The Life of Florence Nightingale*, 1913, Vol. 1, p. 63

On Thursday last we had 1,715 sick and wounded in this Hospital (among whom 120 cholera patients), and 650 severely wounded in the other Building called the General Hospital, of which we also have charge, when a message came to me to prepare for 510 wounded ... arriving from the dreadful affair from Balaklava ... I always expected to end my days as Hospital Matron, but I never expected to be Barrack Mistress. We had but half an hour's notice before they began landing the wounded. Between one and 9'o'clock we had the mattresses stuffed, sewn up, laid down—alas! only upon matting on the floor—the men washed and put to bed, and all their wounds dressed ... The operations are all performed in the ward—no time to move them; one poor fellow exhausted with haemorrhage, has his leg amputated as a last hope, and dies ten minutes after the Surgeon has left him. Almost before the breath has left his body it is sewn up in its blanket and carried away and buried the same day. We have no room for corpses in the wards.

> Florence Nightingale to Dr Bowman,
> 14 November 1854, loc. cit., p. 185

I am a kind of General Dealer in socks, shirts, knives and forks, wooden spoons, tin baths, tables and forms, cabbage and carrots, operating tables, towels and soap, small tooth combs, precipitate for destroying lice, scissors, bedpans and stump pillows ...

A whole army having been ordered to abandon its kit ... I am now clothing the British Army ... or they must have gone naked ...

The daily routine of the Hospital is now performed, or rather *not* performed, by the Purveyor. I am really cook, housekeeper, scavenger (I go about making the orderlies empty huge tubs), washer-woman, general dealer, store keeper. The Purveyor is supposed to do all this, but it is physically impossible. And the filth, and the disorder, and the neglect, let those describe who saw it when we first came . . .

Florence Nightingale to Sydney Herbert,
4, 8 and 28 January 1855, loc. cit., pp. 200, 224-8

What nonsense people do talk, to be sure, about people finding themselves in suitable positions and looking out for congenial work! I am sure if any body in the world is most unsuited for writing and official work, it is I. And yet I have done nothing else for seven years but write Regulations.

Florence Nightingale to M. Mohl,
1 January 1864, loc. cit., Vol. 2, p. 59

As to my being on the [Suffrage] Society you mention . . . I will say why I have kept off the stage of these things. In the years that I have passed in Government offices, I have never felt the want of a vote—because, if I had been a Borough returning two members to Parliament, I should have had less administrative influence . . .

Florence Nightingale to J. S. Mill,
11 August 1867, loc. cit., Vol. 2, p. 216

3.9.2 *Lady nurses*

The nursing staff consists of two classes—the head nurses and the under nurses ... The head nurses give medicines, attend to the surgical dressings, receive the medical directions for each patient, keep order in the wards, serve out the dinners, and see that the actual attendance upon the patients is given by the under nurses. As a rule, they are skilful, experienced and kindly people, very well suited to their work. They usually belong to the lower section of the middle class, are the widows of small tradesmen or clerks, or less frequently they have been confidential domestic servants. Their salary varies from £20 to £50 a year, with board and residence.

The under nurses wait upon the patients, assist the sister in her duties, and in many cases clean the wards ... They are vastly inferior to the head nurses ... They are commonly below the class of second or even third rate domestic servants; if they were not nurses, one would expect them to be maids-of-all-work, scrubs or charwomen. They receive about £10 or £12 a year, with partial board or board wages.

From them, again, there is an apparent descent to the night nurses ... When they do not live in the hospital, they eke out their scanty incomes by working the best part of the day, and consequently they come to the hospital hoping to be able to sleep the greater part of the night . . .

Admitting the superiority of ladies as nurses, it is still possible to question the wisdom of asking them to take up nursing as a profession

. . . The office of lady superintendent is one which should be held by a trained and qualified person . . . But the employment which this would open to educated women is too limited to justify its advocates in thinking of nursing as a profession for ladies in the sense in which the word 'profession' is used commonly. Two hundred such situations represents the maximum number ever likely to be offered . . .

Elizabeth Garrett, 'Hospital nursing', *Transactions of the National Association for the Promotion of Social Science,* 1866

Miss Nightingale's reply. It is far more difficult to induce a 'middle-class' woman than an 'upper-class' one to go through as Head Nurse the incidental drudgery which must fall to the province of the Head Nurse or be neglected.

No nurses should do the work of 'scrubbers'—that therefore the Nurse whether she be upper, middle or lower class is equally able to go through the training of a nurse . . . 'Upper class' [women] . . . are equally qualified to be Nurses, Head Nurses, to attend an operation or to be Supts. . . . My principle has always been that we would give the best training we could to any woman, of any class, of any sect, 'paid' or unpaid, who had the requisite qualifications, moral, intellectual and physical, for the vocation of a Nurse. Unquestionably, the educated will be more likely to rise to the post of Supt., but *not* because they are ladies but because they are educated.

Florence Nightingale to Dr Farr, 13 September 1866, quoted in C. Woodham-Smith, *Florence Nightingale*, 1950, pp. 482-3

3.9.3 *The image of nursing*

A woman who takes a sentimental view of Nursing (which she calls 'ministering', as if she were an angel), is of course worse than useless. A woman possessed with the idea that she is making a sacrifice will never do; and a woman who thinks any kind of Nursing work 'beneath a Nurse' will simply be in the way. But if the right woman is moved by God to come to us, what a welcome we will give her, and how happy she will soon be in her work . . .

Florence Nightingale to her Nurses, 1875

3.9.4 *Nursing in 1890*

The selection of nurses rests in all cases practically with the matron, and the minimum age at which they are taken is usually about twenty-three. There is no lack of candidates for employment; at the London Hospital, for example, the number of applicants in a single year was said to be 1,600. Nurses are drawn from a well-educated class; many are daughters of professional men, merchants, farmers and tradesmen . . .

The nurse enters into a regular contract of service for a stated period of one, two or three years; during that period she not only assists in the practical work of nursing in the wards, but also attends lectures . . . and is required to pass examinations; and at the end of the period, having passed her examinations, she receives from the hospital a nurses certificate.

The sisters are in a position of considerable responsibility, each having under the matron, the entire charge of her ward; and at some hospitals they are generally selected from among nurses of a superior social position . . .

The work of the nurses is supplemented by ward maids and scrubbers . . . Inquiry was frequently made whether the nurses were called on to perform menial duties. The rule seems to be that it is their business to do everything directly affecting the patients, including a great deal of sweeping and dusting . . .

A probationer in her first year is paid usually at the rate of £1 a month . . . The pay of fully trained nurses in the hospitals . . . ranges from £20 to £40 . . . Sisters usually receive from £35 . . . to £60 . . . Board, lodging, and often some articles of clothing are provided free . . . Provision is sometimes made for pensions . . . The salary of a matron in the leading hospitals seems to run from £100 a year up to £350 . . .

If a ward of 36 beds be taken as an example, it appears that the day staff of nurses will probably consist . . . of a sister in charge, a staff nurse and three probationers . . .

The day nurses come on duty at 7 a.m. . . . The first hours are busily occupied in getting the patients fed and washed, their beds made and the wards put in order for the day. Later . . . the doctors have to be accompanied on their rounds, and the orders for the diet, medicine, and general treatment of each patient carefully noted . . . the nurses go off duty at 9 p.m. The average allowance for meals is from 1 hour to 1½ hours . . . Several witnesses expressed the opinion that the existing hours of duty were too long and the labour unduly arduous . . .

The question of registration. The objects of the British Nurses' Association are (in Mrs Fenwick's words) 'first to unite trained nurses together in a purely professional union; secondly, to provide for the local registration of nurses under the control of medical men; thirdly, to help nurses in times of need or adversity; and fourthly, to improve the knowledge and usefulness of nurses throughout the empire' . . . Their view is that the time has come when nursing should be constituted and legally recognized as a distinct profession, with a central controlling body of its own; in short, that the nursing profession should be governed on much the same lines as the medical profession. The nurses' register would resemble the medical register, and the general nursing council would take cognizance of the conduct of the nurses, and would have the same power to strike their names off the register for misconduct ... The ultimate object appears to be ... to obtain statutory power to prevent any public or private institution sending out women to nurse the sick, who were not registered.

Third Report of the Select Committee of the House of Lords on Metropolitan Hospitals, 1892, Vol. XIII

Earl Catheart, Qu. 9,631: It is said that ... an accomplished nurse is composed of two parts, one consisting of the female medical student, and the other of the ministering angel; and they say that the better part is the ministering angel; and that no record or register would convey any idea of the latter qualities, those of the ministering angel, the sympathy, kindness, and goodness of heart, and all those other qualities which are required to make the perfect nurse ...

Mrs. Fenwick: I do not think that we desire to register personal qualifications of that sort. What we want to do is place the skilled nurse on safe ground; that is, that when she had gone through a certain training, and knows a certain amount, that she should not have to compete in the open market with unskilled nurses; and that the public may be protected from any amateur or bogus nurse who may don a cap and apron with very little training, and take the same amount of fees from the public as are paid for a trained nurse ... With all the enormous amount of training going on now in our large hospitals, which are turning out more nurses than can get work, I think it hard that they should have to compete with so many amateurs ...

First Report, op. cit., 1890, Vol. XVI

The main point alleged against the British Nurses' Association by its opponents is that it places good and bad nurses on a level. It is urged that neither the completion of a period of training nor the passing of a theoretical examination is sufficient guide to the practical fitness of a woman for a nurse's work. Only the institution which has actually trained the nurse, and in which her qualities are recorded after long, personal observation, can be in a position to give such a guarantee of her capacity ... It was further said [in the interests of the medical profession] that the grant of a sort of diploma to nurses would lead many people to seek a nurse in case of illness and not a doctor ... To quote Mr. Rathbone, on behalf of the Nightingale Training School, 'The quality of a nurse depends almost more upon moral than upon intellectual considerations; you cannot test it by examinations'.

Third Report, op. cit., paras 510-13

3.10 Medicine

3.10.1 *The need for women doctors*

More than half of ordinary medical practice lies among women and children ... At present, when women need medical aid or advice, they have at once to go out of their own world, as it were; the whole atmosphere of professional life is so entirely foreign to that in which they live that there is a gap between them and the physician whom they consult, which can only be filled up by making the profession no longer exclusively a masculine one.

Drs Elizabeth and Emily Blackwell, 'Medicine as a profession for women', *English Woman's Journal,* May 1860

It is a woman's admitted prerogative to heal the sick, and nurse the wounded ... Why, then, is it said by some, that it is improper for women to be doctors? Some urge that it is because of the curriculum of study to be passed through, though, surely, that could not be much worse than what a nurse has to learn in point of practical duties. But the means for obtaining medical education, ought to be made quite as easy to women as to men, and it ought to be so arranged that no offence could be given to the most delicately proper nature, by the course of study, even though that study may be a somewhat trying ordeal to pass through ... We do not advocate the mixture of the sexes in medical education, for the world is not fit for it, just yet, but means and ways could be found without that necessity, and without the need of such heavy fees as women are now obliged to pay in Edinburgh for anything like medical lectures ... The question of the impropriety of a woman being a doctor is dispersed to the winds, when we know that as nurses in hospitals and on the battlefields they have to pass through more disagreeable sights and scenes than they would even as doctors. The argument indeed would seem to lie in favour of doctoring as being a more refined profession than nursing, and then there would be the great advantage of better pay for those who entered on the higher profession ...

Many a woman would much prefer a doctor of her own sex, if she could be sure of obtaining a well qualified one, for it is the fear of ignorance and incapacity, that has caused the employment of men in many cases ... for duly qualified women doctors would be much better than uneducated mid-wives.

The last argument in favour of the admission of women to the medical profession is utility ... Women are more numerous than men, and therefore lucrative trades and professions should be opened to those who have to go forth into the arena of life to fight for daily bread ... If more women generally would take up the profession of medicine and carry it into our towns and villages the good to the poorer and even to the richer classes is beyond the telling, for there are out-of-the-way villages where no doctor can be had within some miles. In the large cities where the poor are crowded together, what good a district visitor might do if she were only a doctor as well!

A. Le Geyt, 'Medicine as a profession for women',
Englishwoman's Review, July 1872

3.10.2   *Women not suitable*

Sir,

... I believe most conscientiously and thoroughly that women as a body are sexually, constitutionally and mentally unfitted for the hard and incessant toil, and for the heavy responsibilities of general medical and surgical practice. At the same time I believe as thoroughly, that there is a branch of our profession—midwifery—to which they might and ought to be admitted in a subordinate position as a rule.

In France, and in many other parts of the Continent, this division of labour in Midwifery is fully carried out, and with great advantage to both parties—to the regular practitioner, who is relieved of part of his most arduous, most wearing and most unremunerative duties, and to the women who have a vocation for medicine, to gain a respectable living in the profession which they wish to practise ...

The principal feature which appears to me to characterize the Caucasian race, to raise it immeasurably above all other races, is the power that many of its *male* members have of advancing the horizon of science ... I am not aware that the female members of our race participate in this power, in this supreme development of the human mind ... What right then have women to claim mental *equality* with men? ...

Dr H. Bennet, letter to *The Lancet,* 18 June 1870

Sir,

... After saying that women are unfit for 'hard and incessant toil', Dr. Bennet goes on to propose to make over to them as their sole share ... the 'most arduous, most wearing and most unremunerative duties'. In the last adjective seems to lie the whole suitability of the division of labour according to the writer's view ... Let whatever be well paid be left to the man; then chivalrously abandon the 'badly remunerated' work to the women. This is the genuine view of a trades-unionist ...

But when Dr. Bennet proceeds to dogmatize about what he calls our claim to 'mental equality', he comes to a different and much more important question. I for one do not care in the least either to claim or disown such equality ... We say ... 'State clearly what attainments you consider necessary for a medical practitioner ... put no obstacles in our way ... subject us ultimately to exactly the ordinary examinations and tests and, if we fail to acquit ourselves as well as your average student, reject us; if, on the contrary, in spite of all the difficulties, we reach your standard, and fulfil all your requirements, the question of "mental equality" is practically settled ... give us then the ordinary medical licence or diploma, and leave the question of our ultimate success or failure in practice to be decided by ourselves and the public'. This is our position, and I appeal, not to the chivalry, but to the justice of the medical profession, to show us that it is untenable, or else to concede it at once.

Sophia Jex-Blake, letter to *The Lancet,* 9 July 1870

3.10.3   *The riot at Surgeons' Hall*

Shortly before four o'clock, the hour when the ladies arrive at the College, nearly two hundred students assembled in front of the gate leading to the building ... Their noisy demonstration speedily attracted a large crowd ... The appearance of the ladies was greeted with a howl which might have made those who are supposed to be possessed of more temerity, quail, but it seemingly had no effect on the ladies, for they most unconcernedly advanced towards the gate, the students opening up their ranks to allow them to pass. On reaching the gate it was closed in their face ... The janitor succeeded in opening one leaf of the gate, and the ladies were admitted to the precincts, but not before some of them had been considerably jostled.

The anatomical class-room to which they proceeded was crowded to the door, and, in consequence of the noise and interruption, Dr. Handyside found it utterly impossible to begin his demonstrations. With much difficulty, he singled out those students belonging to his class, and, turning the others out of his room, he was about to proceed, when the pet sheep which grazes at the College was introduced to the room ...

Courant, 19 November 1870

If we happen to meet students on our way home in the evening ... [they] find pleasure in following a woman through the streets, and take advantage of her being alone to shout after her all the foulest epithets in their voluminous vocabulary of abuse ... If the wish of those students is to bar our progress, and frighten us from the prosecution of the work we have taken in hand, I venture to say never was a greater mistake made ... I began the study of medicine merely from personal motives; now I am also impelled by the desire to remove women from the care of such ruffians. I am quite aware that respectable students will say, and truly, that these are the dregs of the profession ... and will have only the treatment of unprotected servants and shop-girls. I should be very sorry to see any poor girl under the care (!) of such men as those, for instance, who the other night followed me through the street, using medical terms to make the disgusting import of their language more intelligible to me. When a man can put his scientific knowledge to such degraded use, it seems to me he cannot sink much lower ...

Edith Pechey, letter to the *Scotsman,* 13 July 1871

3.10.4   *Progress report*
Instead of one examining board we have no less than seven thrown open to women; viz., two Universities, two Irish Colleges, and three Scotch Colleges; but the English Colleges of Physicians and Surgeons still remain closed, as also four out of the five English Universities, and all the Scottish Universities, as well as Trinity College, Dublin, and the Apothecaries' Halls of London and Dublin.

Instead of a single medical school for women we now have three ... and the number of students has risen from less than thirty in 1877, to about a hundred at the present time. The number of registered medical women in 1877 was but nine; at the beginning of 1887, the number who had attained registration was fifty-four ...

A hospital for women and children, managed exclusively by medical women, has now been established in London for more than fifteen years, and larger premises have been needed and obtained at least twice during that period. A small hospital of the same kind in Edinburgh has just completed its second year. In addition to these, dispensaries have been started in London, Clifton, Leeds and Manchester, and in every case the attendance of patients has shown how much the facilities offered have been appreciated ... One of the largest day schools for girls in London has a woman doctor in regular attendance, with a view to preventive rather that curative service ... In these days of educational pressure I know of no more useful function for medical women than the constant and careful supervision of growing girls during their period of study.

Sophia Jex-Blake, 'Medical women',
reprinted 1888 from *The Nineteenth Century,* November 1887

3.11 Clerical work

3.11.1 *Women in the post office*

In the first place they have in an eminent degree, the quickness of eye and ear and the delicacy of touch which are essential qualifications of a good operator. In the second place, they take more kindly than men or boys do to sedentary employment and are more patient during long confinement to one place. In the third place, the wages which will draw male operators from but an inferior class of the community, will draw female operators of a superior class. Female operators thus drawn from a superior class, will, as a rule, write better than male clerks, and spell more correctly; and where the staff is mixed, the female clerks will raise the tone of the whole staff. They are also less disposed than men to combine for the purpose of extorting higher wages, and this is by no means an unimportant matter.

On one other ground it is especially desirable that we should extend the employment of women. Permanently established civil servants invariably expect their remuneration to increase with their years of service, and they look for this increased remuneration ... Women however, will solve these difficulties for the department by retiring for the purpose of getting married as soon as they get a chance ... if we place an equal number of females and males on the same ascending scale of pay, the aggregate pay to the females will always be less than the aggregate pay to the males; that, within a certain range of duty, the work will be better done by the females than the males, because the females will be drawn from a somewhat superior class; and further, there will always be fewer females than males on the pension list.

Evidence of Mr Scudamore,
Report on the Re-organization of the Telegraph System, 1871

3.11.2 *Women clerks*

Do you find that there is a progressive tendency to employ women in various directions?—Yes: it is more easy to get them employed than it was formerly.

Do you know from your experience whether their clerical employment in private establishments is increasing?—Yes; it is very largely increasing as book-keepers ... Those who are employed as book-keepers in shops are generally daughters of the better class of trades-people. Ladies have rather a reluctance to go into shops, but some do so ... We have had book-keepers in warehouses for many years. We have several in a large warehouse in Houndsditch. I think there are five now.

What has been your experience of them: have they been often returned upon your hands as inefficient?—Very seldom. When they once make a fair start we seldom have them back again. Before we send any out we have them examined. We have a class, and the girls attend this class until we think that they are competent, and then Mr. Proctor, of King's College, holds an examination for us ... We are also in the habit of sending temporary clerks for several offices. We send clerks to the Society for the Propagation of the Gospel when they want them, and to about 14 other Societies.

Does not the census of 1871 show a very considerable increase in the number of clerks employed in the Civil Service?—Yes, in the Telegraph Department of the Post Office.

Are most of them that come to you young or old?—They vary: we wish we could get them younger. They generally come to us when they have lost their homes; it is ladies of the middle rank who have had homes until their parents die, and then at 30 or 35 they are thrown upon the world.

Do you take them in married and in unmarried life?—Yes, we take any whose recommendations are perfectly good.

You have law-copying for them in connection with your establishment?—Yes ... but we do not get sufficient work for that branch. We employ seven or eight clerks ...

Does the business come to them from the law-stationer, or from the solicitor?—From the solicitors themselves.

You state in your report that last year 68 of the women obtained permanent employment from your office?—Yes ... Some of the societies to which we send ladies used to employ men, and once they have employed women they continue them. We have sent clerks to them now for several years, and I think that if they were not satisfied with them they would not continue to employ them. I have never had any means of comparing the work.

> Evidence of Gertrude King, Secretary of the Society for
> Promoting the Employment of Women, to the (Playfair)
> *Civil Service Inquiry Commission,* 1874

3.11.3 *Women telegraphists*

The English Government has employed women as telegraphists since January 1870 ... They receive eight shillings a week to begin with, the highest scale of pay being thirty shillings a week; and they work eight hours a day between the hours of 8 a.m. and 8 p.m. They formerly worked in separate galleries, but it was found desirable to place them in the same galleries as the men and boys, and their society and mutual influence has been productive of beneficial results. The female telegraphists belong to the class from which assistants behind the counters of shops are recruited: these posts, however, are open to women of all grades. Great accuracy, general intelligence and quickness are required for the work, which is, as a rule, satisfactorily accomplished. It is deemed inexpedient to employ females in night work. At the present time 968 female telegraphists are employed by Government in London, Edinburgh, and Dublin. A large number of women of the same class are employed as counter-women and returners of undelivered letters. These situations are all most eagerly sought for. Years sometimes pass before candidates obtain appointments.

In the year 1875 the thought occurred to Sir John Tilley, K.C.B. then Secretary, that the clerkships in the Post-Office Savings-bank might be filled by gentlewomen of limited means, daughters of officers in the Army and Navy, of civil officers of the Crown, of those engaged in the clerical, legal, and medical professions, of literary men and artists . . .

The numerous applications for nomination prove how the opportunity is valued. The appointments, made by competitive examination among the nominated candidates, are only confirmed after a six months' satisfactory probation ... It was solely on the ground of proved merit, that the branch was organized, in 1876, into two classes, with two or three principal clerks, and a Lady Superintendent, who holds the position of a staff officer. Since then, also, all promotions have been made by merit ... The public has been well served by ladies, to whom the work has furnished an honourable independence.

J. Manners, 'Employment of women in the public service',
Quarterly Review, Vol. 151, 1881

3.12 Survey of the field of women's work

In all England and Wales, then, the proportion of women who may be expected to remain unmarried is, roughly speaking, one in six; in London it is one in five. These statistics have been called startling and alarming ... If all these spinsters had to be shut up in convents the outlook would be gloomy. But as things are, if only we can secure good pay and decent conditions of life, the lot of all women may be immensely improved by this compact band of single women. It would be difficult to overrate the industrial effect of a number of well-instructed, healthy-minded, vigorous permanent spinsters. A man's work is not interrupted but rather intensified by marriage; but in the case of women, not only is the wages question very much affected by the expectation of marriage, but much organised effort on their part, whether for improvement of wages or for provision against sickness and old age, must be wasted unless there be a considerable number of single women to give continuity to the management of their associations ...

[Of working women, 31 per cent belong to Booth's 'poor', 51 per cent to the artisan class, 18 per cent to the middle and upper classes.] From the first of these groups are drawn the lower grades of factory girls in East London, who form the majority of match-girls, rope-makers, jam- and sweetstuff-makers, and a considerable proportion of the box-, and cigar-makers, as well as of the less skilled tailoresses. The factories where the work cannot be given out (as is the case in match, jam, and cigar factories) contain the largest percentage of married women: The great need of this class is training for domestic life, by which I do not mean domestic service. Herein lies the only effective cure for the industrial and social miseries of the poor. Bad cooking, dirty habits, overcrowding, and empty-headedness are the sources of the drunkenness, inefficiency, immorality, and brutality which obstruct progress among so many of the poor, and philanthropic efforts can be better employed in this direction than in any other.

From the second group of working women are drawn our better-paid factory girls, our tailoressses, domestic servants, and a large number of our dressmakers and milliners, shop-assistants, barmaids, clerks, and elementary teachers. Their work is skilled and requires an apprenticeship. They are in the majority of cases brought into direct contact with the consumer, and education, good manners, personal appearance and tact, all raise their market value. In this second group would be included the majority of the Lancashire and Yorkshire weavers ... These girls accept wages which would not be enough to support them if they had not friends to help them; and they endure hard work, long hours, and close rooms because they believe that they are only filling up a brief interval before marriage. The better off their parents may be, the less heed do they give to securing anything but pocket-money wages. Combination is nowhere so much needed, and perhaps is nowhere so unpopular ... skilled hands are not so plentiful that they could easily be replaced, and the girls, if assisted by their friends, could well afford to bide their time quietly at home until they had secured good terms ...

[The third group] form the majority of the shop-assistants in the West End and the richer suburbs, and more than any other class supply the elementary schools with teachers. It is as teachers, and also as Civil Service clerks, that they join the upper middle class, including under that term the professional, manufacturing and trading classes ... [Many of these middle-class] women are not employed to produce commodities which have a definite market value, and have therefore no means of measuring their utility by market price. They nearly all perform services for persons who pay them out of fixed income, and make no pecuniary profit by employing them. And there is no rate at which we can say that the supply of these services will cease; for the desire to be usefully employed is so strong in educated women, and their opportunities of being profitably employed (in the economic sense of the word profitable) are so few, that they will give their services for a year to people as well off as themselves in return for a sum of money barely sufficient to take them abroad for a month or to keep them supplied with gloves, lace, hats, and other necessary trifles ... Two things only I would venture to suggest. One, that instead of supplementing salaries and so lowering them, parents should help their daughters to hold out for salaries sufficient to support them, should assist them in making themselves more efficient, and should help them to make provision for themselves in later life, instead of making self-support impossible. The other, that manufacturers and business men should train their daughters as they train their sons. The better organisation of labour should open a wide field for women, if they will only consent to go through the routine drudgery and hardship that men have to undergo. An educated girl who goes from the high school to the technological college will find full scope for any talents she may possess. As designer, chemist, or foreign correspondent in her father's factory she could be more helpful and trustworthy than anyone not so closely interested in his success. As forewoman in any factory, if she understood her work, she would be far superior to the uneducated man or woman, and some of the worst abuses in our factory system would be swept away.

Clara Collet, 'Prospects of marriage for women',
The Nineteenth Century, April 1892

3.13 Women's Trade unionism

3.13.1 *The Women's Protective and Provident League*

It is seldom disputed that the rate of wages paid to women is, in many occupations, disgracefully low ... Women [are] frequently paid half, or less than half, for doing work as well and as quickly as men ...

Employers alone are not to blame for the evils of underpayment. There are many just and right-minded employers who would gladly pay their workwomen a fair rate of wages; but, however willing they may be to do this, they are almost powerless so long as the women themselves make no stir in the matter. If they were to pay higher wages whilst other less scrupulous employers could, without difficulty, obtain the services of women at about a third or fourth of the fair payment, they would simply be unable to carry on business ...

The present isolated position of working women reacts injuriously on their prospects in many indirect, as well as direct ways ...

So long as women are unprotected by any kind of combination, and are consequently wholly at the mercy of employers for the rate of their wages and the length of their working hours, working men not unnaturally look with suspicion on their employment in trades in some branches of which men are engaged. The fear that the employment of women will lower their wages has led the men to pass rules in many of their trade societies positively forbidding their members to work with women.

They have also carried on and are still continuing, an agitation ... to limit the hours of women's work in factories and workshops. This Bill is intended to apply also to children, with whom working women are classed, thus conveying and endeavouring to perpetuate, the idea that women are entirely unable to protect themselves, a position, to a certain extent, degraded and injurious.

Women, more than ever, urgently need the protection afforded by combination ... as they have no means of making known their collective opinion on the subject.

There can be no doubt that it is desirable, in many cases, to shorten the hours during which women work, but if this is done by legislative enactments instead of by the combined action of the workers themselves, the result may merely be the reduction of wages, already often insufficient, and sometimes complete exclusion from work, thus becoming, in place of protection, a real and grievous oppression. Where there is combined action among the workers, as in the case of men, it has been clearly seen, of late years, that no such legislation is necessary.

It is true that working men ... might invite women to join their trade unions, or assist them to form similar societies. But they do not seem to be inclined to do this. At three successive annual congresses of leaders and delegates of trade unions, the need of womens' unions has been brought before them, and each time some one present has asserted that women *cannot* form unions. The only ground for this assertion appears to be that women *have not* yet formed unions . . .

The following is an outline of a plan . . .

1.   A central council or board, having branches composed of workers in any trade all over the country.
2.   The name of the Association to be the 'National Protective and Benefit Union of Working Women''.
[3, 4, 5, branch secretaries to forward subscriptions]
6.   The subscription to be 1½d. per week, and the entrance fee 4½d.
7, 8,   [entrance fees to cover office expenses, subscriptions to be banked for benefits]
9.   No member to be entitled to receive sick or out of work benefits until she has paid subscriptions for six months; the sum then granted to depend on the amount of funds accumulated.
10.   Strict investigation to be made into applications for benefit payments.

It must be borne in mind that the main object in view is to accustom women to the idea of union . . .

By way of encouragement, women may be reminded of what has been done by that, until recently, worst paid and most isolated class of men, the agricultural labourers ... If men whose circumstances were so unfavourable to combination as those of most agricultural labourers, have been successful in this effort, there is every reason to hope for the success of unions of women.

With regard to the low wages of women (we are told) that 'all cheap production is a benefit to the producers'. Does it, however, benefit women or indeed men either, that cigars, for instance, should be made for 4d. per 100 ... or that the production of cartridges, in which women are largely employed, should be cheapened; or that artificial flowers should be sold at 1½d. per spray; that paper boxes for collars should be sold at so low a price that they are wasted and thrown away as of no value; or that jewel cases can be procured at a very small cost—Even in the case of articles of direct use to working women, cheap production is of but little more benefit. Wages of from 6s. to 12s. per week leave a very small margin for any purchases beyond those of the bare necessaries of life—food and fuel—and are often insufficient for a proper supply of these. Cheap production, which involves, for the producers, want, degradation, and even, occasionally, starvation; or which, when starvation is avoided, throws them upon the poor rates for maintenance, can surely not be beneficial to them or to the community ... Another important advantage is the feeling of strength and mutual sympathy and helpfulness afforded by close association with others in the same position and labouring under the same difficulties as ourselves. Out of such union, too, might grow many movements for still further improving the position of women, such as some kind of co-operative work-rooms, in which women, when temporarily out of employment, might find means of subsistence until they obtained permanent work; educational efforts, emigration clubs, reading-rooms, etc., etc.

The writer earnestly begs all persons interested in improving the social condition of women to communicate with her with a view to action in this matter, and especially invites information and suggestions from women engaged in trades.

Emma Paterson,
The Position of Working Women and How To Improve It, 1874

3.13.2   *A political life*
Trades unions are a kind of beginning of political life ... By such action you are fitting yourselves for having a share in the general protection and defence of all the people's rights ... Thinking and acting together for a common object is an inestimable political education ... No class needs this habit of union and co-operation and this training more than working women; they have interests as a class which they themselves must defend when once they are roused to it and know how.

Arabella Shore, 'What women have a right to',
lecture delivered to members of the Women's Protective
and Provident League, 1879

3.13.3   *The TUC debates*

Women and legislation. Mrs. Paterson (London) said that Factory and Workshop legislation was assuming a different aspect to that which it formerly bore. It was becoming more and more exceptional legislation for women, whereas the first Factory acts applied to men and women alike ... She was somewhat startled the preceding day to hear three delegates declare that when they got this bill passed, they would next try to get a bill to remove women from certain branches of work (agriculture and chain making) altogether ... She asked them to help women by combination to increase their wages, and not to attempt to drive them from work altogether ... No doubt some women were engaged in unsuitable occupations, but let them remove them from these objectionable sphere of labour by persuasion and by the force of public opinion, as had already been done to a large extent. As to chain making ... the heat of the fires was not greater than that of many kitchen fires prepared for roasting, near which cooks had to stand. As to government inspection to prevent over work she had no faith in it, and members of the Societies she represented had often stated at their meetings, how ineffectual such inspection was. She considered that the Reports of the Factory inspectors recently published, were calculated to mislead people as to the position of working women.

Mr. Broadhurst (London): ... They know it was very natural for ladies to be impatient of restraint at any time (Laughter.)—and therefore they might imagine the uneasiness which would be created when the law of the nation prescribed rules and regulations. It was a well-known fact that women had been employed in occupations totally unfitted for them, and they were unable to do anything to help themselves unless someone stretched out a helping hand to them. No doubt they might form unions, but their wages and their ever-changing position in life rendered them unable to do any effective work towards the emancipation of their class from degrading labour. Much good had been done by Mrs. Paterson, and other ladies, in forming and maintaining unions, but they would never be able to lift woman to her proper sphere unless they had some restrictions put upon the greed of those who would work their mothers or sisters like dogs or slaves for the sake of gain. (Applause.) There was another phase of it; they had the future of their country and children to consider, and it was their duty as men and husbands to use their utmost efforts to bring about a condition of things where their wives should be in their proper sphere at home, seeing after their house and family, instead of being dragged into the competition for livelihood against the great and strong men of the world ... (Applause.)

Mr. Wright (Glasgow) said God never intended women to be engaged in trade, but as they had to deal with things as they existed their efforts should be directed towards keeping the hours of work within proper compass, and preventing as far as they could home labour. (Hear, hear.) He thought it would be well to limit by law the hours of labour of men as well as women.

Mrs. Mason, representative of the Society of Seamers and Stitchers in the Hosiery trade, of Leicester and Leicestershire, said that a great deal of their work was done at home by married women, who were of middle age ... Of the advantages of earning this (4s. to 7s. a week) she submitted that they ought not to be deprived. She knew a woman with a family of eight children, all under 17 years of age, and only two of whom could go to work, yet the woman was compelled to work because her husband was too idle to maintain her and the family. (Shame.) If there were laws passed to make idle husbands maintain their families—(applause)—married women could give over working, either at their own houses or elsewhere. (Applause.) She was placed in a position of being compelled to earn a few shillings because her husband was not able himself to maintain the whole of the family, neither did she wish him, in his present state of health ... It would be as reasonable to pass a law to enable inspectors to visit their houses and see that their husbands were out of bed, instead of laying there until what they called luncheon time, as to have these laws for inspecting the work of women. (Laughter and applause.)

Trades Union Congress, September 1877,
reported in the *Women's Union Journal,* October 1877

Women and unionism. Mr. H. R. King said that he considered that women required a large amount of education in the politics of trades unions. (Hear, hear.) Their education on that subject had been very much neglected. He proposed the following resolution:—'That trade unions among women engaged in various industries are necessary for the improvement of the position of such women, and that those present at this meeting pledge themselves to use every effort in their power to promote in their respective localities the women's trade union movement.' ... What women hoped for and sought, was merely help in the first formation of such Unions. Women should be urged and encouraged to carry on the subsequent work themselves. Three years ago, it was proposed to start a Union of women in London, in his trade (bookbinding) and he, being Secretary of one of the Men's Unions in the trade was asked to help. He and a few other Trade Unionists gladly attended meetings, and gave advice in the drafting of the Rules and other matters, but at the first meeting, a Committee of the women was formed, and they soon became able to manage their business alone. The Society had now been paying benefits for two years, was in a good financial position, and had about 300 members ...

Mr. D. Merrick seconded the resolution, and in doing so stated that he had great pleasure in assisting to form the Leicester Union of Seamers and Stitchers (women) in the hosiery trade between two and three years ago. That Union had been instrumental in obtaining a considerable advance in the rates of payment and it hoped to do more in that direction at some future time. He considered the case of the seamers in Leicester as most miserable. He knew instances where women had worked 14 hours a day, and only earned 4s. or 5s. a week. There had been some difficulty in dealing with them on account of their want of courage and apathy which arose to a great extent from their beaten down condition. They had been rather too much inclined to look to men to conduct their business, although some of them had displayed much energy and ability in organizing the Union. Any efforts made by women to protect themselves by Union would always have his warm sympathy and any help he could give.

Mr. Ackrill (London Shoemakers) said that his society had made special laws in order to admit women into their union. They had recognised the advisability of having women's unions, but the women had not availed themselves of the facilities thrown into their way because of their unfortunate tendency to lean for advice upon males. When he was in Hull some few years ago he had succeeded in forming a women's branch of his society there, which prospered for a time, but not what it would have been had the women taken the work more upon themselves. If we wished to have intelligent sons it was requisite that they should have intelligent mothers, and for that reason women should be taught to become self-reliant. He was as anxious as anyone could be that women should be attached to their homes and make home comfortable, but he considered that such teaching would tend to increase their capabilities for their domestic duties, and would give them broader ideas.

Mrs. Paterson: The difference of opinion was only as to the best mode of securing the much needed shortening of working hours—combination or legislation . . . If the work were better paid per piece, women would be glad enough to work shorter hours. What she dreaded was too great a reliance placed upon legislation. She had heard women ask why an Act of Parliament was not passed to give them higher wages (laughter) and with such ideas of the power of law they did not so readily see the urgent need of combination . . . She trusted and believed that wherever women showed a disposition to unite to protect themselves, men who were trade unionists would help and encourage them . . .

Miss Brown wished it to be distinctly understood that women did not want long hours of work any more than men did. They did not like to work any more than they could help; they were like men in that respect (laughter); but there were thousands of women who must work. There was no subject on which greater mistakes were made, or more misunderstanding existed than on the question of the wages of the working-classes. Wherever she went she heard it said that working-men needed only to be provident, and to keep from drinking, in order to live in comfort, and to keep their families almost in luxury. Now this was false. She knew there were thousands of working-men who could not keep their wives, or at any rate, their daughters without work of some kind in addition to their own, therefore such talk was mere clap-trap. (Hear, hear.) So long as women were forced into the labour market, they would say to the men—do not restrict them in any way, give them the right hand of fellowship, and help them in all possible ways to come into the labour market on the same terms as yourselves. (Applause.) With regard to Women's Unions, men could help greatly by using their influence and arguments at home, in favour of Trades Unionism: sometimes when women were asked to come to meetings they refused because their fathers or other male relatives objected. It was for the interest of the men that women should receive high wages. If they could not keep themselves the men would have to keep them. They could not shoot them. It was a very difficult question to find out how far a trade would bear an advance of wages. All they could do was to do as the men did, and ask as much as they could get. (Hear, hear.) If there was any trade which could not afford to pay such wages as would keep the women who worked at it from starving, such a trade had no right to exist. (Hear, hear.)

Mr. Walker said it was a difficult matter for men to set about organising Unions of Women to which he could speak from considerable experience. He and some co-workers attempted it in the Cigar trade in 1872 but there was a fear on the part of the women that the men wanted to turn them out of work. They would probably have succeeded better had they been able to find women who would speak in favour of the proposal and he thought that now there were women ready to do this there was more hope of making progress in the movement. In many cases female labour was introduced into workshops, under the cloak of philanthropy, but really to lessen the cost of production. (Hear, hear.) Men very naturally objected to such competition as this but if women would demand fair payment the objection would be removed.

Mr. Sedgwick (Birmingham) said wherever female labour in his trade had been introduced, the wages of the men had been reduced by one half. He refused to bind himself to support a movement that would make such a result more general.

Mr. H. D. Richardson stated that what the men objected to was to allow the women to manufacture the same articles as the men at half the cost. (Hear, hear.) They were perfectly willing to allow women to enter any trade, and produce any article as long as they did not work for a lower wage than the men.

loc. cit.

3.13.4 *The match-girls' strike*
Bryant and May, now a limited liability company, paid last year a dividend of 23 per cent to its shareholders . . .

The hour for commencing work is 6.30 in summer and 8 in winter; work concludes at 6 p.m. Half-an-hour is allowed for breakfast and an hour for dinner. This long day of work is performed by young girls, who have to stand the whole of the time. A typical case is that of a girl of 16, a piece-worker; she earns 4s. a week, and lives with a sister, employed by the same firm, who 'earns good money, as much as 8s. or 9s. per week'. Out of the earnings 2s. is paid for the rent of one room; the child lives on only bread-and-butter and tea, alike for breakfast and dinner ... The splendid salary of 4s. is subject to deductions in the shape of fines; if the feet are dirty, or the ground under the bench is left untidy, a fine of 3d. is inflicted; for putting 'burnts'—matches that have caught fire during the work—on the bench 1s. has been forfeited, and one unhappy girl was once fined 2s. 6d. for some unknown crime. If a girl leaves four or five matches on her bench when she goes for a fresh 'frame' she is fined 3d. and in some departments a fine of 3d. is inflicted for talking. If a girl is late she is shut out for 'half the day', that is for the morning six hours, and 5d. is deducted out of her day's 8d. One girl was fined 1s. for letting the web twist round a machine in the endeavour to save her fingers from being cut, and was sharply told to take care of the machine, 'never mind your fingers'. Another, who carried out the instructions and lost a finger thereby, was left unsupported while she was helpless. The wage covers the duty of submitting to an occasional blow from a foreman; one who appears to be a gentleman of variable temper, 'clouts' them 'when he is mad' . . .

These 'female hands' eat their food in the rooms in which they work, so that the fumes of the phosphorus mix with their poor meal and they eat disease as seasoning to their bread. Disease, I say: for the 'phossy jaw' that they talk about means caries of the jaw, and the phosphorus poison works on them as they chew their food, and rots away the bone. The foreman have sharp eyes. If they see a girl's face swell they know the sign, and she is sent off and gets no pay during her absence.

Annie Besant, 'White slavery', Link, 23 June 1888

'My dear Lady,—We thank you very much for the kind interest you have taken in us poor girls, and hope that you will succeed in your undertakings ... Dear lady, they are trying to get the poor girls to say that it is all lies that has been printed, and trying to make them sign papers to say it is lies; dear lady, no one knows what we have to put up with, and we will not sign them. We all thank you very much for the kindness you have shown to us. My dear lady, we hope you will not get into any trouble in our behalf, as what you have spoken is quite true; dear lady, we hope that if there will be any meeting we hope you will let us know it in the book. I have no more to say at present, from yours truly, with kind friends wishes for you, dear lady, for the kind love you have shown us poor girls. Dear lady do not mention the date this letter was written or I might have put my or our names, but we are frightened, do keep that as a secret, we know you will do that, dear lady.' [*sic*]

On Friday, a little before three o'clock the meaning of the letter became clear: between one and two hundred girls flocked down Fleet Street, cheered vigorously as they saw Annie Besant's photograph in the window . . .

The Deputation. Three sturdy respectable women soon appeared in the LINK office, and told their story. The foremen had brought round on Wednesday a paper certifying that the girls were well treated and contented and repudiated the statements made on their condition, and this paper was laid to receive signatures during the dinner hour. When the foreman of one department returned, expecting to find it filled, it offered to his angry eyes a white unsullied surface. In vain he threatened and scolded; the girls would not sign . . . A girl pitched on apparently as ringleader was threatened with dismissal, but stood firm. On the following morning she was suddenly discharged for a pretended act of insubordination, and the women, promptly seeing the reason of her punishment, put down their work with one accord and marched out. The news spread, and the rest of the wood-match girls followed their example, some 1,400 women suddenly united in a common cause. An offer was made to take back the girl, but the spirit of revolt against cruel oppression had been aroused, and they declared they would not go in 'without their pennies'.

Link, 14 July 1888

On Tuesday, the Strike Committee—Mrs. Naulls, Mrs. Mary Cummings, Sarah Chapman, Alice Francis, Kate Slater, Mary Driscoll, Jane Wakeling, and Eliza Martin—accompanied members of the London Trades' Council into the presence of the directors, and put their own case. It was finally agreed that (1) all fines should be abolished; (2) all deductions for paint, brushes, stamps, etc., should be put an end to; (3) the 3d. should be restored to the packers; (4) the 'pennies' should be restored, or an equivalent advantage given in the system of payment of the boys who do the racking; (5) all grievances should be laid directly before the firm, ere any hostile action was taken; (6) all the girls to be taken back. The firm hoped the girls would form a union; they promised to see about providing a room for meals away from the work; and they also promised to provide barrows for carrying the boxes, which have hitherto been carried by young girls on their heads, to the great detriment of their hair and their spines.

It is small wonder that these terms were enthusiastically endorsed by the girls as a whole, when they were submitted to them at a meeting held at 6 p.m. on the same day. The girls feeling that they had won a victory which would materially better their conditions.

Link, 21 July 1888

3.13.5 *Women's Unions in 1893*

There are three classes of women's unions—one which enrols men and women upon equal terms; another which, while having separate rules and subscriptions, and keeping its business distinct, is looked after by the men of the trade, and is, in a measure, affiliated to the men's union; and a third class which is composed of women alone.

Enrolled in Men's Unions

	1893
Boot and shoe operatives	3,216
Card and blowing-room operatives	21,000
Gasworkers and general labourers	1,350
Glasgow Trades Council	1,000
Midland Trades Federation	1,500
Scottish mill and factory union	2,500
Weavers	45,496
	76,062

Affiliated to Men's Unions

Bedstead painters, Birmingham	700
Cigarmakers, Nottingham and London	1,600
Denton, hatters and wool formers	4,000
Total	82,362

The case is widely different when we turn to those unions which are composed of women only. After twenty years of effort, London counts fourteen branches, having in all about 2,250 members.

The match-makers is still the largest, though it has very much decreased. The book-folders have formed a strong body, and, though suffering from a temporary check, they promise well. The bookbinders, the oldest society, formed eighteen years ago, numbers 250. The ropemakers are 300. No others exceed 100. Printers refuse to combine at all, though, being skilled workers, they might do so with good effect. It is next to impossible to influence dressmakers, milliners, and shop assistants, though few classes need protection more, while numbers of the small trades have not even been approached.

In the provinces it is the same story. The Leeds tailoresses, of whom there are about 8,000 started, during a strike, a thousand strong; they then nearly died out, but have since risen to 150, and are gradually increasing. In Nottingham, the lacemakers are 370. In Manchester, where women are very badly paid, the shirtmakers are 400, and it is the only union there worthy of the name. In Birmingham I can obtain no tidings of those which formerly existed. In Bristol, organization is struggling for life. In Aberdeen, out of 8,000 women, only 250 are combined. In the Potteries, where thousands are employed, about 400 have banded themselves together since last autumn. I can only make out about 2,600 in the provinces, making a total of under 5,000 members of women's unions proper.

In the north we find the fish-curers of Aberdeen, toiling as even slaves have scarcely done, in open sheds, exposed to all weathers, wet through, pushing and lifting immense weights, starting so early from home and returning so late that they constantly do not see their families from one week's end to another. When great takes of fish come in they often work thirty-six hours at a stretch, while men in the same city are clamouring for a forty-eight hour week. They earn 12s. a week, and nothing for overtime, and this is far from being the only industry where women sometimes work all day and all night and all the next day. In the confectionery trade the hours are long, wages low, and fines heavy. Girls are fined sometimes 1s. out of a 6s. wage, for such trivial offences as looking out of window, talking, eating a piece of bread. In some factories they take their meals in rooms where the oranges are sorted and the coconuts smashed up. These are often very rotten, and the stench is such that the girls are sick and have sometimes even been attacked by typhoid fever.

In Manchester, in the great shirt factories, those who formerly made shirts at the steam sewing machines at 11½d. a dozen (all except button holes), are now beaten down to 7½d. Such examples could be quoted in many trades. In workshops things are even worse, and in home employment the lowest level is reached. The match-box makers earn a bare subsistence wage, 2¾d. a gross (six dozen boxes), and they find their own paste. Competition is so keen that, as a woman said, you have to beg and pray to get six gross to make, and if any work were declined on the score of low pay hundreds would rush in to take it up.

Nor are these the worst features. In a great many trades women are stepping in and underselling men, dragging down their wages and throwing them out of work, till it is imperative that the wife and mother should leave her home and her little children to spend her days in the workshop or the factory, while the children at the earliest opportunity scramble into some ill-paid employment in which they can earn a shilling or eighteenpence a week, 'working in the play-time of others', never properly trained to a calling but growing up to swell the helpless army of the unskilled. In the Potteries we find women doing work for 13s., for which men used to receive 30s. In the tailoring trade the tailoresses are in many places taking the trade entirely out of men's hands, doing it 50 per cent. cheaper. I have just heard of a well-known fashionable ladies' tailor, who this season is employing nothing but women, paying them 18s. where he used to pay men £2. The female printers work for 5d. an hour where the men get 8d. In the badly organized parts of Yorkshire, a man and a girl weaving side by side, doing work of precisely the same quality and quantity, find a difference of one-third between their wages at the week's end, so that an old weaver said he 'went in daily fear o'being jostled o'one side by a lass'. Female labour is beginning to affect the furniture and French polishing trade, among others, so that more French polishers than usual have been out of work last winter.

[Why are women apathetic about trade unionism?] First and most obvious is the fear of employers ... In the unskilled and ill-paid trades more especially, girls are constantly dismissed for joining ... Secondly the system of home employment, with its isolation and deplorable conditions ... where the losing of the ill-paid work is the one haunting fear ... The sweater's best friend [however] ... is that girls usually marry by the time they are twenty, and have not yet learned to reckon with the fact that as often as not they are obliged to return to the factory or take in home work ... In getting up a meeting, bills may be distributed by the thousand, home visits may be paid and assurances of attendance secured, but at the appointed hour it does not follow that anyone will appear ... At one meeting a man who was speaking turned away in despair. 'What can we do with these women?' he said; 'it is impossible to get any hold over them.'

We come to the conclusion, firstly that combination requires the stimulus afforded by large bodies working together, and that this condition is only to be ensured by the support of legislative regulation; secondly, that women only combine successfully when they join forces with men ... [who can supply] the perseverance ... and doggedness ...

There will still remain a mass of workers with which men are not legitimately concerned. The prospect of dressmakers combining is doubtful; perhaps their best remedy will be an efficient staff of female inspectors. Laundresses, together with paper-makers and some others, are agitating to be included in the Factory Acts ... Other trades almost exclusively confined to women are the making of envelopes, steel pens, paper bags and boxes, sacks, threads, tape, artificial flowers, corsets, trimmings and embroideries, gloves, nets, match-boxes, straw-plaiting, feather-dressing, and metal burnishing. These home industries employ about 83,000 hands ... The skilled workers are showing greater willingness than ever before to stand by the unskilled.

Evelyn March-Phillipps, 'The progress of
women's trades unions,' *Fortnightly Review*, vol. 60, 1893

3.13.6 *And in 1900*
In our union about 20 per cent of the members are women, and the thing which has greatly helped to organize them is the fact that men and women have equal rights and duties, and are equally eligible for election to any official position in the Union. At the branch meetings they discuss things in common, and find an identity of interests ... But the largest proportion of women wage-earners do not organize [because] ... they look upon it as a temporary occupation to be superseded by marriage! They fail to see any need for bothering themselves about the wages and general conditions obtaining in their trade ... Until girls are taught independence and a trade ... women wage-earners in the aggregate will remain where they are today—outside the ranks of Trade Unionism.

> Margaret Bondfield, Assistant Secretary, National
> Amalgamated Union of Shop Assistants, from articles
> collected by Isabella Ford, *Women's Trade Union Review*,
> January 1900

In 1889 our union enrolled women as members ... at the india-rubber works at Silverton [due to] Mrs. Aveling ... At one time we had a branch at Norwich of girls and women in the boot and shoe trade ... and women cotton workers at Bristol ... But women collectively do not seem to grasp the real need for unions ... They did not attend to the branch business ... But a married woman has children ... housework ... washing to do, which all tends to take the spirit out of women workers. Then in many cases, the single girl helps the mother to do the housework ... When a man has done his day's work he becomes free, but that is not so with women. I am strongly of the opinion that legislation is the strongest weapon that can be used for the benefit of all women workers. Give them the franchise and they will help to solve the problem for themselves ...

> W. Thorne, General Secretary, National Union of
> Gas Workers and General Labourers, loc. cit.

Of course, in common with everyone who has had much experience in the struggle of organizing women on Trade Union lines, I consider the struggle a most disheartening and painful one. but I hold very strongly that the fault does not lie with the women themselves. Those women who really grasp the aim of Trade Unionism, grasp it, I think, more firmly, even than men, because more religiously. No battle can be fought successfully that has not a religious spirit or meaning within it, and this meaning, which exists in Trade Unionism, appeals more strongly to women than the merely economic side of the cause. Of course, when I use the word 'religious', I use it in its widest sense, and as in no way connected with dogma or sects. This religious side has never been sufficiently emphasised to women.

All the orthodox religious world, broadly speaking, is against Trade Unionism for women (except theoretically), because Trade Unionism means rebellion, and the orthodox teaching for women is submission in this world in order to gain happiness in the next world . . .

The political world preaches to women submission, so long as it refuses them the Parliamentary franchise, and, therefore, ignores them as human beings.

Society encourages selfish indifference amongst women in that it considers a woman's home must make her sacrifice to it everyone else's home, and all public honour. Those are the forces we have to fight, and it is only when we have fought them successfully that the Trade Union movement will widen out into a really great and saving power.

The indifference, and more than indifference of parents and husbands about their daughters and wives being Trade Unionists is wide spread . . . as is also the still surviving remnant of the old jealousy and rivalry between the sexes. It sometimes seems to me as if we had the whole world to fight; certainly every form of conventional thought must be fought; particularly amongst the workers themselves. Real Trade Unionism for women means a moral and industrial revolution, and many people dread a revolution. They prefer stagnation, particularly for women.

Isabella Ford, 'Women as trade unionists', loc. cit.

3.14 State Intervention

3.14.1 *The opposition of the Vigilance Association*
The Chairman said the Association was formed to protect the
personal rights both of men and women; and as women were the
weakest and the most exposed to danger, and had no share in the
representation of the country, it was only natural that the defence of
their rights should be especially an object of the Association. The
attention of the Conference would be directed mainly to the injustice
which women suffered from restrictions upon their employment.

Miss Lucy Wilson (Leeds) ... desired them to notice the policy of
the advocates of restriction. Having obtained a concession of the
principle of interference with women, on the specious ground that
some work was too hard for them they now proceeded to demand
interference with them whatever their occupation was, provided that it
was not domestic labour, done without pay, which women might
follow as long as individual circumstances and individual taskmasters
might decree. So long as women worked much and got nothing, they
might work as much as they liked; it was only when, if they worked
much, they would get much, that they were to be restricted. As to the
proposed restrictions on the labour of married women, she considered
these would be more serious almost than the others were; and she was
less hopeful of their being able to make any fair fight against them on
account of the popular theory, that married women existed only for
their families, and therefore anything that was said to be good for
their families might be inflicted on them. She maintained that women
knew as well as men what it was well for them to do, and that they did
not do that which was unwise, either for themselves or their families,
except under strong pressure; and that they had a right, each for
herself, to judge of the circumstances of her particular case, and
decide whether the undesirable work or the undesirable starvation
were the worse alternative. Did men really believe that compulsion to
restrain the doing of wrong, and to compel to the doing of duty was
required more for women than for themselves, even in domestic
matters? Was it true that women were guilty of more crimes, and
greater crimes to their families than men? One had heard of drunken
husbands reducing their families to misery ... The plea that women
ought to stop at home and mind their families, was not an excuse for
legislation of this kind, because there was already a law which
provided for cases of parental neglect ... and it might apply to the
Duchess who neglected her children to go to State Balls and
fashionable vanities, as much as to the poor woman who left her

children to get bread for them. (Applause.) ... All the women who were married at the present time, had entered into the marriage contract, knowing that they had the power, if their husbands did not provide for them, to work for themselves. If such laws as were proposed were passed, women would be stripped of that power without any ability to revoke the contract into which they had entered on the faith of possessing that power. If any such proposal was made regarding the rights of men, it would be scouted in an instant, as grossly unjust. If anybody could think it was wise or right to reduce a wife to a condition of greater slavery, of more utter and helpless and hopeless dependence on her husband, good or bad, than she was at the present time, let it be done openly and avowedly, as a change in the law of marriage, and let people consider it as such; but it ought not to be done by the way of a law proposing to regulate labour. The province of law was to maintain personal rights, not to invade them. Its business was to protect the life and property of each individual, and not to rob anybody of that which he or she possessed ... They must try to get rid of the notion that women existed only for their usefulness to the other sex; until this was done, she saw no hope of getting rid of the interference with their work and their liberty. (Hear, hear.)

Dr. Ewing Whittle: Any proposal to forbid married women from returning to work until a certain time after their confinements ... was quite unnecessary as a protection to women ... The question of returning to work rested with the women; surely they must be the best judges as to when they were able to do this.

Mr. Thomas Snape (Liverpool): The parties who demanded this legislation ... are Trades Unions of Men, whose interest it is to restrict the labour of women, because by restricting the employment of women, they increased the demand for the employment of men.

Report of the Conference of the Vigilance Association for the Defence of Personal Rights, 25 November 1875, Liverpool, presided over by the Rev. G. Butler

3.14.2 *Women and the Factory Acts*

The discussions on the Factory Act of 1895 raised once more all the old arguments about Factory legislation ... This time legal regulation was demanded, not only by all the organizations of working women whose labour was affected, but also by, practically, all those actively engaged in Factory Act administration. The four women Factory Inspectors unanimously confirmed the opinion of their male colleagues ... Only the employers were ranged against the Bill, and that not unanimously. But the employers had the powerful aid of most of the able and devoted ladies who have usually led the cause of women's enfranchisement, and whose strong theoretic objection to

Factory legislation caused many of the most important clauses in the Bill to be rejected.

The ladies who resist further legal regulation of women's labour usually declare that their objection is to special legislation applying only to women. They regard it as unfair, they say, that women's power to compete in the labour market should be 'hampered' by any regulation from which men are free. Any such restriction, they assert, results in the lowering of women's wages, and in diminishing the aggregate demand for women's work ... But it is curious that we seldom find these objectors to unequal laws coming forward to support even those regulations which apply equally to men and to women. Nearly all the clauses of the 1895 Bill, for instance, and nearly all the amendments proposed to it, applied to men and women alike. The sanitary provisions; the regulations about fire-escapes; the pre-eminently important clause making the giver-out of work responsible for the places where his work is done; the power to regulate unhealthy trades or processes; all these made no distinction between the sexes ... It is clear that there lurks behind the objection of inequality an inveterate scepticism as to the positive advantages of Factory legislation ...

Let us concede to the opponents of Factory legislation that we must do nothing to impair or limit the growing sense of personal responsibility in women; that we must seek, in every way, to increase their economic independence, and their efficiency as workers and citizens, not less than as wives and mothers; and that the best and only real means of attaining these ends is the safeguarding and promoting of women's freedom. The only question at issue is how best to obtain this freedom. When we are concerned with the propertied classes—when, for instance, it is sought to open up to women higher education or the learned professions—it is easy to see that freedom is secured by abolishing restrictions. But when we come to the relations between capital and labour an entirely new set of considerations come into play. In the life of the wage-earning class, absence of regulation does not mean personal freedom. Fifty years' experience shows that Factory legislation, far from diminishing individual liberty, greatly increases the personal freedom of the workers who are subject to it. Everyone knows that the Lancashire woman weaver, whose hours of labour and conditions of work are rigidly fixed by law, enjoys, for this very reason, more personal liberty than the unregulated laundry-woman in Notting Hill. She is not only a more efficient producer, and more capable of associating with her fellows in Trade Unions, Friendly Societies, and Co-operative Stores, but an enormously more independent and self-reliant citizen. It is the law, in fact, which is the mother of freedom.

The Factory Acts ... are based upon a fundamental economic fact

... —the essential and permanent inequality between the individual wage-earner and the capitalist employer ... If the capitalist refuses to accept the workman's terms, he will no doubt, suffer some inconvenience as an employer ... But slow starvation forces the labourer to come to terms ... Unfettered individual bargaining between capitalist and workman results, not in the highest wage that the industry can afford, but the lowest on which the workman and his family can subsist ...

But this is not all ... What hours he works, when and where he shall get his meals, the sanitary conditions of his employment, the safety of his machinery, the atmosphere and temperature to which he is subjected, the fatigue or strains which he endures, the risks of accident or disease which he has to incur: all these are involved in the workman's contract and not in his employer's. Yet about the majority of these vital conditions he cannot bargain at all ...

We may indeed leave them to be determined by the employer himself: that is to say, by the competition between employers as to who can most reduce the expenses of production. What this means we know from the ghastly experience of the early factory system ... The worker knows by experience that there is no question of his ever settling these matters for himself. There are only two alternatives to their decision by the employer ... collective bargaining—in short Trade Unionism—or the settlement by the whole community of questions which affect the health and industrial efficiency of the race ... Factory legislation ... There is no more individual choice in the one than in the other ... Trade Unionism is just as much founded on the subordination of the individual whim to the deliberate decision of the majority as any law can be ... Rates of wages, for instance, are best settled by collective bargaining; and sanitation, safety, and the prevention of overwork by fixed hours of labour are best secured by legal enactment.

But this question of the relative advantages of legislative regulation and Trade Unionism has unhappily no bearing on the women employed in the sweated industries ... Before wage-earners can exercise the intelligence, the deliberation, and the self-denial that are necessary for Trade Unionism, they must enjoy a certain standard of physical health, a certain surplus of energy, and a reasonable amount of leisure. It is cruel mockery to preach Trade Unionism and Trade Unionism alone, to the sempstress sewing day and night in her garret for a bare subsistence; to the laundrywoman standing at her tub 18 hours at a stretch; or to the woman whose health is undermined with 'wrist-drop', 'potters-rot', or 'phossy-jaw' ... If we wish to see the capacity for organization, the self-reliance and the personal independence of the Lancastrian cotton weaver spread to other trades, we must give the women workers in those trades the same legal fixing of hours, the same effective prohibition of overtime, the same legal security against accident and disease ... that they enjoy ...

Capitalists' wives and daughters seek to alarm working women by prophesying, as the result of further Factory legislation, the dismissal of women and girls from employment, and their replacement by men. The opposition to Factory legislation never comes from workers who have any practical experience of it. Every existing organization of working women in the kingdom has declared itself in favour of Factory legislation. Unfortunately, working women have less power to obtain legislation than middle-class women have to obstruct it ...

It is frequently asserted as self-evident that any special limitation of women's labour must militate against their employment. If employers are not allowed to make their women work overtime, or during the night, they will, it is said, inevitably prefer to have men. Thus, it is urged, any extension of Factory legislation to trades at present unregulated must diminish the demand for women's labour ...

The first assumption is, that in British industry today, men and women are actively competing for the same employment ... We are so accustomed, in the middle-class, to see men and women engaged in identical work, as teachers, journalists, authors, painters, sculptors, comedians, singers, musicians, medical practitioners, clerks, or what not, that we almost inevitably assume the same state of things to exist in manual labour and manufacturing industry. But this is very far from being the case. To begin with, in over nine-tenths of the industrial field there is no such thing as competition between men and women: the men do one thing, and the women do another. There is no more chance of our having our houses built by women than of our getting our floors scrubbed by men. And even in those industries which employ both men and women, we find them sharply divided in different departments, working at different processes, and performing different operations. In the tailoring trade, for instance, it is often assumed that men and women are competitors. But in a detailed investigation of that trade I discovered that men were working at entirely separate branches to those pursued by the women. And when my husband, as an economist, lately tried to demonstrate the oft-repeated statement that women are paid at a lower rate than men, he found it very difficult to discover any trade whatever in which men and women did the same work.

The second assumption is, that in the few cases in which men and women may be supposed really to compete with each other for employment, the effect of any regulation of women's hours is pure loss to them, and wholly in favour of their assumed competitors who are unrestricted. This, I believe, is simply a delusion. Any investigator of women's work knows full well that what most handicaps women is their general deficiency in industrial capacity and technical skill.

Where the average woman fails is in being too much of an amateur at her work, and too little of a professional ... The real enemies of the working woman are not the men, who always insist on higher wages, but the 'amateurs' of her own sex. So long as there are women, married or unmarried, eager and able to take work home, and do it in the intervals of another profession, domestic service, we shall never disentangle ourselves from that vicious circle in which low wages lead to bad work, and bad work compels low wages. The one practical remedy for this disastrous competition is the extension of Factory legislation, with its strict limitation of women's hours, to all manufacturing work wherever carried on. It is no mere coincidence that the only great industry in which women get the same wages as men— Lancashire cotton weaving—is the one in which precise legal regulation of women's hours has involved the absolute exclusion of the casual amateur. No woman will be taken on at a cotton mill unless she is prepared to work the full factory hours, to come regularly every day, and put her whole energy into her task ...

This evolution of industry leads inevitably to an increased demand for women's labour. Immediately we substitute the factory, with its use of steam power, and production on a large scale, for the sweater's den or the domestic workshop, we get that division of labour and application of machinery which is directly favourable to the employment of women ... It is therefore infinitely more important for the friends of women's employment to enquire how an extension of the Factory Acts would influence our progress towards the factory system, than how it would affect, say, the few hundred women who might be engaged in night-work book-folding.

If there is one result more clearly proved by experience than another, it is that the legal fixing of definite hours of labour, the requirement of a high standard of sanitation, and the prohibition of overtime, all favour production on a large scale ... Factory legislation is, therefore, strenuously resisted by the 'little masters', who carry on their workshops in the back slums; by the Jewish and other subcontractors who make a living by organizing helpless labour; and by all who cherish a sentimental yearning for domestic industries. But this sentiment must not blind us to the arithmetical fact that it is the factory system which provides the great market for women's labour. Those well-meaning ladies who, by resisting the extension of Factory legislation, are keeping alive the domestic workshop and the sweaters' den, are thus positively curtailing the sphere of women's employment. The 'freedom' of the poor widow to work, in her own bedroom, 'all the hours that God made'; and the wife's privilege to supplement a drunken husband's wages by doing work at her own fireside are, in sober truth, being purchased at the price of the exclusion from regular factory employment of thousands of 'independent women'.

Beatrice Webb, 'Women and the Factory Acts',
Fabian Tract No. 67, 1896

Part Four

Education

Introduction

The education question for the women's movement was the provision of secondary and higher education for (mainly) middle-class girls. Elementary education for working-class girls and boys had already developed under the auspices of the two great voluntary societies, the National Society, and the British and Foreign Schools Society, aided from the 1830s by government grant and government inspection, augmented from 1870 by the rate-financed board schools permitted by the 1870 Education Act. Elementary schools enjoyed trained and certificated teachers (see 3.8 above); and elementary school girls enjoyed co-educational classes and therefore essentially a co-educational curriculum. By contrast, middle-class girls had the choice of very small private boarding schools, offering mainly accomplishments (French, music, drawing, deportment); or ill-paid and ill-trained home governesses. There was nothing equivalent to the boys' great public schools and universities. The circle of women around Barbara Leigh Smith, Bessie Parkes and Emily Davies, who were trying to open up occupations for women, were fully aware that they could not carve out careers for girls without education; but equally parents would not educate girls if there were no subsequent careers open to them. As Emily Davies remarked in 1861, 'Untrained women are as unfit for the colonies as they are for home life. It is indeed no wonder that people who have not learnt to do anything cannot find anything to do.'

Governessing was perhaps the most overstocked and pitiable of (middle-class) occupations (see 3.8.1 above). The Governesses' Benevolent Institution, offering pensions and alms to distressed gentlefolk, quickly found that it was at least as urgent to train governesses for their work, and thereby to improve their prospects. Out of the evening lectures offered by F. D. Maurice, the Christian Socialist professor of King's, developed in 1848 (4.1) Queen's College and shortly after the more secular Bedford College. Their early students included Barbara Leigh Smith, Sophia Jex-Blake, Miss Buss and Miss Beale, Octavia Hill.

Two years later Miss Buss founded the North Collegiate School for girls, in London, and in 1858 Miss Beale founded Cheltenham Ladies' College, both of them pioneering day high schools. Miss Beale's paper (4.2.1) to the Social Science Association pointed out that working-class girls received a better education from their elementary schools than did the twelve-year-olds who entered her school. And she, together with Emily Davies and Miss Buss, gave evidence to the Taunton Commission of Inquiry into Endowed Schools in 1865 (the third of the three great Commissions, following the Clarendon Commission on public schools and the Newcastle Commission on elementary schools: see above, 3.8.3). Girls' schools needed trained teachers, public examinations and parental support (4.2.2).

Parents remained ambivalent about girls' education. Members of the Social Science Association might favour education unlimited (4.3.1). But Elizabeth Sewell spoke for many when she wrote that women's separate sphere and irregular health necessitated an education different from that available to boys (4.3.2 and 4.3.3; see also the 'Biology her destiny' debate, above, 1.4). Women must be educated to be wives and mothers.

To this Mrs Maria Grey crisply replied that women unfortunately were not educated to be wives and mothers, but to get husbands. She urged that the main function of education was to train the reason and the conscience (4.3.4).

Elizabeth Wolstenholme, herself headmistress of a small boarding school in Manchester and highly active in the Manchester suffrage committee, mapped out the educational provision needed by girls—high schools, colleges, extra-mural lectures, co-education and co-endowment (4.4).

The Taunton Commission had shown that girls' education was superficial, showy and sparse. Maria Grey and her sister Emily Shirreff had been writing on education since the 1840s; Emily had recently been temporary mistress of Girton College, Maria had stood but failed to be elected to the new school boards. With the support of the Social Science Association, and the North of England Council for Promoting Women's Higher Education (founded by Anne Clough), they formed the National Union in November 1871 (4.5) which in mid 1872 sponsored the Girls' Public Day School Trust—a company which raised capital by shares and founded its first school in Chelsea in 1873. Undenominational, its fees of four to eight guineas a term attracting a wide range of girls, and its hours from 9.15 a.m. to 1.15 p.m., the GPDST by the 1890s had almost forty schools and 7,000 pupils from Norwich to Newcastle. In 1878 the National Union opened the first training college for non-elementary school teachers, the Maria Grey. Girls' public boarding schools followed, with prefects, houses, games and team spirit. Where in 1864 there had been just twelve endowed schools in the country, by 1890 there were eighty, including those of the GPDST.

Meanwhile Emily Davies had been bringing women teachers together in schoolmistresses' associations; and in 1863 she persuaded Cambridge University to open its local examinations, established five years before, to girls; at six weeks' notice her circle entered eighty-three girls, who did respectably in literature and scripture, dismally in mathematics. By 1869 her schoolmistresses' associations were entering 241 girls at junior and 160 for the senior local examinations (a form of 'O' and 'A' levels). By 1900 there were 3,000 junior and 1,366 senior entrants. Girls had obtained their public examinations. In 1869 she opened her women's college at Hitchin with five girls, which in 1873 moved to Girton. She insisted from the start that whatever their private inclination, girls must study the same subjects and take the same examinations as men. Different would be seen as inferior.

At the same time, ladies' educational associations in certain northern cities, in Liverpool (led by the Butlers), Manchester, Sheffield, Leeds, Birmingham, Wolverhampton, had been negotiating with progressive university men to establish extra-mural lectures for women, particularly teachers. From this came the university extension movement. Anne Clough, sister of Arthur Clough, became the organising secretary (4.6) of the North of England council for women's education; James Stuart, later professor of mathematics at Cambridge, offered in 1867 lectures on astronomy, thus beginning, in his words, his 'peripatetic university'. By the mid 1870s, the universities had created University Extension Delegacies, most of whose clients remained women. Henry Sidgwick organised the women's lectures at Cambridge; and when Emily Davies was preparing to move her women's college at Hitchin nearer to Cambridge, to ease the problems of visiting lecturers, he tried to persuade her to build in Cambridge to help accommodate women attending the Extension lectures. She refused (4.7), and therefore with the aid of the Fawcetts he established Newnham Hall in 1870. Anne Clough became its Principal.

The differing origins of Girton and Newnham were reflected in their very different educational philosophies (4.7). Girton continued to insist that their students followed the existing three-year men's degree; Newnham, that women's education should not be forced into the anachronistic Anglican curriculum of mainly classics and mathematics; women should obtain a higher education that suited their needs and resources, whether they stayed a term or a year. By 1879 Girton had received 100 students, Newnham 230, most of them returning to girls' schools as teachers. In 1878 London University was opened to women; the following year, Lady Margaret Hall and Somerville College were established at Oxford, and in 1881 Cambridge degrees were opened to women as of right.

Suggestions for further reading:
Barbara Stephen, *Emily Davies and Girton College,* 1927; J. Kamm, *Hope Deferred,* 1965; *Indicative Past,* 1971; M. MacWilliams-Yullberg, 'Women and degrees, 1862-1897', in M. Vicinus (ed.), *The Widening Sphere,* 1977.

4.1 Founding of Queen's College

Queen's College was opened on the 1st May, 1848. It was an offshoot from the Governesses' Benevolent Institution; which is a Society having for its design to benefit an important and very interesting class of our countrywomen, not only by affording assistance to them when in difficulty, sickness and old age, but by raising the standard of their accomplishments and thus entitling them to higher remuneration. With a view to these latter objects, the conductors of that Institution were led to the plan of examining into the attainments of governesses in quest of situations, and granting certificates of approval to those who could stand the test. But they soon discovered that 'to do any real good they must go farther; they must fit the governesses for their examination; they must provide an education for female teachers'. Finally, they came to the resolution that it was expedient to extend that instruction beyond the governess in fact and the governess in prospect, to all and sundry who might choose to avail themselves of it.

The result has been the establishment of Queen's College in its present form; an institution, namely where lectures are given in the various branches of female education, according to the enlarged requirements of the present day, in classes open to all ladies of twelve years old and upwards, on payment of a moderate fee per quarter. About two hundred and fifty are understood to be now on the list of pupils, the number in each class averaging about twenty, and the number of classes which each individual attends varying at pleasure ... There are preparatory classes for young ladies from nine to twelve years of age; and also evening classes for governesses already engaged in the duties of their profession. In these last the instruction given is entirely gratuitous: 'they have been attended by above seventy ladies engaged in tuition, for the most part every evening: many of them at the head of schools, some connected with public institutions, some governesses of considerable standing'.

'Queen's College', *Quarterly Review,* vol. 86, 1850

.2 The need for educational reform

.2.1 *The state of middle-class girls' education*

he education of girls has too often been made showy, rather than eal and useful—accomplishments have been made the main thing, ecause these would, it was thought, enable a girl to shine and attract, while those branches of study especially calculated to form the udgment, to cultivate the understanding, and to discipline the haracter (which would fit her to perform the *duties* of life), have been eglected; and thus, while temporary pleasure and profit have been ought, the great moral ends of education have too often been lost ight of.

To the poorer classes the daily toil and struggles of their early life lo, to some extent, afford an education which gives earnestness, and trength, and reality; and if we would not have the daughters of the igher classes idle and frivolous, they too must be taught to appreciate he value of work. We must endeavour to give them, while young, uch habits, studies, and occupations, as will brace the mind, improve he taste, and develop the moral character. They must learn, not for he sake of display, but from motives of duty. They must not choose he easy and agreeable, and neglect what is dull and uninviting. They nust not expect to speak language without mastering the rudiments; ot require to be finished in a year or two, but impatiently refuse to abour at a foundation . . .

I have a set of papers written by girls much younger in St. Paul's listrict school here, which are greatly superior . . . We may well ask iow is such a state of things possible? How is it that the daughters of he higher middle class are more ignorant and untrained than the :hildren of the national schools? I think one cause is that parents have oo often trusted, when they should have inquired; they frequently pend from £100 to £200 a year on sending their daughters from iome; during the holidays they hear the piano, they see the drawings not always the pupils' own) but how often do they institute any nquiry into the progress made in any other branches; or, if unable to undertake it themselves, how rarely do they care that there should be a ystem of examination to see whether the work is properly done. They are afraid of popular outcry, afraid of the excitement, afraid that their :hildren should take a low place, forgetting that (if the examination be conducted without any of the improper excitement of publicity) it is also a test and means of moral training, since those who work from the right motives simply do their best, and are not over anxious about results. I do not desire that there should be a system of competitive

examination, but a general testing of the work done, and if this cannot
be responded to in a quiet lady-like manner, it does not speak well for
the moral training of the school.

Another cause is that girls are often placed in an inferior school, or
under incompetent governesses, or allowed to work in a desultory way
until they are 14 or 15. Plans and governesses and schools are changed
for a passing fancy.

I ask whether a boy educated on this plan would be good for much;
would he or would he not be likely to have acquired habits of lazy
self-indulgence? And is a girl so trained likely to prove a diligent and
wise and thoughtful woman?

Lastly a girl usually leaves school altogether, and too often throws
aside serious occupations at an age at which her brother enters on his
college life. When she is just beginning to see the use of much she had
previously found dull and monotonous, when more than at any
previous time, a taste for good reading and useful pursuits might be
developed.

Dorothea Beale, 'The Ladies' College at Cheltenham',
*Transactions of the National Association for the Promotion
of Social Science,* 1865

4.2.2   *The Taunton Commission*

You attach importance to a system of giving certificates generally to
schoolmistresses? ...—I think the most useful thing would be a
system of examinations for women generally, not specially for
schoolmistresses.

By what authority do you think such a system would best be
instituted and managed?—I think the examinations of the University
of London would answer the purpose . . .

I think you yourself had an opinion that if any special standard
were set up for girls, nobody would believe that their arithmetic was as
good as the boys' arithmetic, however carefully it might be examined
into? ... I think that a special certificate would always be assumed to
be less strict and less exacting, whether it was so or not.

Are there any subjects which are almost universally taken up, or is
there any remark you wish to make on the subjects?—The subjects
most taken up are religious knowledge, English, and French, but the
senior students also take up every subject that may be taken by boys
except Greek and applied mathematics. They take Latin, pure mathematics, chemistry, zoology, botany, geology, and all the other things,
except Greek and applied mathematics. They take pure mathematics.

Can you suggest any means by which that defect which seems to be
very much at the root of the want of good schoolmistresses generally
can be remedied?—I should think that the real cause of the low
stipends of schoolmistresses is that there are too many. There are not

too many well qualified, of course, but the inferior ones compete with the good ones, and there are no means of distinguishing between them, at least very little means, so they bring each other down.

Is there any other way you could mention of raising the standard and power of instruction in governesses and female teachers beyond the opportunity of obtaining a certificate, which is what you have chiefly brought before us?—I think if colleges were multiplied it would be a great advantage. There are two in London, but they are kept down very much by the ignorance of the girls who come to them. They are not able to carry on the instruction so high as they would because of the girls coming so young and so ignorant. If they stayed longer, which they would be encouraged to do if examinations were open to women, the standard of instruction might be raised. Probably more colleges would be wanted. It is, I think, rather an inconvenience that they should be only in London, because some people do not like to send their daughters to London.

Should I be right in concluding that your view is that the male and female mind should run exactly in the same groove as regards education!—Yes; I think they might be educated in the same things ... I do not suppose the results would be exactly the same, at least, I do not think one knows what the result would be.

You think that the sexual difference of mind is so slight that you would not make any difference essentially in the higher education of a man and the higher education of a woman?—I do not know what the difference may be, but I do not think it is the sort of difference that would lead one to make a difference in the subjects of education.

> Evidence of Emily Davies, 30 November 1865,
> to the (Taunton) *Schools Inquiry Commission*

Do you think any means could be taken for improving the class of schoolmistresses by any system of certificates, or in any other mode?—I think most strongly that every one who teaches ought to go through some course of training in the art of teaching after having received a certificate of attainment ... I only know of one place at the present moment where a governess of the middle class can get training, and that is at the Home and Colonial.

[Dr Storrar:] From what sources do you usually draft your assistants?—We have tried to get them from those who have been educated in the school and subsequently trained in the Home and Colonial. By that means we have secured a certain amount of power of teaching.

Have you been able to get a sufficient supply from your own school?—Not always, on account of the difficulty of age. Of course the girls are too young at 20 or 21 to be entrusted with the charge and moral training of a large class ... My belief is that we should do better with certificated mistresses trained in the National schools, than with such mistresses as we can get.

[Lord Lyttelton:] You are not allowed to have certificated mistresses?—No; Government will not allow it. It does occasionally happen that one can get a mistress who has been trained, but who has fallen short of the certificate, or who from change of circumstances has resigned a Government school.

How have they done with you?—They generally do extremely well, in so far that they are able to govern the children and impart a good English education, but they are very deficient in accomplishments. In such cases we are obliged to supplement French and higher drawing by some other teacher ... We find it answers extremely well with the young children, where accomplishments are not so necessary ... For them, I do not think there is any better teaching than is given by the Government trained mistresses, and that if we can secure one of those mistresses she is perfectly capable of making the teaching interesting, discarding text books almost entirely, and making the teaching oral.

You attach great importance then to getting rid of the habit of merely learning bits of books by heart?—Yes. All our teaching for years past has been almost entirely oral, that is to say, we do not use text books and do not set lessons to be learnt, except in facts, such as geographical names, which must be committed to memory.

Do you mean that you give what are called gallery lessons, and then call upon the children to reproduce them; or do you mean that you take a book and require the girls to master it and catechise them upon it?—In the lower classes we require the teachers to draw up sketches of their lessons, as they would have to do in the National schools, to make the lesson oral, and to reproduce the teaching from the children by rapid questions, of course combining with these a certain amount of home lessons. The teaching of the more advanced pupils necessarily involves books. In languages and literature, for instance, there must be books to be read, but as a rule we entirely discard lessons from mere text books.

[Lord Lyttelton:] How many teachers have you?—We have 11 governesses in daily work and 19 assistants, making a total of 30 for 200 pupils.

Evidence of Frances Buss (North London Collegiate),
30 November 1865, to the (Taunton) *Schools Inquiry Commission*

It cannot be denied that the picture brought before us of the state of middle-class female education is, on the whole unfavourable ... want of thoroughness and foundation; want of system; slovenliness and showy superficiality; inattention to rudiments; undue time given to accomplishments, and these not taught intelligently or in any scientific manner; want of organization ... a very small amount of professional skill, an inferior set of school books, a vast deal of dry, uninteresting work, rules put into the memory with no explanation of their principles, no system of examination worthy of the name ... a reference to effect rather than to solid worth, a tendency to fill rather than to strengthen the mind ...

Findings of the (Taunton) *Schools Inquiry Commission*

4.3   An appropriate education

4.3.1   *No sex in mind*
Dr. Hodgson,
It is for those who object to the equalisation of the instruction of boys and girls to show in what respects the two ought to differ, and in what respects the characters of the two sexes are so widely distinct as to involve the necessity of a separate education for each ... Now let us ask ourselves for a moment what are the subjects, if any, on which boys should, and girls should not, be taught. I have not been able to hear from anyone the suggestion of even a single subject ... I would draw no line of demarcation, so as to limit the extent of knowledge which either boy or girl may acquire. I would throw open the portals of knowledge freely to both. Let each sex acquire what it can. Circumstances will draw a line of demarcation: so will ability and opportunity. There is no necessity for our drawing any other line, and there is extreme injustice in our doing so. I would apply to those differences between the male and female sex, the very same principle I would apply to the different classes of society, the rich and the poor. I say it is unwise and unjust to fix any arbitrary limit to the education the poor are to get. Their poverty already more than sufficiently limits it; and it is for us rather to try and extend the amount of instruction than to endeavour arbitrarily and intentionally to limit it. So with the female sex, I say, let us throw open the gates through which the temple of knowledge is to be entered, and let us allow fair play to every one who enters it, being satisfied that difference of capacity, difference of means, difference of opportunity, will fully maintain that inequality of knowledge, that difference of mental state which I confess is desirable ...

Dr. Hancock,
It appears to me that the reason of the neglect of the education of girls in the upper and middle schools is that we do not carry out with regard to them the principles which prevail in other departments of education. With regard to the poorer classes, wherever the government recognises the necessity of interfering it interferes equally. Wherever they found boys' schools they found girls' schools; and in every parish school founded by the state over the three kingdoms both sexes are taught alike. But when we come to the middle and upper schools it is otherwise ... If we hold that universities and grammar-schools are unnecessary, abolish them; but if they are maintained as advantageous to men, we ought to give the same advantages to women

... Now I think this inequality in our educational system produces some very unsatisfactory results. We live in an age when men's opinions are modifying and changing, and it is a serious disadvantage when, in the same family, the women are not educated equally with the men. We labour under the disadvantage of the men having more advanced views than the women.

Mr. Joseph Payne,
Where we have to deal with a common mind, both the subjects taught and the mode of teaching must be in a great degree common. We are not teaching a different, but the same kind of human being. The mind has properly no sex. It is the mind of the human being, and consequently there must be of necessity a similarity in the instruction of both sexes.

'The education of girls', *Transactions of the National Association for the Promotion of Social Science,* 1865

4.3.2 *Special education for girls*
The aim of education is to fit children for the position of life which they are hereafter to occupy. Boys are to be sent out into the world, to buffet with its temptations, to mingle with bad and good, to govern and direct. The school is the type of the life they are hereafter to lead. Girls are to dwell in quiet homes, amongst a few friends; to exercise a noiseless influence, to be submissive and retiring. There is no connexion between the bustling mill-wheel life of a large school and that for which they are supposed to be preparing . . .

This idea, of making a boy's attainments the standard by which to measure the girl's is indeed obviously unfair ... Not one girl in a hundred would be able to work up the subjects required for an Indian Civil Service examination in the way which boys do. Her health would break down under the effort: and health is the obstacle which, even under the most favourable circumstances, must stand in the way of a girl's acquiring the intellectual strength which at this age is so invaluable to a boy. He had been tossed about in the world, left in a great measure to his own resources, and been inured to constant physical exertion. He has been riding and boating and playing at cricket, and both body and mind have been roused to energy; and so, when he comes to study, he has a sense of power which acts mentally as well as physically, and enables him to grasp difficulties and master them. The girl, on the contrary, has been guarded from over-fatigue, subject to restrictions with regard to cold and heat and hours of study, seldom trusted away from home, allowed only a small share of responsibility;—not with any wish to thwart her inclinations, but simply because, if she is not thus guarded, if she is allowed to run the risks which to the boy are a matter of indifference, she will probably develop some disease which if not fatal, will at any rate be an injury to her for life. The question of health must be a primary consideration with all persons who undertake to educate girls. It will be a perpetual interruption to their plans for study and mental improvement, but it is one which can never be put aside.

Elizabeth Sewell, *Principles of Education,* 1865

4.3.3 *Special education for women*

The one thing men do not like is the man-woman, and they will never believe the College, or University, woman is not of that type. Sensible men will always like sensible and cultivated women; but they will always prefer that their good sense and cultivation should have come through channels which they recognise as suitable for the womanly character. The learned woman does not make the best educator of children. We require the well-trained and well-balanced woman. The duties of women do not to any great extent lie in the intellectual direction. Their sprightly intuition is often, in practical matters, worth far more than the reasoning faculty which a laborious education has developed in man ... But whatever Mr. John Stuart Mill may think, England is not prepared for either female suffrage or a female Parliament, for women as Poor law guardians, attendants at vestries, public lecturers, public speakers, doctors, lawyers, clergy, or even, to any much greater extent than at present, as authors. The attempts of Miss Becker and her friends to prepare the country for this change simply defeat their own object. They are received with unmitigated disgust by all but an isolated few. The sphere of women is home. Such a cultivation as will make a really good wife, sister, or daughter, to educated men, is the thing to be aimed at, and this must be something which recognises woman not as a 'fair defect of nature,' something which may be brought up to the same point as man by education, and taught to be his rival; but rather as the complement of man, perfect in herself, and intended to hold an entirely different place in the world, a something which is expressed in such words as these:-

> 'For nothing lovelier can be found
> In woman than to study household good,
> And good works in her husband to promote;'

But, if it is conceded that a special training is necessary for school teachers and governesses, the advantages may well be held to outweigh the disadvantages. May we give a word of kindly advice? We would say let it be a *true College for women*. Let its promoters give up the ambitious notion of an institution on the same footing as a man's College ... Let all the arrangements be made with reference to the special work of the College, the training of teachers ... Thus simplicity of living, the strictest economy, so as to suit governesses; training in housekeeping, regular needlework, and, if possible, actual schoolteaching, should be parts of a system to which all should with very slight exceptions conform ... If the College is to succeed, there will be no such thing as free permission to read as much and as late as enthusiastic students may desire. The health of women cannot stand much evening reading. Nature is imperative in these matters. Reading aloud should be cultivated and might be made exceedingly useful if some were to read out to others, who, in various self-arranged sets, practised making their own dress, or worked for others as in the mission-working parties now happily becoming common in many places. Nothing could be more useful to governesses, who seldom at present possess this often necessary and alway feminine accomplishment; while the relief from the constant strain upon minds ill prepared for hard and regular study, as most of them will be, may make the whole difference in the bill of health.

With all respect for the ladies who are about to make this interesting experiment, no one of the slightest experience can contemplate without very great alarm the effect of indiscriminately applying the system of men to women. As we have already said in regard of boys and girls, the former have gone through a mingled discipline of physical and mental labour which enables them, when they have reached manhood, to grapple with the tasks of the real student, to apply any amount of patient study, and to suffer but little from the strain of the stiffest examinations. Even among them it is well-known how many, from want of proper care, break down before they arrive at the goal. It is an ascertained physiological fact that the actual capacity of the average male brain is considerably greater than that of the female ...

Then, further, consider that, say what we please about 'accomplishments', the young woman must necessarily have been heavily weighted in comparison with the young man during the years of her preparation for College life ... There is reason in the general demand that women should be 'accomplished'. Society requires some power in the sex of pleasing others, yes, and of being useful to others in social life, over and above what it requires of men, who are necessarily trained to earn their bread or to govern ...

But it may be said that we have occupied our space without grappling with the half-million-superfluous-women problem ... We confess it; but ... for one woman who will beat the man out of the sphere he now occupies there will be two who will frighten him out of matrimony.

Keep the male and female types essentially distinct. For those young ladies who cannot obtain 'a higher education' through their parents, brothers, friends, and books at home, or by means of Lectures in cities, let a refuge be provided with the training governesses; but for heaven's sake, do not let us establish the 'University-woman' as the modern type. We want to entice our 'golden youth' into matrimony, not by wiles and plots and match-making warfare, but by the exhibition of a true, modest, retiring, useful, womanly character.

M. Burrows, 'Female education',
Quarterly Review, vol. 126, 1869

4.3.4   *All education, moral education*

Let men and women alike, then, be educated as human beings. Here, however, I must guard against the fatal confusion so common in this country, between education and instruction or preparation for the special profession or work of life. It is owing to this confusion that we hear of elementary education, consisting of the 'three R's', of the necessity of technical education supseding classical, etc., etc., of women, or of the working classes being enough educated already, and being thus unfitted for the duties of their position. But the true meaning of the word education is not instruction, technical or otherwise. It is intellectual, moral, and physical development, the development of a sound mind in a sound body, the training of reason to form just judgments, the discipline of the will and the affections to obey the supreme law of duty, the kindling and strengthening of the love of knowledge, of beauty, of goodness, till they become governing motives of action. This alone is truly education, to be begun in the first twenty years of life, to be carried on through time, and as I trust, through eternity; and this is the education which should be given, or at any rate aimed at, in the case of every human being. Once accept this view of education, and there is an end of all the distracting talk about this education being good for a man, that for a woman, this for working men, that for tradesmen or professional men, or men of fortune. The technical education may be different for all these, but the education of reason, and conscience, and will, and affections, must be the same for all; and the test to be applied to every proposed system will be this:—Does it tend to form a sound judgment, an enlightened conscience, a disciplined will, a heart loving whatever things are true, honest, just, pure and lovely? . . .

[The remedies for improving girls' education:]

1. The creation of a sounder public opinion respecting the need and obligation of educating girls.
2. The re-distribution of educational endowments, so as to give a fair share of them to girls.
3. The improvement of female teachers by their examination and registration according to fixed standards.

Maria Grey, *On the Education of Women,* 1871

4.4   A map of provision

Women should speak for themselves, and claim to be considered, not as a separate community, but as a part of the whole . . .

We want first, in every considerable town in England, a High school for girls . . . which would offer the best possible education on very moderate terms . . . We need the establishment first of one, and ultimately of many such institutions as the Hitchin College of Women . . . That there are many among us who would gladly have profited by this higher education we know too sadly. That there are those now eager and desirous to avail themselves of it, is perfectly certain; but whether such a demand exists or not, it is plain that it ought to exist and that we ought to set about creating it if it did not . . . The difficult social problems of to-day are not to be solved by mere native kindness of heart, still less by unassisted common sense. Never was there a time when there was so much work waiting to be done which demanded the highest faculty, perfected by the best possible training. Our schools cannot supply this want of good training. They are not adequate to the work already imposed upon them.

But for the multitude of women who cannot avail themselves of such an institution, or who would not if they could, who want systematic instruction brought to their own doors, or who have only time and opportunity for some measure of the higher culture, which fragment they would yet most highly prize,—for these, for the young mothers seeking instruction, for the teachers engaged in their profession and wishing to continue their studies and to supplement their own fragmentary education—for all these we must look to the development of the Lecture system at work in many of our large towns. These courses of lectures, distinctly educational in character and supplemented by examinations, have already proved of essential service. Whether ultimately these lectures will develop themselves into genuine local colleges, offering the highest instruction attainable to women, whether they will form an important part of those educational agencies of the future which are to affect not only our women but our men, it is premature to say. Those who work most earnestly for them, and are most interested in their success, are of all people the most unwilling that they should be prematurely systematized, or should ever become crystallized or stereotyped . . . As a matter of natural right it might be fairly argued that girls have a claim to a full half of whatever money is nationally devoted to educational purposes . . . The practical exclusion of girls from the highest educational advantages offered to this class is in very many cases equivalent to a sentence of lifelong pauperism and dependence. It is to the last degree indecent that women should be dependent on marriage for a professional maintenance. It is highly inexpedient that they should be restricted to a few avocations for which it is presumed that the slightest possible education—or none at all—is adequate. Yet such is the practical result of the exclusion of girls from the higher education ... It is clear that men do not know the material destitution which so largely exists amongst this class of women. It is assumed in the face of the most patent facts that all women marry and are provided for by their husbands; whilst nothing is more plainly to be seen by those who will open their eyes, than these three things:—1. That a very large minority of women do not marry. 2. That of those who do marry, a very considerable proportion are not supported by their husbands. 3. That upon a very large number of widows (more than one-third of the widows in the country), the burden of self-maintenance and of the maintenance of their children is thrown. It is an absolute necessity of our present social condition that women should have as free admission to professional and industrial training as men; that there should be no monopoly of sex, and no protective duty on either side. Natural differences and natural fitnesses would then assert themselves, and men need not for one moment fear that in any work for which they have special natural advantages they will ever be driven out of the field by women. The injustice to women consists in appropriating to men all the artificial and acquired advantages of education and training. Of the economic gain to the community it is not necessary here to speak. But equality of education must precede equality of industrial training. The former is the foundation upon which the latter must rest. Experience has conclusively shown that in cases where it has been sought to give a sound industrial training to girls or women, their defective early education has always been the most miserable but the most effectual hindrance ... Nor again is it for those who boast of the sanctity of our domestic institutions to admit that a slighter culture on the part of women than of men is the just basis of such institutions. The influence of the mother is probably the most real and pervading influence in the world ... Nobody wants to deprive boys of any educational advantages to be derived from endowments. But is it quite necessary that what is given to the girls should be taken from the boys? If there cannot be the good school for boys and the good school for girls, it seems reasonable to conclude that the one good school ought to be equally for boys and girls. To many of us mixed education appears the only rational solution of our educational difficulties. On the economic ground the gain is plain. The expense of a double staff of teachers and a double set of school-buildings is at once saved. But the only objections to such an experiment rest on moral and social grounds. Why it should be considered so dangerous and doubtful for boys and girls or for men and women to share each other's serious pursuits whilst they are allowed freely to share each other's frivolities, is a matter of perpetual surprise to those who accustom themselves to look beyond the range of tradition or convention . . .

We plead the cause of women. We ask that the gifts of God may not be wasted, that women themselves may not be robbed of some of the purest joys of life, those of intellectual effort and achievement, and that society which needs their help so much may not be defrauded of their best and worthiest service. Give us knowledge, power and life. We will repay the gift a hundred-fold.

Elizabeth Wolstenholme, 'The education of girls, its present and its future', in Josephine Butler (ed.), *Woman's Work and Woman's Culture,* 1869

4.5   The National Union

The objects of this Union are:

1. To bring to communication and co-operation all individuals and associations engaged in promoting the Education of Women and Girls, so as to strengthen and combine their efforts; to collect and register for the use of members, information on all points connected with such education.

2. To promote the establishment of good and cheap day-schools, for all classes above those attending the public elementary schools, with boarding-houses in connection with them, when necessary, for pupils from a distance.

3. To raise the social status of female teachers by encouraging women to make teaching a profession, and to qualify themselves for it, by a sound and liberal education and by thorough training in the art of teaching; to supplement training-colleges by attaching, where possible, a class of student teachers to every large school and by such other means as may be found advisable; also to secure a test of the efficiency of teachers by examinations of recognised authority and subsequent registration.

4. To extend the existing system of itinerant lectures on special subjects, for all places not of sufficient size to maintain a permanent staff of efficient teachers.

5. To endeavour to form classes for girls in connection with grammar schools, making the teaching staff available for both.

6. To endeavour to restore to the use of girls the endowments originally intended for their benefit, and to obtain for them a fair share in the other endowments applied to education.

7. To promote the increase of the number of girls and women attending the University Local Examinations and likewise the number of centres for such examinations, and to endeavour to diminish the cost of attending them.

8. To aid all measures for extending to women the means of higher education beyond the school period; and to facilitate the preparatory and supplementary studies by forming classes for students and libraries where required, and enlarging the system of instruction by correspondence, already begun at Cambridge and elsewhere.

9. To assist the establishment of evening classes for young women already earning their own livelihood, and to obtain for women, when possible, admission to classes for technical instruction; thus helping them to fit themselves for better and more remunerative employments than are now accessible to them.

10. To create a sounder public opinion with regard to education itself, and the national importance of the education of women, by means of meetings, of lectures, and of the press; and thus to remove the great hindrance to its improvement, the indifference with which it is regarded by parents, and by the public.

Women's Education Union, quoted in Emily Shirreff,
The Work of the National Union, 1873

4.6 University Extension

In large towns some twenty or twenty-five lectures might, in the course of three months, be delivered by one professor to a number of schools, collected in groups according to situation ... These lectures would be for older pupils ... A system of this kind would be an immense help to teachers, and an enlivenment to pupils. It would be the means of bringing both the teachers and the taught under the influence of superior men, who would probably be led to take a greater interest in female education with such increased opportunities of knowing something about it, and using their influence in directing it. Some intercourse with University men who carry on the highest education in the country, would be a great boon to many teachers, who are doing their best under great difficulties ...

Anne Clough, 'Hints on the organization of girls' schools', 1866, quoted in B. A. Clough, *Memoir of Anne Jemima Clough*, 1897, pp. 114-15

4.7 Girton and Newnham

I must speak first of some objections [to a women's college in Cambridge] to which I do *not* attach much weight. These are: 1. the undergraduate difficulty, i.e., the supposed danger of annoyance to the students when out walking. 2. The mothers' fears ... 3. The possible loss of supporters ...

My difficulty is, the impossibility for women to carry on a free, healthy, undisturbed student-life in a town at all, and especially in a University town ... One way [is to have] ... restrictive rules ... the other would trust to the strength of mind of the students ... The students come because they like it and feel that it gives them what they want ... and they emphatically assert that they do *not* want anything like a grown-up boarding school. But supposing that we succeeded in getting a different kind of student—say girls fresh from school, to whom restrictions would not be galling—we should still feel that we were sacrificing one of our chief aims, that of giving to women an opportunity of laying out their own lives, in circumstances which may help them to lay them out wisely. Women have plenty of practice in submitting to little rules. We want to give them the discipline of deciding for themselves and acting upon their own responsibility. Then, it may be said, why not choose the other plan, which would give them such abundant opportunities of practising self-control? ... Our students would [not] feel the interest in their work that they do now, if they were constantly being diverted from it by interests of a different sort ... Then too in the case of women, much visiting means much time and thought bestowed upon dress, especially by those who are not rich and have not maids to do things for them. And this would tell upon the tone of the College generally ...

Hitherto, the singularly good health of our students has been one of our strongest points ... I trace it in great part to the quiet, regular, unperplexed life. And I cannot believe that we should sacrifice this to at all the same extent at two or three miles off [at Girton] as we should in the town itself. There would not be the morning calls and the dropping in and the servants coming with notes to wait for an answer, and the general victimization by idle ladies ...

Emily Davies to Mr H. Sidgwick, 31 December 1870, refusing to
build in Cambridge, quoted in Barbara Stephen,
Emily Davies and Girton College, 1927, pp. 251-2

All separate schemes for women are undesirable ... drawing lines of demarcation and setting up artificial distinction. And it seems to me that tho' there is an increasing disposition to give women fair play, there is also some tendency to increasing separation. We have not yet come to it in religion, but with Ladies' Committees, Ladies' Associations, Lectures to Ladies, and the rest, one does not quite see why we should not soon also have Ladies' Churches and Chapels, in which the duties of women as such should be specially inculcated. We have the principle already, in the double moral code, which most people believe in ... You know of course my feeling against raising barriers between men and women has nothing to do with the assertion of equality or identity, in neither of which I believe ...

Emily Davies to Mr Tomkinson, 6 January 1869,
quoted in loc. cit., p. 195

The position of the Girton Committee on this question [of examinations] was perfectly clear and logical. They believed that it would be of great service to the cause of women's education generally if they could prove conclusively that women were capable of the same intellectual work as men, and it seemed to them that any difference in the conditions observed would weaken their case in the judgement both of the University and of the world outside.

The view taken by the [Newnham] Association was that it was undesirable in the interests of the individual students concerned, to insist on the regulations enforced on undergraduates ... In the first place, Mr. Sidgwick and others did not wish to encourage women to use the Previous Examinations, because they disapproved of making classics compulsory either for men or women. In the second place, they knew that few of the women students had received an education which would serve as preparation for a University course; and it seemed, therefore, reasonable, and for their advantage educationally, to allow them a longer time at Cambridge before taking the final examination than was granted to undergraduates ... Because many women were not able ... to be long away from their homes or other occupations ... Newnham accordingly accepted and provided for many students who could only stay for two or three terms or even less; and though most of them worked for the Higher Local Examinations, they were not required to take any examination, and no subjects were made compulsory.

B.A. Clough,
Memoir of Anne Jemima Clough, 1897, pp. 175-7

Part Five
Birth Control

Introduction

Contraceptive literature ('neo-malthusianism') had been quietly circulating in England since the late 1820s when radicals such as Francis Place, Richard Carlyle and the young John Stuart Mill had been urging women to use the sponge as a primitive diaphragm, a method recommended by Drysdale in the 1850s. Charles Knowlton, on the other hand, in his *Fruits of Philosophy* (1832) favoured women douching with vinegar. In 1876 a Bristol bookseller was imprisoned for publishing Knowlton, and other booksellers began to withdraw it. So Charles Bradlaugh and Annie Besant published their own edition and challenged the courts to prosecute them. In three months they sold 125,000 copies.

Bradlaugh and Annie Besant were comrades working to advance free thought—secularism, republicanism, neo-malthusianism, and for Annie Besant Fabianism and theosophy a few years later. Their periodical, the *National Reformer*, and their missionary lecture tours disseminated their views. At their trial, the book was found obscene but they were not, and they were subsequently acquitted on a technicality. Annie Besant then replaced Knowlton's out-of-date book with her own *The Law of Population* (5.1) which sold 175,000 copies in the next three years before she withdrew it under theosophical influence. She was never prosecuted; but was to be more severely punished in that her husband had her declared unfit to care for their daughter because of her neo-malthusian views (5.1.2; also 6.3.3).

Dr Henry Allbutt's *The Wife's Handbook*, published ten years later, favouring pessaries and diaphragms, was to sell nearly 400,000 copies in twenty years, for which he was struck off the medical register.

Along with the democratisation of knowledge about contraception, other trends were encouraging couples to limit their families. Children were becoming more costly as they were dependent longer, many from 1876 staying on at school until 14 years old; wives were buying more medical attention to their health. By 1906 the Webbs estimated that between half and two-thirds of all families practised some form of limitation. The birth rate which was 35.5 per thousand in 1871 fell to 14.4 by 1914.

The desperation of working-class women, whose health and family finances were wrecked by unwanted pregnancies, is clear in their letters on maternity (5.2) published by the Women's Co-operative Guild as part of their campaign to secure maternity benefits. Writing in 1911 of their married life in the 1880s and 1890s, for these women birth control is still illicit. Mrs Mona Caird, a staunch feminist, had no such hesitations (5.3). Marriage was bondage, women were breeding animals (see also 1.4.2 above). But other feminists had doubts about birth control (much as they had about emigration), fearing that it would not 'free' women but free men to indulge their vices without penalty. The women's movement remained silent, if not openly hostile, to the birth control movement. They wanted to end the double standard: men and women alike should live lives of greater purity.

Suggestions for further reading:
J. A. Banks, *Prosperity and Parenthood,* 1954; J. A. and O. Banks, *Feminism and Family Planning,* 1964; P. Fryer, *The Birth Controllers*, 1965; P. Branca, *Silent Sisterhood*, 1975; A. Mclaren, *Birth Control in Nineteenth Century England*, 1978.

5.1   Annie Besant

5.1.1   *Her advice*

All thinkers have seen that since population increases more rapidly than the means of subsistence, the human brain should be called in to devise a restriction of the population, and so relieve man from the pressure of the struggle for existence ... Malthus proposed ... the delay of marriage ... The more marriage is delayed, the more prostitution spreads ... Later thinkers, recognizing at once the evils of over-population and the evils of late marriage ... have advocated early marriages and small families ... How is this duty to be performed? It is clearly useless to preach limitation of the family, and to conceal the means whereby such limitations may be effected ...

The check we will take first is 'natural laws' ... Women are far less likely to conceive midway between the menstrual periods than either immediately before or after them. [*sic*]

The preventive check which is so generally practised in France ... consists simply in the withdrawal of the husband previous to the emission of the semen, and is, of course absolutely certain as a preventive ...

The preventive check advocated by Dr. Knowlton is, on the other hand, entirely in the hands of the wife. It consists in the use of the ordinary syringe immediately after intercourse, a solution of sulphate of zinc or of alum being used instead of water. There is but little doubt that this check is an effective one, a most melancholy proof of its effectiveness being given by Dr. J. C. Barr to the Commission on the working of the Contagious Diseases Act ... These women are not meant to bear children, they are to be kept 'fit for use' by her Majesty's soldiers.

Apart altogether from this sad, but governmentally authorized use of this check, there are many obvious disadvantages connected with it as a matter of taste and feeling. The same remark applies to the employment of the *baudruche*, a covering used by men of loose character as a guard against syphilitic diseases, and occasionally recommended as a preventive check.

The check which appears to us to be preferable, as at once certain, and in no sense grating on any feeling of affection or of delicacy, is that recommended by Carlile many years ago in his 'Every Woman's Book' ... To prevent impregnation, pass to the end of the vagina a piece of fine sponge ...

There is a preventive check attempted by many poor women which is most detrimental to health, and should therefore never be employed, namely, the too long persistence in nursing one baby in the hope of thereby preventing the conception of another. Nursing does not prevent conception . . .

Another class of checks is distinctly criminal, i.e. the procuring of abortion. Various drugs are taken by women with this intent, and too often their use results in death, or in dangerous sickness . . .

If this system of preventive checks were generally adopted, how happy would be the result both to the home and to the State! The root of poverty would be dug up, and pauperism would decline and at last vanish. Where now overcrowded hovels stand, would then be comfortable houses; where now the large family starves in rags, the small family would live on sufficient food, clad in decent raiment; education would replace ignorance, and self reliance would supersede charity. Where the workhouse now frowns, the busy school would then smile, and care and forethought for the then valuable lives would diminish the dangers of factory and of workroom. Prostitution would cease to flaunt in our streets, and the sacred home would be early built and joyously dwelt in . . . No longer would transmitted diseases poison our youth, nor premature death destroy our citizens. A full possibility of life would open before each infant born into our nation, and there would be room, and love, and cherishing, enough for each new-comer . . .

Many people, perfectly good hearted, but somewhat narrow-minded, object strongly to the idea of conjugal prudence, and regard scientific checks to population as 'a violation of nature's laws' . . . Nature sends typhus fever and ague to slay us; we frustrate her ends by purifying the air, and by draining the marshes . . . 'Immoral'. But what is morality? It is the greatest good of the greatest number. It is immoral to give life where you cannot support it . . . Conjugal prudence is most highly moral . . . To reject preventive intercourse is in reality to choose the other three true population checks—poverty, prostitution and celibacy . . .

But the knowledge of these scientific checks would, it is argued, make vice bolder, and would increase unchastity among women by making it safe. Suppose that this were so, it might save some broken hearts and some deserted children; men ruin women and go scatheless, and then bitterly object that their victims escape something of public shame . . . Are mothers to die slowly that impure women may be held back, and wives to be sacrificed, that the unchaste may be curbed? . . . Englishwomen are not yet sunk so low that they preserve their loyalty to one, only from fear of the possible consequences of disloyalty . . . Shame on those who slander England's wives and maidens . . .

Another class of objectors appears . . . Why not emigrate? Because emigration is impracticable to the extent needed for the relief of the labour market. Emigration caused by starvation pressure is not a healthy outlet for labour . . . Emigration for penniless agricultural labourers, and for artizans, means only starvation abroad instead of at home ... One great evil connected with emigration is the disproportion it causes between men and women, both in the old country and in the new ... 1,173 infants are born daily, and to equalize matters about 1,000 emigrants should leave our shores daily . . .

Annie Besant, *The Law of Population*, 1877, pp. 3-48

5.1.2 *Annie Besant's punishment*
Even Mrs. Besant would probably admit that an infant daughter might properly be taken from her mother, supposing that this mother advocated prostitution or infanticide as useful and praiseworthy practices. In the opinion of the great majority of Englishmen and Englishwomen there is no appreciable difference between this and the kind of advocacy to which Mrs. Besant has devoted herself.

Saturday Review, 12 April 1879

5.2 Letters on Maternity

Restriction Advocated. I feel that I must write and explain why I advocate educating women to the idea that they should not bring children into the world without the means to provide for them. I know that it is a most delicate subject, and very great care must be used in introducing it, but still, a word spoken sometimes does good. Someone has said that most of the trouble with delicate children were caused by women trying to destroy life in the early days of pregnancy. I do not, of course, recommend that sort of thing. It is absolutely wrong. But it is terrible to see how women suffer, even those that are in better conditions of life. I will quote one or two personal experiences. My grandmother had over twenty children; only eight lived to about fourteen years, only two to a good old age. A cousin (a beautiful girl) had seven children in about seven years; the first five died in birth, the sixth lived, and the seventh died and the mother also. What a wasted life! Another had seven children; dreadful confinements, two or three miscarriages, an operation for trouble in connection with same. Three children died and the mother also quite young. There are cases all around us much worse. You find in the majority of cases that in large families a certain number die and the others have less strength. Of course there are exceptions. The trouble is that it takes so very long in England for things to be changed, and you are told to mind your own business and let people do as they like; but I am pleased to see that many men and women are getting wiser, to the benefit of the wives and families for whom the poor husband has to provide.

> Anon. (no. 32), *Maternity*, Letters from working women
> collected by the Women's Co-operative Guild, 1915

I think I have been very fortunate ... [eight children, two still-born, three miscarriages] but I could not afford help during pregnancy, and I suffer from valvular disease of the heart ... leaving me a complete wreck at those times ... No one who has not been placed in a similar position can realize how horrible it is to be so placed. I have resorted to drugs, trying to prevent or bring about a slip. I believe I and others have caused bad health to ourselves and our children. But what has one to do?

> loc. cit., no. 15

5.3 Breeding Her Bondage

Dependence, in short, is the curse of our marriages, of our homes, and of our children, who are born of women who are not free—not free even to refuse to bear them. It would be interesting, though probably not a little painful, if we could learn what proportion of children enter the world, whose mothers are perfectly willing and able to bear them: willing, in a strict sense, apart from all considerations of duty, or fear of harbouring unsanctioned feelings. A true answer to this question would shake down many brave edifices of sentiment which are now flying holiday flags from their battlements.

Nervous exhaustion and many painful forms of ill-health among women are appallingly common, and people try to find roundabout explanations for the fact. Do we need explanations? The gardener takes care that his very peach-trees and rose-bushes shall not be weakened by over-production (though to produce is *their* sole mission). Valuable animals are spared in the same way and for the same reason. It is only women for whom there is no mercy.

Mona Caird, *The Morality of Marriage*, 1897, pp. 134-5

Part Six
Law

Introduction

The inferior position of women was nowhere more visible than in law. Blackstone in 1765 had made it clear that 'By marriage the very being or legal existence of woman is suspended, or at least is incorporated and consolidated into that of her husband, under whose wing, protection and cover she performs everything'. More popularly, 'husband and wife are one and that is he'. Barbara Bodichon's *Brief Summary of the Laws* (6.1) was originally drawn up in 1854 as part of the campaign for a Married Woman's Property Act. Until marriage, a woman had control of her earnings and property, if any; once married, they passed to her husband (unless she was protected by a settlement); the children of the marriage were the property of the husband—the wife did not have any legal right even to see them; divorce was virtually impossible—only in four cases in the last century had women obtained a divorce, and in two of these it was on the grounds of incest. Her husband controlled her body too; until 1891 he could imprison her in her own home. As the wife had no independent legal existence, she could obtain no legal redress from him.

Mrs Bodichon's pamphlet was much influenced by the case of Caroline Norton (6.2) who experienced most of the rigours of the law. The granddaughter of Sheridan (and the *Diana of the Crossways*), she was unhappily married and left her husband, whereupon he took the children from her; at the same time urged on by his Tory friends, he proceeded in 1836 to sue Lord Melbourne for criminal conversation. This was thrown out by the jury but Caroline was unable to clear her name; but as she had accepted her husband back after some previous cruelty, she had 'condoned' his behaviour and had therefore no grounds for divorce. Libelled about her behaviour in the *British and Foreign Quarterly*, she could not sue as she had no legal existence. Nor could she prevent his obtaining her mother's property. The greatest heartbreak was over the children; the death of one of them in 1842 sufficiently shook her husband that he allowed her full access to them subsequently. But not until his own death in 1875 was Caroline free to remarry with an old family friend.

Caroline Norton was propelled into challenging the law because of her own experiences, and accordingly more abstract feminists, like Harriet Matineau, viewed her with suspicion. Indeed the first bill to give mothers access to their children in 1837 was actually withdrawn when the Nortons appeared to be reconciled, and was reintroduced when they were not.

Child custody was the most bitter issue at stake: the property rights of the father clearly outweighed the mere sentiment attached to the notions of motherhood. The Hansard debates (6.3.1) make it clear that members feared that if women did not risk losing their children, they would more readily leave an unhappy marriage; children were the chains of silk binding a woman to her marriage. The Act of 1839 allowed the Lord Chancellor to make appropriate arrangements for the care and custody of the children, usually that an innocent mother would have their care until they were 7 years old. The extent to which the wishes of even a mentally disturbed father remained paramount (6.3.2) meant that they overruled the welfare of the child or the wishes of the mother. Not until 1873 could the innocent mother have the care of her children until 16 years of age: and from 1886 the welfare of the child, rather than the guilt or innocence of its parents, was supposed to determine the issue of custody. However, the father remained the sole guardian at law; and only after 1886, and only after the death of the father, could the mother become a joint guardian of the child along with a guardian of the father's appointment (6.3.4).

Annie Besant (6.3.3) found that these changes did not protect her. On her husband's petition her daughter was taken from her because of her views on birth control (see 5.1.1 above), and though she fought back to obtain rights of access she relinquished them when she found they distressed her child.

The Act permitting husbands to divorce their wives had a rather easier parliamentary passage than the Act permitting mothers to have access to their children. As it was widely held that adultery destroyed the marriage vows, husbands needed an easier method of divorce than was currently available. Before 1857, men had first to prove their wives' adultery by suing for criminal conversation in the civil courts; they had then to obtain a divorce *a mensa et thoro* (effectively legal separation) from the ecclesiastical courts; and finally to obtain a private Act of Parliament granting them a divorce *a vinculo matrimonii*, which permitted remarriage. Two or three such Acts a year were obtained. The Act of 1857 brought all these processes together before a single matrimonial court, allowing poorer men to enjoy the privileges of the rich; only Gladstone consistently argued that women might want to enjoy the privileges of men. In the original bill, the husband obtained divorce on the grounds of his wife's adultery; the wife could obtain it only on the grounds of incest; under pressure, this was enlarged to allow divorce for adultery with desertion, adultery with cruelty, and adultery with unnatural offences. And it did allow the innocent wife to petition for maintenance arrangements, and to keep any subsequent property she might obtain. From 1883, even the guilty wife might petition for maintenance. Much of the Hansard debate (6.4) was devoted to justifying the double standard at law; biblical texts such as Matthew 5.32, permitting the husband to set aside his wife for adultery, were much favoured. By the 1860s, there were some 150 divorces a year; by 1890, this had risen to some 600 a year. But not until 1923 could women obtain divorce on the same grounds, of simple adultery, as men.

Throughout the period, there were regular parliamentary bills to legalise marriage to a deceased wife's sister (6.5). Many unmarried women lived in their sister's household and often became the natural guardian of the children on their sister's death in childbirth. Many husbands wished to marry them, and where the couple had the resources they could be married abroad, these marriages then being recognised at home. Such marriages were not possible in England: for scriptural reasons, because at marriage the husband and wife became one, the wife's sister became the husband's sister, and marriages prohibited by consanguinity were equally prohibited by affinity. It would be incest. A second reason was the fear that if such a marriage should be possible, the sister would become a 'sexual' object to the husband with all the resulting domestic strain; and should the wife die and marriage become possible but not desired, then the sister could not remain in her brother-in-law's home, and the children lost their guardian. The arguments were on the advantages and disadvantages to men: as Lord Lyveden commented, no one proposed to legalise the widow's marriage to her deceased husband's brother. The bill was eventually passed in 1907.

The last area of legal reform was the Married Woman's Property Act (6.6). Before 1870, the wife's personal property (everything except freehold land) passed on marriage to her husband unless, under principles of equity, it was secured on the wife by a trust. One wife in ten it was estimated enjoyed a marriage settlement. Any subsequent earnings passed to the husband. Barbara Bodichon's *Brief Summary* (6.1) interested the Law Amendment Society (founded in 1844) to seek a change in the law. And the first known feminist committee (Barbara Bodichon, Bessie Parkes, Maria Rye) organised a petition to Parliament; but the bill was swamped by the Divorce Act of 1857 securing their property to divorced or legally separated women.

J. S. Mill's great suffrage speech of 1867 (see below, 9.2.4) made much of women's property disabilities; bills were introduced in 1868, 1869 and finally passed in 1870, allowing women to retain their property or earnings acquired after marriage, and from 1882 any property possessed at the time of marriage. It was in this field that women made their greatest legal gains, mainly because the law of equity which protected the rich and the common law which neglected the poor were so clearly in conflict. And the great judicial reform movement of the later nineteenth century sought to fuse these systems, and to ensure that equity prevailed.

Suggestions for further reading:
O. McGregor, *Divorce in England,* 1957; H. Burton, *Barbara Bodichon*, 1948; R. Graveson and F. Crane (eds), *A Century of Family Law 1857-1957*, 1957; A. Acland, *Caroline Norton*, 1948; L. Holcombe, 'The Married Woman's Property Acts', in M. Vicinus (ed.), *The Widening Sphere*, 1977.

*Miss Garrett did obtain the diploma of L.S.A., but it is now no longer given to women. Those who wish to enter the medical profession must go to Zurich or to Paris. The Medical School of the University of Paris is free to women. There are also many Medical Colleges for female students in America, which have charters from the legislature granting power to give degrees.

**On Saturday Mrs. Sarah Wooster was appointed by the Aylesbury magistrates to the offices of overseer of the poor and surveyor of highways for the parish of Illmore; and last year four women filled similar offices in the Aylesbury district. Among other places for which it has been held that women are eligible are those of high chamberlain, high constables, common constable, sexton, and returning officer at an election to Parliament.

Pall Mall, March 30th, 1868

6.1   Brief Summary of the Laws

The Queen Regnant in all respects fills the office of King; she has the same rights, prerogative and duties; and all that is said in the words of the law of the regal office, is as applicable to the Queen Regnant as to a King.

A Queen Consort is considered by the law as unlike other married women. She can herself purchase land and make leases, receive gifts from her husband, and sue, and be sued alone. She is the only wife in England who has these rights.

Legal Condition of Unmarried Women or Spinsters. A single woman has the same rights to property, to protection from the laws, and must pay the same taxes to the state, as a man . . .

A woman duly qualified can vote upon parish questions, and for parish officers, overseers, surveyors, vestry clerks, etc.

If a woman's father or mother die intestate (i.e. without a will) she takes an equal share with her brothers and sisters of the personal property (i.e. goods, chattels, moveables, leases for years of houses or land, stock shares, etc.), but her eldest brother, if she have one, and his children, even daughters, will take the real property (i.e. not personal property, but all other, as freehold houses and lands, etc.) as the heir-at-law, males and their issue being preferred to females; if, however, she have sisters only, then all the sisters take the property equally. If she be an only child, and has no parent surviving, she is entitled to all the intestate real and personal property.

The Church and nearly all offices under government are closed to women. The Post Office affords some little employment to them; but there is no important office which they can practically hold with the single exception of that of sovereign. The professions of law and medicine, whether or not closed by law, are in England closed in fact.* Women may engage in trade, and may occupy inferior situations, such as matron of a charity; sextoness of a church; and some parochial offices are open to them. Women are occasionally governors of prisons for women, overseers of the poor,** and parish clerks. A woman may be a ranger of a park . . .

Any person guilty of certain fraudulent practices to procure defilement of any woman or girl, under the age of twenty-one, commits a misdemeanor, and may be imprisoned with or without hard labour for a term not exceeding two years. Unless a promise of marriage has been made in writing, or overheard, a seduced woman has no remedy against her seducer.

Her father may maintain an action against the seducer, it being supposed that he stands in the place of a master, and sustains a loss of service in consequence of the pregnancy of his daughter.

There is no direct punishment for seduction, but the use of violence is visited with penal servitude for life, or not less than five years; or, with imprisonment for not exceeding two years, with or without hard labour. All persons aiding in the perpetration of rape are punishable by penal servitude or imprisonment.

If any person take away a girl under 16 years of age out of the possession of her natural guardians, he is liable to imprisonment for not more than two years.

If a man, from motives of lucre, forcibly take away a woman, he and all who abet him are guilty of felony.

Laws concerning the Children of Single Women. Illegitimate children belong to the mother, and the father, even if avowed, cannot take possession of them. If a woman who is able to maintain her bastard child, fails to do so and it becomes chargeable to the parish, she may be punished as a rogue and a vagabond.

If a woman can give corroborated testimony, to the satisfaction of the Justices at the Petty Sessions that a certain man is father of her child, she can obtain from him ten shillings for the midwife, and ten shillings for the burial if the child is dead. If application be made by the mother before birth, or within two calendar months after birth, a sum, not exceeding five shillings per week, may be obtained for the first six weeks. In other cases two shillings and sixpence is the largest sum the law can oblige the putative or reputed father to pay. If he fail to pay, his goods may be seized for payment, or if he have no goods he may be imprisoned for not more than three calendar months.

But if a woman allows more than thirteen weeks' payments to remain due, she can only claim thirteen weeks. The money is paid to the mother. When the child has attained the age of thirteen all payment ceases.

If a man marry a single woman having a child he is bound to support it, as if it were legitimate, till it attains the age of sixteen.

Laws Concerning Women in Other Relationships. A single woman can act as agent for another person, and as an agent, legally execute delegated authority. A wife can so act if her husband do not dissent.

An unmarried woman can be invested with a trust, but if she marry, the complexities and difficulties are great, from her inability to enter alone into deeds and assurances.*

---

*Her husband's name must always be joined with hers, and his assent given to everything which she does as trustee.

A single woman can act as executrix under a will, but a wife cannot accept an executorship without her husband's consent.

A woman can hold the office of administratrix to an intestate personality, that is to the personal property of a deceased person dying without a will; and administration will be granted to her if she be next of kin to the intestate. But a wife cannot so act without the consent of her husband.

If a man place a woman in his house, and treats her as his wife, he is responsible for her debts to the same extent as if she were married to him.

Recent Laws in Which Women are Specially Named. All females are included in the restrictions of the Factory Act; that is to say, women of all ages, married or single, are forbidden to work above a certain number of hours, by the same Act which regulates the hours of work of children and young persons. This Factory Act is extended to rope works, lace factories, etc., etc., with many special provisions, some for the sending of children to school, etc. These are the most important provisions of this Act.

No young person or woman shall be employed during any period of the four-and-twenty hours for more than twelve hours, with intervening periods for taking meals, and rest—amounting in the whole to not less than one hour and a half and such employment shall take place only between the hours of five in the morning and nine at night. No such person (that is no woman or young person) shall be employed on Sunday, or after two o'clock on Saturday afternoon, except in cases where not more than five persons are employed in the same establishment, and where such employment consists in making articles to be sold by retail on the premises, or in repairing articles of a like nature.

In some counties of England, men, called gang-masters, hire a number of women and children, and contract to get a certain amount of work done for farmers. A law has been made [1867] regulating this description of labour; the following are two of the provisions regarding women:—

No females are to be employed in a gang with males. No female shall be employed in any gang under a male gang-master, unless a female, licensed to act as gang-master, is also present with that gang. Then follow the penalties.

Laws Concerning Married Women. Matrimony is a civil and indissoluble contract between a consenting man and woman of competent capacity.

These marriages are prohibited:—A widower with his deceased wife's sister; a widow with the brother of her deceased husband; a widower with his deceased wife's sister's daughter, for she is by affinity in the same degree as a niece to her uncle by consanguinity; a widower with a daughter of his deceased wife by a former husband; and a widower with his deceased wife's mother's sister. Consanguinity or affinity, where the children are illegitimate, is equally an impediment.

A lunatic or idiot cannot lawfully contract a marriage; but insanity after marriage does not invalidate a marriage.

A lunatic may contract a marriage during a lucid interval. Deaf and dumb persons may marry by signs.

It is a punishable offence for an infant (a person under twenty-one) to marry without the consent of the father or guardians. The consent of the mother is not necessary if there be a father, or unless she is the guardian.

A second marriage, while a husband or wife is living, is absolutely void, and, except under certain circumstances, which raise a presumption of ignorance of the fact of the former husband or wife being alive, is felony, and punishable by imprisonment or penal servitude.

An agreement to marry made by a man and woman who do not come under any of these disabilities, is a contract of betrothment, and either party can bring an action, upon a refusal to complete the contract, in a superior court of Common Law.

Marriages may be celebrated as a secular form, or as a religious ceremony after the requisite public proclamations or banns, or by licence . . .

Lawful marriages in foreign countries are valid in England, save such marriages of persons domiciled in England as are forbidden by the law of England. Marriage with a deceased wife's sister is valid in England, if it has been celebrated in a country where such marriage is legal, provided the parties were at the time of the marriage domiciled there.

A man and wife are one person in law; the wife loses all her rights as a single woman, and her existence is, as it were absorbed in that of her husband. He is civilly responsible for her wrongful acts, and in some cases for her contracts; she lives under his protection or cover, and her condition is called coverture.

In theory, a married woman's body belongs to her husband; she is in his custody, and he can enforce his right by a writ of habeas corpus; but in practice this is greatly modified.

The belief that a man can rid himself of his wife by going through the farce of a sale, and exhibiting his wife with a halter round her neck is a vulgar error. This disgusting exhibition, which has often been seen in our country, is a misdemeanor, and can be punished with fine and imprisonment.

The author of a recent publication asserts that a man may lend his wife; a man may not lend, let out, or sell his wife; such transactions are considered as being against public decency, and are mis-demeanors.

A wife's personal property before marriage (such as stock, shares, money in hand, money at the bank, jewels, household goods, clothes, etc.) becomes absolutely her husband's, unless when settled in trust for her, and he may assign or dispose of it at his pleasure, whether he and his wife live together or not.

A wife's chattels real (i.e. estates held during a term of years, or the next presentation to a church living, etc.) become her husband's by his doing some act to appropriate them; but, if he does not and the wife survives, she resumes her property. Her choses in action (property which she can obtain by means of an action or suit) may be sued for and obtained by her husband; but if he fails to do so, they revert to her on his death.

While the Common Law gives the whole of the wife's personal property to her husband, the Courts of Equity, when he proceeds therein to recover property in right of his wife, oblige him to make a settlement of some portion of it upon her, if she be unprovided for and virtuous.

A husband is liable for the price of such goods as he allows his wife, as his agent, to order; she may have more power than any other agent, but her power is of the same kind; for if a wife orders goods without the knowledge of the husband, it is not at all certain that a legal decision will oblige him to pay for them; it mainly depends on what the jury thinks are domestic necessaries, or requisite for the position of the family.

Neither the Courts of Common Law nor of Equity, have any direct power to oblige a man to support his wife. But the Divorce or Matrimonial Court, on granting a judicial separation may decree that the husband shall pay alimony to the wife for her support, and when a wife becomes chargeable to the parish, the magistrate may, upon application of the parish officers direct the husband to pay for her maintenance.* A wife, whose husband without valid reason refuses to support her, may rent lodgings, take up goods etc., suitable to her station, for which the creditors can compel the husband to pay.

A husband has the possession and usafruct of his wife's freehold property during the joint existence of himself and her; that is to say he has absolute possession of them as long as they both live. If the wife dies without children, the property goes to her heir, but if she has borne a child capable of inheriting, her husband holds possession until

*When a married woman requires relief from her parish without her husband, the justices in petty sessions may summon such husband before them, and make him pay some sum weekly towards the cost of the relief of the wife.

his death, when it passes to her heir; but on surviving her husband, her freeholds revert to her.

Money earned by a married woman belongs absolutely to her husband; that and all sources of income, excepting those mentioned above, and included in the term personal property. And her receipt for the earnings is not legal. The husband can claim the money notwithstanding such payment.

By the express permission of her husband, a wife can make a will of her personal property; for by such a permission he gives up his right. But he may revoke his leave at any time before *probate* (i.e., the exhibiting and proving a Will in Court).

The legal custody of children belongs to the father. During the life time of a sane father, the mother has no rights over her children, except limited power over young infants, and the father may take them from her and dispose of them as he thinks fit. If there be a legal separation of the parents, and there be neither agreement nor order in Court, giving the custody of the children to either parent, then the *right to the custody of the child* (except for the nutriment of infants) belongs legally to the father.

A married woman cannot sue or be sued for contracts, nor can she enter into them except as the agent of her husband; that is to say, neither her word nor her deed is binding in law, and persons giving a wife credit have no remedy against her. There are some exceptions, as where she contracts debts upon estates settled to her separate use, or where a wife carries on trade separately, according to the custome of London, etc.

A husband is liable for his wife's debts contracted before marriage, and also for her breaches of trust committed before marriage.

Neither a husband nor a wife can be witness against or for the other in criminal cases, not even after the death or divorce of either.

A wife cannot bring actions unless the husband's name is joined.

As the wife is presumed to act under the command and control of her husband, she is excused from punishment for certain offences, such as theft, burglary, house-breaking, etc. if committed in his presence, unless it is proved that she did not act under his influence. A wife cannot be found guilty of concealing her felon husband, or of concealing a felon guilty with her husband. She cannot be convicted of stealing from her husband or of setting his house on fire, as they are one person in law. A husband and wife cannot be found guilty of a conspiracy to which they themselves only are parties, as that offence cannot be committed by one person.

A married woman cannot be bound apprentice except by the permission of her husband, and will, in the indenture, stand in the same position to her, as a father or guardian to an apprentice who is a minor.

Usual Precaution against the Laws Concerning the Property of Married Women. Where a woman has consented to a proposal of marriage she cannot dispose or give away her property without the knowledge of her betrothed; if she make any such disposition without his knowledge, even if he be ignorant of the existence of the property, the disposition will not be legal.

It is usual before marriage, in order to secure a wife and her children against the power of the husband, to make with his consent a settlement of some property on the wife, or to make an agreement before marriage that a settlement shall be made subsequently. It is in the power of the Court of Chancery to enforce the performance of such agreements.

Although the Common Law does not allow a married woman to possess any property, yet in respect of property settled for her separate use, equity endeavours to treat her as a single woman. She can acquire such property by contract before marriage with her husband, or by gift from him or other persons, and can, unless forbidden by the settlements, deal with it as she pleases.

There are great difficulties and complexities in making settlements, and they should always be drawn by a competent lawyer.

When a wife's property is stolen, the property (as it legally belongs to the husband) must be laid as his in the indictment.

Separation and Divorce. A husband and wife can voluntarily separate upon a deed containing terms for their immediate separation, but they cannot legally agree to separate at a *future* time. Trustees must be parties to the deed which must provide what property the wife is to take.

The Divorce and Matrimonial Court decrees either a judicial separation or a divorce.

Judicial separation may be decreed at the suit of the husband for adultery, or upon any of the grounds for which he might, if he be pleased, sue for a divorce. At the suit of the wife, it may be decreed for cruelty, adultery, etc., also for the grounds on which she might, if she pleased, sue for a divorce.

Divorce is an absolute dissolution of the marriage, after which the parties are free to re-marry.

At the suit of the husband it may be decreed for adultery; and at the suit of the wife for adultery coupled with cruelty or desertion, and for certain aggravated cases of adultery.

A woman who has been deserted by her husband can obtain an order from the Divorce and Matrimonial Court, or from a magistrate, freeing her subsequent earnings and subsequently acquired property from the husband and his creditors. This protection to a wife is most valuable to working women.

Upon a judicial separation all the property subsequently acquired by the wife, becomes her own, and devolves after her death as if she were single. She is considered to be a single woman for purposes of contract, bringing actions; and her husband is not liable for what she does. If she and her husband live together again (which they may do if they please) the property belonging to her at the commencement of re-cohabitation is considered as settled to her separate use, but in other respects the separation comes to an end. Judicial separation does not enable the parties to marry again.

Laws Concerning a Widow. A widow recovers her real property, but if there be a settlement she is restricted by its provisions. She recovers her chattels real, if her husband has not disposed of them by will or otherwise.

A wife's paraphernalia (i.e. her clothes and ornaments) which her husband owns during his life-time, and which his creditors can seize for his debts, becomes her property on his death.

A widow is liable for any debts which she contracted before marriage, and which have been left unpaid during her marriage.

The widow is not bound to bury her dead husband, that being the duty of his legal representative.

If a man die intestate, his widow, if there are children, is entitled to one-third of the personalty; if there are no children, to one half; the other half distributed among the next of kin of the husband, among whom the widow is not counted.

If there is no next of kin, the moiety goes to the Crown.

A husband can, by will, deprive a wife of all right in his personalty.

A right is granted in Magna Carta to a widow to remain forty days in her husband's house after his death, provided she do not marry during that time.

A widow, married before the passing of the Dower Act, has by law *dower* of her husband's freehold lands, which is a right to the possession of a third of them during her life, and *free-bench* of a portion of his copyholds, but these rights are generally taken away by settlements or conveyances. If she accept a jointure she has no claim to dower. A widow, who was married since the Dower Act, had dower only of her freeholds, etc., which her husband possessed at his death, and died intestate of; but unlike the widow married before the passing of the Dower Act, she has also dower of equitable estates.

Barbara Leigh Smith Bodichon,
Brief Summary of the Laws of England Concerning Women,
1854 (1869 edn)

6.2 The Case of Caroline Norton

So long as a husband is not guilty of incest,—a wife, (according to Lords Cranworth and Campbell) has nothing to complain of which she might not 'condone'. Yet God knows it seems difficult to imagine what shade of torment, insult, or injury, could be added to what has been endured in my own case. I have learned the law respecting women, piece-meal, by suffering from every one of its defects of protection. I married very young and my marriage was an unhappy one. My family interfered earnestly and frequently in my behalf: and as for me, I forgave and resented—resented and forgave—till at length I left my husband's for my sister's house. He wrote them adjuring me to pardon him; beseeching me, by all that was holy, 'not to crush him', but 'to trust to him', to return! ... To my lasting injury—(even now I will not write, to my lasting regret,)—I 'condoned'. I knew I was not myself faultless; I was deeply touched by his imploring phrases; and I returned to the home and the husband I had abjured. My family, however, did not choose to resume terms of intimacy with him; and he quarrelled with me on that account. I insisted on my right to take my children to my brother's house, though my brother would not receive him. Those children were kidnapped while I was with my sister, and sent by my husband to a woman who has since left him money, and of whom he knew I had the worst opinion.

At that time the law was, (and I thank God I believe I was greatly instrumental in changing that law), that a man might take children from the mother at any age, and without any fault or offence on her part. There had been an instance in which the husband seized and carried away a suckling infant, as his wife sat nursing it in her own mother's house. Another, in which the husband being himself in prison for debt, gave his wife's legitimate child to the woman he cohabited with. A third (in which the parties were of high rank), where the husband deserted his wife, claimed the babe born after his desertion (having already his other children); and left her to learn its death from the newspapers! A fourth, in which the husband living with a mistress, and travelling with her under his wife's name, the latter appealed for a separation to the Ecclesiastical Court; and the adulterous husband, to revenge himself, claimed from her his three infant girls. In all these cases, and in all other cases, the claim of the father was held to be indisputable. There was no law then to help the mother, as there is no law now to help the wife. The blamelessness of the mother signified nothing in those days, as the blamelessness of the wife signifies nothing in this present day. The father possessed

precisely the right the husband still possesses—namely to do exactly
what he pleased. Mr. Norton, then took my little children (aged two,
four and six years); and I traced them to the house of that vile woman,
who threatened to give me 'to the police' when I went there and
claimed them.

It was not till six weeks after the stealing of my children . . . that Mr.
Norton took higher ground than his real cause of anger,—and
appeared before the world in the character of 'an injured husband'.
He brought an action against Lord Melbourne; who was in no way
connected with our quarrel; who had been a most kind friend to us;
and with whom the last time I had ever seen him in my home—my
husband was on the best possible terms, endeavouring to procure
from him a loan of money! The infamous opportunity afforded to
unscrupulous men, in the English 'Action for Damages' . . . was
suggested as a temptation and a bait. Lord Melbourne declared that,
so far as Mr. Norton was concerned, he believed the action to be
brought entirely as a means of obtaining money . . .

At the trial it was proved that the witnesses for the 'injured
husband' had received money, and had actually resided till the time of
trial at the country-seat of Lord Grantley, Mr. Norton's elder brother.
The jury listened with incredulity and disgust to the evidence; and
without requiring to hear a single witness for Lord Melbourne, or
leaving the jury-box, they instantly gave their verdict against Mr.
Norton; a verdict which was received with cheers which the judge
could not suppress: so vehement was the expression of public
contempt and indignation . . .

One of my children was afterwards killed, for want of the
commonest care a mother would have given to her household. Mr.
Norton allowed this child to lie ill a week before he sent to tell me he
was dying; and, when I arrived, I found the poor little creature already
in his coffin.

When it was not a case of death, I was not allowed to hear at all.
Once, when they were ill, I wrote to ask news of them; and my own
letter was refolded and sent back to me. That husband, whose petition
for pardon had touched me so easily, never pitied me. What I
suffered respecting those children, God knows, and He only: what I
endured, and yet lived past,—of pain, exasperation, helplessness, and
despair, under the evil law which suffered any man, for vengeance or
for interest, to take baby children from the mother, I shall not even try
to explain.

I believe men have no more notion of what that anguish is, than the
blind have of colours; and I bless God that at least mine was one of the
cases which called attention to the state of the law as it then existed.

After the action against Lord Melbourne (in which, according to the
preposterous English code, I could have no personal defence, nor any

means of showing how I had been treated as a wife): I consulted counsel whether I could not now divorce my husband: whether a divorce 'by reason of cruelty' might not be pleaded for me; and I laid before my lawyers the many instances of violence, injustice, and ill-usage, of which the trial was but the crowning example. I was then told that no divorce I could obtain would break my marriage; that I could not plead cruelty which I had forgiven; that by returning to Mr. Norton I had 'condoned' all I complained of. I was an ENGLISH WIFE, and for me there was no possibility of redress. The answer was always the same. The LAW, 'Have I no remedy?'—'No remedy in LAW. The LAW 'can do nothing for you: your case is one of 'singular, of incredible hardship; but there is 'no possible way in which the LAW could assist you' . . .

One of the episodes of my 'non-existence' in law, at this time, consisted in my having to endure a libel of immoderate length and bitterness, in the 'British and Foreign Quarterly Review' . . .

No less than one hundred and forty-two pages were devoted to the nominal task of opposing the Infant Custody Bill, and in reality to abusing me. Not being the author of the paper criticised, I requested my solicitor to prosecute the Review as a libel. He informed me that being a married woman, I could not prosecute of myself; that my husband must prosecute: my husband—who had assailed me with every libel in his power! There could be no prosecution: and I was left to study the grotesque anomaly in law of having my defence made necessary,—and made impossible,—by the same person.

'Oh! but',—say those who have not studied and suffered under the law, as I have,—'in return for all this, the husband is responsible for his wife's debts; that we all know!' Do you? I will shew that not only he is not responsible for his wife's debts to others—but he is not responsible for his own covenanted debts to her. He is, as I have said, legally responsible for nothing, but that she shall not come upon the parish.

In 1848, my husband required ready money to improve the estate left him by the woman to whom my children were at first taken.

In order to raise this money on the trust funds of our marriage settlements, my signature was necessary. To obtain my signature, Mr. Norton drew up a contract. He dictated the terms of the contract himself; vehemently urged its completion; and reproached my solicitor for the delay, distrust, and reluctance, which I shewed before I signed it. I did eventually sign it; and so did Mr. Norton ... The effect of my signature was, that Mr. Norton immediately raised the loan from our trust fund, to employ in his estate. The effect of his signature, and the signatures of the Marquis of Normanby's brother, and the solicitor who drew it up, was absolutely nil.

In 1851 my mother died. She left me (through my brother, to guard it from my husband) a small annuity, as an addition to my income. Mr. Norton first endeavoured to claim her legacy, and then balanced the first payment under her will, by arbitrarily stopping my allowance. I insisted that the allowance was secured, by his own signature and those other signatures, to a formal deed. He defied me to prove it,—'as, by law, man and wife were one, and could not contract with each other; and the deed was therefore good for nothing'.

I confess I thought the fear of exposure would prevent his disputing the contract ... by availing himself of the legal fiction of my 'non-existence', to escape from a written bond, which anyone not his wife might have prosecuted upon.

I was mistaken. Not only Mr. Norton held by the quibble that man and wife could not contract with each other; not only he did this,—but he had the base and cruel hypocrisy to once more drag forward Lord Melbourne's name, in order to make that seem my shame and my disgrace, which was in fact his shame and his disgrace; and to pretend wrong, where he knew he had been the wronger. Once more, for the sake of money,—as in the action for 'damages',—he endeavoured to cover me with opprobrium! . . .

Now I will pray your Majesty's attention to the effect of this non-existence in law . . .

And first I will take Mr. Norton's position. From the date of my mother's death, he has witheld entirely, and with perfect impunity, my income as his wife. I do not receive, and have not received for the last three years, a single farthing from him. He retains, and always has retained, property that was left in my home—gifts made to me by my own family on my marriage, and to my mother by your Majesty's aunt, H.R.H. the Duchess of York;—articles bought from my literary earnings,—books which belonged to Lord Melbourne; and, in particular, a manuscript of which Lord Melbourne himself was the author, (when a very young man) which Mr. Norton resolutely refused to give up.

He receives from my trustees the interest of the portion bequeathed me by my father ... If my father lived, it is to be presumed there is no man he would see with greater abhorrence than Mr. Norton (considering what the fate of his daughter has been), yet such portion as he was able to leave me, goes from the 'non-existent' wife, to the existent husband, in the general trust-fund of our marriage.

I have also (as Mr. Norton impressed on me, by subpoenaing my publishers) the power of earning, by literature,—which fund (though it be the grant of Heaven, and not the legacy of earth) is no more legally mine than my family property.

Now again, I say, is or is not this a ridiculous law (if laws be made to conduct to justice)? I cannot divorce my husband, either for adultery, desertion, or cruelty; I must remain married to his name; he

has, in right of that fact (of my link to his name), a right to everything
I have in the world—and I have no more claim upon him, than anyone
of your Majesty's ladies in waiting, who are utter strangers to him! I
never see him:—I hear of him only by attacks on my reputation:—and
I do not receive a farthing of support from him . . .

The natural position of woman is inferiority to man. Amen! That is
a thing of God's appointing, not of man's devising. I believe it
sincerely, as a part of my religion: and I accept it as a matter proved to
my reason. I never pretended to the wild and ridiculous doctrine of
equality. I will even hold that (as one coming under the general rule
that the wife must be inferior to the husband), I occupy that position,
Uxor fulget radiis Mariti; I am Mr. Norton's inferior; I am the
clouded moon of that sun. Put me then—(my ambition extends no
further)—in the same position as all his other inferiors! In that of his
housekeeper, whom he could not libel with impunity, and without
possible defence; of an apprentice whom he could not maltreat
lawlessly, even if the boy 'condoned' original ill-usage; of a scullion,
whose wages he could not refuse on the plea that she is legally 'non-
existent'; of the day-labourer, with whom he would not argue that his
signature to a contract is 'worthless'. Put me under some law of
protection; and do not leave me to the mercy of one who has never
shewn me mercy. For want of such a law of protection, all other
protection has been in vain! . . .

If Mr. Norton, a magistrate and member of the aristocracy, had
cheated at a game of cards in one of the clubs of London, all England
would have been in a ferment. Nay, even if he had refused to pay a
'debt of honour'—to a man—it would have been reckoned a most
startling and outrageous step! But, because the matter is only between
him and his wife,—because it is 'only a woman'—the whole
complexion of the case is altered. Only a woman! whom he can libel
with impunity, to find a loophole for escape or excuse . . .

There is needed in England, what is established by law in other
countries; a tribunal for marriage and divorce cases, with full power
of control; and why that power cannot be vested in the Court of
Chancery (as the Lord Chancellor Proposed), it is for the legists who
contradicted him to shew.

Hon. Caroline Norton,
*A Letter to the Queen on Lord Chancellor Cranworth's
Marriage and Divorce Bill*, 1855

6.3   Custody of Children

6.3.1   *The House of Commons debate on Serjeant Talfourd's Bill*

Mr. Serjeant Talfourd,

The subject has reference to the rights of parents in relation to their children, when the natural state of joint superintendence and protection is broken by unhappy differences, which compel or induce them to separate, without involving any breach of the marriage tie on the part of the mother . . . Not only may the mother be prevented from bestowing upon them in their early infancy those solicitudes of love for the absence of which nothing can compensate—not only may she be prevented from tending upon them in the extremity of sickness, but she may be denied the sight of them; and, if she should obtain possession of them, by whatever means, may be compelled by the writ of *habeas corpus* to resign them to her husband or to his agents without condition—without hope. That is the law—at least such is its recent exposition by the highest authorities; and how is it enforced? By process of contempt, issued at the instance of the husband against his wife, for her refusal to obey it, under which she must be sent to prison, there to remain until she shall yield or until she shall die . . . In Skinner's case (9 Moore 278) the husband had treated his wife with barbarity; they were separated, he cohabited with a woman named Deverall, and his child of six years of age remained in its mother's care. He sued out a writ of *habeas corpus* to take it from her, and on the case being heard before Mr. Justice Best, then one of the judges of the Court of King's Bench, a recommendation was made that the rigour of the law should not be enforced, and the child was, by arrangement of the parties, placed in the care of a third person agreed on by them. From this person the father took it by fraud, and gave it into the care of the woman with whom he cohabited, while he himself was a prisoner for debt in Horsemonger-lane gaol, to which place this prostitute resorted with the child. In this state of things the mother applied for a writ of *habeas corpus*; the case was heard and the court ordered the child to be delivered to its father. In M'Clellan's case (I Dowling's Practical Cases, 81) the child had been placed at a boarding-school by her father; the mother removed it thence because the child was in declining health, and afflicted with a disease by which she had already lost an elder child, and yet Mr. Justice Patteson said he had no option but to take it from her—he, one of the kindest and most simple-hearted of men, feeling himself compelled to deny to a mother, whose anxieties had been sharpened by the loss of one of her children, the mournful pleasure of watching over the survivor affected by a similar disease. 'It might be better (said that learned and excellent person) as the child is in delicate health, that it should be with the mother, but we can make no order' . . .

But it is not to these extreme cases (in which despair has made a feeble and timid woman bold) that the present law is most to be dreaded. It is the silent operation of its power—the threat which the husband dares scarcely utter—by which he may compel an innocent wife to resign property, or to submit to disgrace, on pain of being excluded for ever from the sight of those who are dearer to her than life . . .

With these feelings I move that leave be given to bring in a Bill to provide for the access of parents who live apart from each other to their children of tender age.

Mr. Leader,
. . . As it stands at present the law is entirely in favour of the husband and oppressive to the wife. A man who may be drunken, immoral, vicious and utterly brutalized, may place his wife, who seeks to live separately from him, in this cruel dilemma—'You shall either continue to live with me, or you shall be deprived of your children.' The wife, in such a case, has no redress. It may be notorious that she has just grounds for complaint, that it would be misery for her to live with her husband; it may be well known that she possesses her children's sympathy and affection, and that the husband disregards his children, and is disregarded if not disliked by them. It may be admitted that the wife is the fitter person to have the care of the early education of her children, to form their habits to minister to their childish wants to soothe them in trouble, and to tend them in sickness. All this may be admitted: but the law sternly refuses to listen to the pleading of natural sympathies and affection, gives to the husband the charge and possession of the children, and denies even the sight of them to the beloved and loving mother. How many mothers, rather than submit to such a deprivation, are driven to choose the other alternative, and endure a life of harassing ill-treatment and vexation and misery? . . . There are hundreds of women now suffering in silence, pining for the children whom a stern law has torn from them, now looking anxiously to the decision of this House—now eagerly hoping that the representatives of the people will save them from the terrible alternative which forces them to choose between being the abject slaves of a brutal husband or of being deprived of the very sight of their own children.

Access of Parent to Children Bill,
House of Commons, *Hansard,* 14 December 1837

Sir E. Sugden,

A wise legislature, as it appeared to him, would seek to bind married persons by a common interest, and certainly no wise Legislature would hold out facilities for separation. It frequently happened that very trifling differences were the subject of dispute between married persons, and, assuredly, so far as the mother was concerned, the love of offspring formed the great means of preventing in such cases a separation of the parents. The great tie which prevents the separation of married persons is their common children. A wife, was, in general glad to have that excuse for submitting to the temper of a capricious husband. It was some satisfaction for an angry woman, indignant at the treatment of her husband, to say, 'I would leave him immediately but for my children.' What was the consequence of this reflection? that her anger gradually cooled down; that the clouds which for a while brooded over her happiness were dispersed, and that after a short lapse of time, she was herself the first to admit the absurdity of which she would have been guilty had she left the protection of her husband's home. Now this Bill, by providing the wife with the means of always commanding access to her children, removed many of the obstacles which stood at present in the way of separation. In married life, the differences between the parties generally arose from their not giving way mutually to each other in the earliest stages of the dispute. Some time generally elapsed before husband and wife accommodated themselves to each other's temper. If you opened a facility to separation between husband and wife at the very commencement of their union, you opened a door to divorces and to every species of immorality.

Sir V. Smith,

... The right hon. and learned Gentlemen had said that one of the finest principles of human nature was the attachment of a mother to her child. He (Mr. Smith) admitted that it was so, and implored the House not to take advantage of it to compel a woman to reside with a husband who treated her with neglect and cruelty. That would be a compulsion inflicted on the weak for the benefit of the party who was strong enough already. All the difficulties of separation were at present on the side of the woman, and therefore in all the bickerings of married life the wife felt it expedient to yield, as she was the party on whom punishment must fall ... What did the husband suffer from this state of things? Did any man refuse to associate with a husband living separate from his wife unless it was charged against him that he had exercised some enormous cruelty against his wife? But was the rule the same with regard to the wife living separate from her husband? No. There was a scandal abroad which deprived her of the position she formerly occupied in society. She was tried with far greater severity than the man. She was tried at a tribunal where slander was her accuser, and vulgar credulity was her judge ... His impression was, that the House ought to provide for the protection of the weaker party in the marriage union; for in many, indeed he might say in the majority, of the cases of separation between husband and wife, the fault arose either from the neglect, or from the carelessness, or from the viciousness of the husband.

Custody of Infants Bill, House of Commons,
Hansard, 14 February 1838

6.3.2   *The welfare of the father*

A wife obtained separation on account of cruelty ... the children were handed over to the father who ... in 1862 had locked her into the drawing room, and behaved in a very violent manner ... [and] in 1869 ... struck her with several violent blows upon the head with his clenched fist. She fell, and was taken up insensible ... [The judges granted separation] but refused custody of even the youngest child ... 'To leave the wife with the defender were to subject him to an influence exciting and tempting him to violence towards her. To leave his little child in his house is, or may well be, to introduce a soothing influence to cheer the darkness and mitigate the bitterness of his lot, and bring out the better part of his nature' ... Observe that even the separation is granted, not as a protection to her, but rather because 'to leave her with her husband were to subject him to an influence exciting him to violence'. She must therefore be removed; but his little girl of four will be left with him, in the hope that its 'soothing influence' will prevent him breaking any more heads than his wife's, and as a means to 'cheer the darkness and mitigate the bitterness' which his own vile temper has produced ... The desirability of 'cheering the darkness and mitigating the bitterness' of the wife's lot does not seen to have crossed the judicial mind at all ... The only excuse one can discover for this extraordinary judgement is that the man had at one time been temporarily bereft of his reason ... Many a mother in such a case would deliberately elect rather to run the risk of future violence than to leave her children in the clutches of a man whose cruelty has driven her from his home ...

'Law in relation to women', *Westminster Review,* vol. 128, 1887

6.3.3   *The unfitness of a mother*

I received notice in January 1878 that an application was to be made to the High Court of Chancery to deprive me of my child ... arguing that my Atheism and Malthusianism made me an unfit guardian for my child ... I claimed the child's custody on the ground that the deed of separation distinctly gave it to me, and had been executed by her father after I had left the Christian Church, and that my opinions on the other side were not sufficient to invalidate it. It was admitted on the other side that the child was admirably cared for, and there was no attempt at attacking my personal character ... However [the judge] deprived me of my child ... No access to her was given me, and I gave notice that if access was denied me, I would sue for a restitution of conjugal rights, merely that I might see my children ... The money due to me was stopped ... Finally the deed of separation executed in 1873 was held to be good as protecting Mr. Besant from any suit brought by me, whether for divorce or for restitution of conjugal rights, while the clauses giving me the custody of the child were set aside. The Court of Appeal in April 1879 upheld the decision, the absolute right of the father as against a married mother being upheld.

Annie Besant, 'The Knowlton pamphlet', *Autobiography,* 1893

6.3.4 *The reforms of 1886*

Our country is to be congratulated on this achievement, and on the liberality of our law, which discerned fully four years ago that a child generally has two parents, and that one of them, though comparatively unimportant—even verging on the superfluous—might feel hurt if her existence and wishes were altogether ignored ... Yet even now their position is subordinate. The woman who bears, suffers, risks her life, rears, trains, watches—of whom, indeed, public opinion *demands* these things; she whose body and soul have been subjected to this terrible service, has still only secondary rights to her children ...

Consider this in conjunction with the tremendous rigour with which maternal duties are pressed upon a woman; with the demand that she shall surrender to her children health, happiness, and all hope of self-development; with the unbounded, merciless condemnation which is heaped upon her if she prove a neglectful or unenthusiastic mother ... Father and mother are to share pleasantly between them the rights and duties of parenthood—the father having the rights, the mother the duties ...

Mona Caird, *The Emancipation of the Family*, 1890, pp. 56-7

6.4 Divorce

The Lord Chancellor,
It was the common feeling of mankind that, if a husband repented and treated his wife with kindness, the sin on the part of the husband was not necessarily an unpardonable offence. There were cases in which a wife might and ought to condone, but the common feeling of mankind told them that this must be on the part of the wife only ... When parties felt that they must continue husband and wife, that feeling induced them to become good husbands and good wives. He did not propose, therefore, to enable this court to grant divorce at the instance of the wife merely on the ground of the husband's infidelity.

House of Lords, *Hansard,* 20 May 1856

The Lord Chancellor,
He had set out by stating that he thought no measure could be more injurious, more calculated to interfere with the social welfare of the country, than one which tended to shake the solidity of marriage and the strength of the marriage tie ... But all experience showed that when marriage was held to be indissoluble in cases of the adultery of the wife, some subterfuge was resorted to in order to supply the defect of the law; in Roman Catholic times, by pretending that the marriage was invalid, and recently by the parties obtaining a private Act to give the relief which the Ecclesiastical Courts could not give ... The law should be made to adapt itself to the practice and what had been shown to be the wants of the community, and that a competent tribunal should be constituted to do that which the Legislature had heretofore been in the habit of doing.

House of Lords, *Hansard,* 19 May 1857

Mr. Drummond,
His object was to have perfect equality between the two sexes. The laws of England were more severe against the woman than were those of any other country in Europe. That House was a body of men legislating for women, and they had by a code of their own invention, and for their own purposes, contrived to establish the general notion that unchastity in a man was a much less evil that unchastity in a woman.

Mr. Puller,
The inference he drew was that in legislating on the subject of adultery they could not, viewing it as a social question, be guided by the same

principles with respect to women as with respect to men. He agreed with Mr. Drummond in thinking that in the sight of God unchastity was as great a sin on the part of men as on the part of women; but viewing it as a social question, as regards injury to society, he must affirm adultery to be a far greater injury to society when committed by women than when committed by men, in consequence of being attended with uncertainty as to the parentage of the offspring.

Mr. Gladstone,
I believe that the evil of introducing this principle of inequality between men and women is far greater than the evil which would arise from additional cases of divorce *a vinculo* ... It is the special and peculiar doctrines of the Gospel respecting the personal relation in which every Christian, whether man or woman, is placed to the person of our Lord that form the firm, the broad, the indestructible basis of the equality of the sexes under Christian law ... If adultery really constitutes in the sight of God that right to release from the marriage tie, and absolutely abolishes the marriage tie, so that those of whom one party has committed adultery are no longer married—if that be so, where do you find your title to withhold from women the remedy which you give to men? Is it to be found in considerations of social expediency? ... I believe that a very limited proportion of the offences committed by women are due to the mere influence of sensual passion. On the other side, I believe that a very large proportion of the offences committed by men are due to that influence. If you punished in men the act of sensual passion, you would make a law which in many instances would, I believe, be operative to prevent that act; but you decline to make such a law ... You are going to enact that law, however, as against women ... [whose motives are] less impure and less ignoble than those which actuate the man. It is commonly because aversion has been contracted to the husband, or because attachment—and though a guilty, yet not a gross attachment—has been conceived for another object. That aversion is often grounded in the neglect or cruelty of the husband, even where there is nothing worse; that attachment is grounded in the attentions of another admirer, and has no immediate or direct reference in its early passages to the commission of sin. You, therefore, punish in a woman that which she does not contemplate; and as it is not usually in her contemplation when she enters on the downward road, the punishment which you are about to inflict will have little of a deterring effect. But with the man just the reverse is the case; for there is the direct action of sensual desires that causes him to offend, and there, where you might strike directly at the offence by giving the means of remedy to the wife, you refuse to do it. I must confess that it appears to me that a measure so framed is not so much designed in the spirit of preventing a particular

sin as by way of the assertion—I must add, the ungenerous assertion—of the superiority of our position in creation ... [which] results from the exclusive possession of power and from the habits of mind connected therewith.

Mr. Buxton,
The distinction drawn by this clause was consistent with the intuitive feeling of mankind. In all ages it had been felt that the adultery of the wife brought ruin on the married state, but no so much the simple unfaithfulness of the husband. This was evident from the general prevalence of polygamy except where Christianity had introduced a purer standard. But polygamy, though permitted to the male sex, both in the animal world and in human societies, had never been conceded to the female. From this and other circumstances, it appeared that nature drew a distinction in this matter between the husband and the wife, and he deemed it the first and most fundamental principle of statesmanship to adapt human laws so as to chime in with the dictates of intuitive common sense.

Divorce and Matrimonial Causes Bill,
House of Commons, *Hansard,* 7 August 1857

6.5 Marriage to a Deceased Wife's Sister

Mr. Walpole,
Remember the state of society in which we live. By what may be called an instinctive sense of propriety and delicacy of feeling, no single woman can ever live in the house or under the roof of a man she may eventually marry. The wife's sister may do so now, because the wife and the husband know there is no possibility of their future union. Repeal the law, however, and when the wife dies the wife's sister can no longer undertake the guardianship of her orphaned nieces, can no longer live on the same terms of intimacy with the widowed husband, and cannot render those services to the children which are attended with such advantage to the motherless family. Now, I ask you this—will you for the sake of a few exceptional circumstances change the law, and ... deprive large numbers of persons of the advantage they now enjoy in obtaining for their family the guardianship of the aunt, which the deceased wife would probably herself desire, and which, after all, is the best substitute for a mother's love and a mother's care?

> Marriage of a Deceased Wife's Sister Bill,
> House of Commons, *Hansard,* 25 April 1855

Viscount Bury,
This was emphatically a poor man's question. A poor man with three or four children who lost his wife, and who was dependent on weekly wages, could not leave his children without some female supervision; and, in many cases, the person to whom he could most readily turn was the sister of his deceased wife; but, in a house with limited sleeping accommodation, it was not decent that an unmarried sister of the late wife should be allowed to remain in the home unless her presence there had been consecrated by marriage.

Solicitor General,
If any question in the world was a woman's question, this was a woman's question ... and he asked the House whether it would be a reasonable thing or a generous thing to legislate on the marriage law against the will and the feelings of one of the sexes concerned in the matter? But it was also a man's question ... narrowing the circle of that affection [for him] into which passion could not enter ... It was in truth a Bill for the abolition of sisters-in-law to please some few who wanted to marry them.

> House of Commons, *Hansard,* 21 April 1869

Lord Lyveden,
It was well to suppose the tenderness of a wife's sister; but of what much greater value to a widow would be the assistance of a husband's brother. Yet this marriage was never proposed for the advancement in life of the children. If a man might marry his wife's sister, he must marry her; for society would never tolerate their residence together unmarried.

House of Lords, *Hansard,* 19 May 1870

6.6 Married Women's Property

Mr. Lopes,
The bill will affect the existing relations between husband and wife, and introduce discomfort, ill-feeling, and distrust where hitherto harmony and concord had prevailed.

Mr. Karslake,
... objected to it on two grounds—in the first place, because it would effect an entire revolution in the social status of husband and wife; and in the next, because it would work a like revolution in regard to the law of property; and it was difficult to say under which head it was most open to objection.

Mr. Lowe,
If a woman possesses property and is married, the law, being no doubt afraid the husband might tyrannically take it from her, puts that temptation out of his reach by taking the property away and giving it to him all at once. That is the simple state of the law. Every marriage settlement that is made is a tacit protest against it. Well, now, what is the duty of the law?—for we sitting here as legislators have just as much a duty to perform as fathers or guardians. The only occasion when our duty comes into play is when from any reason, whether accident or improvidence, no marriage settlement is made; and what ought we to do? Why, surely we ought to put ourselves *in loco parentis*, and show towards the persons we are bound to protect just the same feelings of kindness and beneficence and the same wish to protect and spare them from injury, which the parent or guardian is bound to show to his child or ward. We cannot make the same provision that they can, because we do not know the circumstances of each case, and can only deal with cases generally; but I maintain that where a change of condition has not been provided for by special contract it is the duty of the law to make as just a settlement as it can for the generality. And what is the most just settlement? Is it to give over the whole of her property to her husband? Is that discharging the duty we undertake?

Married Women's Property Bill,
House of Commons, *Hansard,* 10 June 1868

Mr. Shaw Lefevre,
It was essentially a poor woman's Bill, and was designed for the

benefit of that large proportion of the population to whom the system of equity and marriage settlements was altogether inapplicable. That system was really one for the rich, while the Common Law, giving all the wife's property to the husband, was one for the poor.

Mr. C. O. Morgan,
The Bill would secure to the wife of the poor man the savings of her industry. He wanted to know why the savings of a woman should not be as sacred in the eyes of the law as the savings of her husband. She had probably struggled harder for them than the man.

Married Women's Property Bill,
House of Commons, *Hansard,* 14 April 1869

Mr. Russell Gurney,
There is probably not a Member of this House who, upon the marriage of a daughter, does not pronounce his condemnation of the principle of our common law by securing to her, by means of a settlement, the enjoyment of her property ... They will protect the rich woman's Consols, but they will not protect the poor woman's mangle. [If they pass this bill, Members] will receive the blessing of multitudes of toiling women who now, when they see the hard earnings of a fellow-workwoman swept away, gather together in the streets, saying—'What is the use of a body striving.' And they will have the higher reward of witnessing the great improvement in the working classes, which will be the natural and necessary consequence of increased self-respect, arising from increased sense of responsibility among the women, and increased respect for womanhood among the men. I have reason to know that the women of this country feel deeply on this question; the poor women, especially, feel that they are suffering a grievous wrong. I have to appeal on their behalf to a Legislature elected exclusively by men. I trust that it will appear that the Members of a Legislature, so elected, are as keen to discern the evil, and as earnest in applying a remedy, as if the appeal were made on behalf of those whose voices could be heard at elections, and whose votes could be recorded at the hustings.

Mr. Raikes,
... deprecated the passing of this measure, on the ground that it would disturb the peace of every family, and destroy for ever that identity of interests at present existing between husband and wife, which had hitherto been regarded as the basis of the Christian family, and the peculiar characteristic of English society. The House was asked to create a factitious, an artificial, and an unnatural equality between men and women. But he also objected to the Bill, on the ground that it created an inequality between husband and wife; it

retained to the wife the sole use of her property, and yet still obliged the husband to support the family.

Married Women's Property Bill,
House of Commons, *Hansard,* 18 May 1870

Part Seven

The Social Evil

Introduction

The police estimated that there were 6,000 prostitutes in London and 25,000 in the country as a whole in the 1860s; many philanthropists thought the figure was up to ten times that. All agreed, however, that full-time professional prostitutes were only a proportion of the whole. Many were girls formerly in domestic service who had lost their character and taken temporarily to the streets; or were dressmakers and milliners whose prostitution eked out desperately low wages (7.1.1). An extensive network of befriending societies sought to aid and reclaim girls at risk (see below, 8.9.5). The demand for prostitutes reflected the lack of other legitimate sexual outlets for men. Late marriages for professional men whose early earnings were low (7.1.2); the denial of marriage to most of the Service ranks; and presumably the demand from married men whose wives were exhausted and incapacitated from frequent pregnancies. Lecky saw the prostitute as the abused guardian of domestic virtue (7.1.2). Revealingly, when *Meliora* deplored prostitution for its effect on families (7.1.3), its compassion was not for the seduced and pregnant daughter but for the seduced and syphilitic son. William Acton's survey of prostitution (7.1.4) challenged the stereotype of the bedraggled butterfly dying in the gutter. Prostitution was a transitory phase, a temporary trade, from which most women passed back into respectable society. He therefore supported the Contagious Diseases Act as a useful form of medicare, mitigating the worst effects of their activity.

The Contagious Diseases Acts (7.2) were introduced quietly in 1864 to the garrison towns (Plymouth, Portsmouth, Woolwich, Chatham, Sheerness, Aldershot, Colchester, Shorncliffe). If a woman was believed to be a common prostitute, the special police could lay information against her to a JP who could require her medical examination, and if she was infected, her treatment in hospital. If she refused she was liable to imprisonment. In 1866 and again in 1869 the Acts were extended to Windsor, Canterbury, Dover, Gravesend, Maidstone, Southampton, and their ten-mile radius. Knowledge about the Acts spread only slowly; and it was not until 1869 that Josephine Butler, wife of the Rev. George Butler, Principal of Liverpool College, formed the Ladies' National Association which published the Women's Protest (7.2.1). Drawing on Liberal provincial Dissent, opponents of the Acts were to organise 17,000 petitions with 2½ million signatures in the next fifteen years, and upwards of 900 public meetings. Their itinerant missionaries encouraged girls to resist arrest; their periodical, the *Shield*, was explicitly feminist in tone.

Josephine Butler argued that the Contagious Diseases Acts were class legislation (upper-class men using 'publicly cleansed' working-class women), and sex legislation (in which woman the victim was made woman the villain) (7.2.2). Supporters of the Acts replied that prostitutes were traders and the customer should be protected from 'faulty' goods; that they actually diminished prostitution; and that the taxpayer had the right to ensure that public expenditure on defence was not wasted by the hospitalisation of its men, a third of whom were suffering from VD. Josephine Butler was unshaken. As she told the Royal Commission on the working of the Acts (7.2.3), the statute book should reflect the moral order of the community; in Stansfield's words, 'Law and government ought to be on the side of virtue'. More particularly, the Acts both publicly labelled loose-living girls and then brutalised them with physical examination by speculum, and so hardened them beyond redemption and reclamation. Above all, the Acts sanitised poor women so that men could take their pleasures without risk (7.2.4). If men wanted to protect themselves against prostitution, they should instead denounce the double standard, expand economic opportunities for poor girls and allow women the protection of the vote.

But though women might lack the vote, they did not lack political power. Scorning parliamentary lobbying, Mrs Butler turned to direct action and, with immense courage, took the battle into Colchester's by-election of 1870 (7.2.5). The government candidate, General Storks, had implemented the Contagious Diseases Acts in Malta; by running an abolitionist candidate in the teeth of the two most powerful interests in Colchester, the army and the brewers, they split the Liberal vote and Storks was defeated. In 1872, the women opposed the re-election of Mr Childers at Pontefract, since he had administered the Acts at Plymouth and Portsmouth. In 1883 the Acts were suspended, in 1886 repealed.

By that time, Josephine Butler was working to expose and to end perhaps the most sickening variety of Victorian sexuality: its taste for children. Until 1875 the age of consent was 12; it was then raised to 13 years. The age of puberty for under-nourished working-class girls was often much later than this. Mrs Butler joined with the Salvation Army, Benjamin Scott, and the journalist W. T. Stead to campaign to raise the age of consent to 16 years. Stead's article in the *Pall Mall Gazette*, 'The maiden tribute to modern Babylon', showed how he bought a 13-year-old, Eliza Armstrong, from her mother for £5. As the child was (of course) the property of her father, whose consent he had neglected to obtain, Stead was imprisoned for abduction. (It was later revealed that Eliza was illegitimate and that therefore the father's consent had never been necessary.) In 1885, as a result, the Criminal Law Amendment Act raised the age of consent to 16 years.

Suggestions for further reading:
On prostitution see E. Sigsworth and T. J. Wyke, 'Victorian prostitution and V.D.', in M. Vicinus (ed.), *Suffer and Be Still,* 1973; J. Walkowitz, 'Prostitution in Plymouth and Southampton', in L. Banner and M. Hartman (eds), *Cleo's Consciousness Raised,* 1974; J. Walkowitz, 'The making of an outcast group', in M. Vicinus (ed.), *The Widening Sphere,* 1977. More generally, S. Marcus, *The Other Victorians,* 1969. On Josephine Butler, see G. Petrie, *Singular Iniquity,* 1971, and more generally, C. Rover, *Love, Morals and the Feminists,* 1970.

7.1 Prostitution

7.1.1 *Prostitution: supply*

She told her tale with her face hidden in her hands, and sobbing so loud that it was difficult to catch her words . . .

I used to work at slop work—at the shirt trade—the fine full-fronted white shirts; I got 2½d. each for 'em . . . By working from five o'clock in the morning to midnight each night I might be able to do seven in the week. That would bring me in 17½d. for my whole week's labour. Out of this the cotton must be taken, and that came to 2d. every week, and so left me 15½d. to pay rent and living and buy candles with. I was single and received some little help from my friends; still it was impossible for me to live. I was forced to go out of a night to make out my living. I had a child and it used to cry for food. So, as I could not get a living for him and myself by my needs, I went into the streets and made a living that way . . .

My father was an Independent preacher, and I pledge my word that it was the low price paid for my labour that drove me to prostitution. I often struggled against it, and many times I have taken my child into the streets to beg rather than I would bring shame on myself and it any longer. I have made pin cushions and fancy articles—such as I could manage to scrape together—and taken them into the streets to sell, so that I might get an honest living, but I couldn't. Sometime I should be out all night in the rain, and sell nothing at all, me and my child together; and when we didn't get anything that way we used to sit in a shed, for I was too fatigued with my baby to stand, and I was so poor I couldn't have even a night's lodging on credit. One night in the depth of winter his legs froze to his side. We sat down on the step of the door. I was trying to make my way to the workhouse, but was so weak I couldn't get any further. The snow was over my shoes. It had been snowing all day, and me and my boy out in it. We hadn't tasted any food since the morning before . . . A lady saw me sitting on the door-step, and took me into her house, and rubbed my child's legs with brandy. She gave us some food, both my child and me, but I was so far gone I couldn't eat.

I got to the workhouse that night. I told them we were starving but they refused to admit us without an order; so I went back to prostitution again for another month. I couldn't get any work . . . I then got an order for the workhouse, and went in there for two years. The very minute we got inside the gate they took my child away, and allowed me to see it only once a month. At last I and another friend left the 'house' to work at umbrella covering, so that we might have our children with us ... I then made from 3s. to 4s. a week, and from that time I gave up prostitution ... Had I remained at shirt making, I must have been a prostitute to this day.

H. Mayhew, 'Prostitution among needlewomen',
Morning Chronicle, 13 November 1849

There is not one young girl that works at slop work that is virtuous ... Could I have honestly earnt enough to have subsisted upon, to find me in proper food and clothing, such as is necessary, I should not have gone astray; no, never ... But no one knows the temptations of us poor girls in want. Gentlefolks can never understand it. If I had been born a lady it wouldn't have been very hard to have acted like one. To be poor and to be honest, especially with young girls, is the hardest struggle of all.

H. Mayhew, loc. cit.

7.1.2 *Prostitution: demand*
We forbid a wife except to very few gentlemen, and to the very many gentlemen, the harlot has taken her place ... Our harlots exist in the numbers they do in London because young gentlemen and young ladies cannot and dare not marry without ceasing to be gentlemen and ladies ...

J. C. Whitehorne, *The Social Evil Practically Considered,* 1858, p. 20

There has arisen in society a figure which is certainly the most mournful, and in some respects the most awful upon which the eye of the moralist can dwell. That unhappy being whose very name is a shame to speak; who counterfeits with a cold heart the transports of affection and submits herself as the passive instrument of lust; who is scorned and insulted as the vilest of her sex, and doomed for the most part to disease and abject wretchedness and an early death, appears in every age as the perpetual symbol of the degradation and sinfulness of man. Herself the supreme type of vice, she is ultimately the most efficient guardian of virtue. But for her, the unchallenged purity of countless happy homes would be polluted and not a few who, in the pride of their untempted chastity, think of her with an indignant shudder, would have known the agony of remorse and despair. On that degraded and ignoble form are concentrated the passions that might have filled the world with shame. She remains, while creeds and civilizations rise and fall, the eternal priestess of humanity, blasted for the sins of the people.

W. E. H. Lecky,
The History of European Morals, 1869, Vol. II, p. 299

7.1.3 *Prostitution: its domestic consequences*
It is impossible to form anything like a correct estimate of the extent

and magnitude of the evils produced by this detestable system of prostitution. The amount of physical suffering, in the shape of loathsome and ghastly disease, is prodigious. The records of our hospitals bear hideous testimony to the ravages of this frightful system. The number of victims who are sacrificed every year to our public allowance of brutal sin is enormous. The ramifications of mischief and misery produced by prostitution are almost countless. There is probably not a single family in England that has not suffered in some way from this national sin. Many young lads and young men are sent from the country to our great towns as apprentices, or students, or shopmen, or labourers. Virtuous, amiable, unsullied as yet by the grosser vices, but inexperienced in the ways of the world, multitudes of them fall into the pit of ruin prepared for them by the allurements of prostitution. Of those that escape bodily and physical ruin, very many contract such habits as are no less ruinous. There is a peculiar moral degradation which accompanies and marks this sin: companionship with abandoned women breaks down all the finer feelings and affections of the heart absolutely and often irretrievably. Many a young man, from being the companion, learns to be the accomplice of a strumpet, and gradually becomes as dishonest; and he who, before his fatal connection with prostitutes, was upright, honourable, and noble in his disposition, not seldom ends his days in the felon's prison! Who can tell how many parents have died heart-broken in consequence of prostitution being publicly permitted, or at least not publicly checked? How many youths, who might have been the pride, the comfort, and the blessing of their family, are consigned year by year to dishonoured and untimely graves, the victims of legislative toleration of exorbitant national sin!

'The vices of the streets', *Meliora*, vol. 1, 1859, pp. 70-9

7.1.4   *The career of a prostitute*

What is a prostitute? She is a woman who gives for money that which she ought to give only for love; who ministers to passion and lust alone, to the exclusion and extinction of all the higher qualities, and nobler sources of enjoyment which combine with desire, to produce happiness derived from the intercourse of the sexes. She is a woman with half the woman gone, and that half containing all that elevates her nature, leaving her a mere instrument of impurity; degraded and fallen she extracts from the sin of others the means of living, corrupt and dependent on corruption, and therefore interested directly in the increase of immorality—a social pest, carrying contamination and foulness to every quarter to which she has access ... Such women, ministers of evil passions, not only gratify desire, but also arouse it. Compelled by necessity to seek for customers, they throng out streets and public places, and suggest evil thoughts and desires which might otherwise remain undeveloped. Confirmed profligates will seek out the means of gratifying their desires; the young from a craving to discover unknown mysteries may approach the haunts of sin, but thousands would remain uncontaminated if temptation did not seek them out. Prostitutes have the power of soliciting and tempting. Gunpowder remains harmless till the spark falls upon it; the match, until struck, retains the hidden fire, so lust remains dormant till called into being by an exciting cause.

The sexual passion is strong in every man, but it is strong in proportion as it is encouraged or restrained; and every act of indulgence only makes future abstinence more hard, and in time almost impossible . . .

. . . [It is widely but wrongly believed]

1. That once a harlot, always a harlot.
2. There is no possible advance, moral or physical, in the condition of the actual prostitute.
3. That the harlot's progress is short and rapid.

. . . The order may be divided into three classes—'the kept woman' . . . who has in truth, or pretends to have, but one paramour, with whom she, in some cases resides; the common prostitute, who is at the service, with slight reservation, of the first comer, and attempts no other means of life; and the woman whose prostitution is a subsidiary calling . . . adopting prostitution only when their slender wages become insufficient for their legitimate wants . . .

[Few die of syphilis.] In London only 127 deaths are noted during the 156 weeks, out of a population amounting to more than 3,000,000, or on the average less than one a week . . . The fact of a girl's seduction generally warrants her possession of youth, health, good looks, and a well proportioned frame—qualifications usually incompatible with a feeble constitution. She, at least, meets the world with power of resistance beyond the average of women in her station. Notwithstanding all her excesses (and legion is their name), the prostitute passes through the furnace of a dissipated career less worse from wear than her male associates; and when she withdraws from it—as withdraw she will in a few years, for old prostitutes are rarely met with—she is seldom found with her nose sunk in, her palate gone, or nodes upon her shins . . .

If we compare the prostitute at thirty-five with her sister, who perhaps is the married mother of a family, or has been a toiling slave for years in the over-heated laboratories of fashion, we shall seldom find that the constitutional ravages often thought to be necessary consequences of prostitution exceed those attributable to the cares of a family and the heart-wearing struggles of virtuous labour.

How then is the disparition of this class of women to be accounted for, as they are neither stricken down in the practice of harlotry, nor by their own hands, nor by intemperance and venereal disease, nor would seem to perish of supervening evils in any notable proportion? Do they fall by the wayside, as some assume, like leaves of autumn, unnoticed and unnumbered, to be heaped up and to rot? ... I have every reason to believe that by far the larger number of women who have resorted to prostitution for a livelihood, return sooner or later to a more or less regular course of life ... The better inclined prostitutes become the wedded wives of men in every grade of society, from the peerage to the stable, and as they are frequently barren, or have but a few children, there is reason to believe they often live in ease unknown to many women who have never strayed, and on whose unvitiated organization matrimony has entailed the burden of families. Others who, as often happens, have been enabled to lay by variable sums of money, work their own reclamation as established milliners, small shop-keepers, and lodging-house keepers, in which capacities they often find kind assistance from ci-devant male acquaintances, who are only too glad to second their endeavours. Others again devote their energies and their savings to preying in their turn, as keepers or attaches of brothels and other disorderly establishments, upon the class of male and female victims they themselves have emerged from . . .

I repeat that prostitution is a transitory state, through which an untold number of British women are ever on their passage. Until preventive measures ... have been adopted ... it is the duty, and it should be the business of us all, in the interest of the commonwealth, to see these women through that state, so as to save harmless as may be of the bodies and souls of them. And the commonwealth's interest in it is this—that there is never a one among all of these whose partners in vice may not sometime become the husbands of other women, and fathers of English children; never a one of them but may herself, when the shadow is past, become the wife of an Englishman and the mother of his offspring ... If the race of the people is of concern to the State ... then arises the necessity for depriving prostitution not only of its moral but of its physical venom also.

The control and relief of prostitutes. A woman who knows herself to be diseased, is free to invite all comers to the enjoyment of her person, and to spread among them deadly contagion ... But if we can ill excuse the laws, which afford no protection to those who, after all, are comparatively free agents, what shall we say of them, if we find them placing thousands of men every year in the utmost jeopardy, compelling them almost, for the convenience of the State, to have recourse to the prostitution by which they are surrounded, and yet providing for them no means of safety or adequate relief? It is hardly credible that, until a few years ago, this was the case in England. At length in 1864 the injury inflicted by this apathy on our soldiers and sailors, and the loss sustained by the public purse, seems to have touched the conscience or the cupidity of the legislature, and in that year an Act was passed ... followed in 1866 ... the Contagious Diseases Act.

W. Acton, *Prostitution Considered in its Moral, Social and Sanitary Aspects, in London and other large cities: with proposals for the mitigation and prevention of its attendant evils,* 1870 edn

7.2 Contagious Diseases Acts

7.2.1 *The ladies' protest*

On the 1st January, 1870, was published the famous Women's Protest, as follows:

'We, the undersigned, enter our solemn protest against these Acts.

'1st.—Because, involving as they do such a momentous change in the legal safeguards hitherto enjoyed by women in common with men, they have been passed, not only without the knowledge of the country, but unknown, in a great measure, to Parliament itself; and we hold that neither the Representatives of the People, nor the Press, fulfil the duties which are expected of them, when they allow such legislation to take place without the fullest discussion.

'2nd.—Because, so far as women are concerned, they remove every guarantee of personal security which the law has established and held sacred, and put their reputation, their freedom, and their persons absolutely in the power of the police.

'3rd.—Because the law is bound, in any country professing to give civil liberty to its subjects, to define clearly an offence which it punishes.

'4th.—Because it is unjust to punish the sex who are the victims of a vice, and leave unpunished the sex who are the main cause, both of the vice and its dreaded consequences; and we consider that liability to arrest, forced medical treatment, and (where this is resisted) imprisonment with hard labour, to which these Acts subject women, are punishments of the most degrading kind.

'5th.—Because, by such a system, the path of evil is made more easy to our sons, and to the whole of the youth of England; inasmuch as a moral restraint is withdrawn the moment the State recognises, and provides convenience for, the practice of a vice which it thereby declares to be necessary and venial.

'6th.—Because these measures are cruel to the women who come under their action—violating the feelings of those whose sense of shame is not wholly lost, and further brutalising even the most abandoned.

'7th.—Because the disease which these Acts seek to remove has never been removed by any such legislation. The advocates of the system have utterly failed to show, by statistics or otherwise, that these regulations have in any case, after several years' trial, and when applied to one sex only, diminished disease, reclaimed the fallen, or improved the general morality of the country. We have, on the contrary, the strongest evidence to show that in Paris and other

Continental cities where women have long been outraged by this system, the public health and morals are worse than at home.

'8th.—Because the conditions of this disease, in the first instance, are moral, not physical. The moral evil through which the disease makes its way separates the case entirely from that of the plague, or other scourges, which have been placed under police control or sanitary care. We hold that we are bound, before rushing into experiments of legalising a revolting vice, to try to deal with the *causes* of the evil, and we dare to believe that with wiser teaching and more capable legislation, those causes would not be beyond control.'

This Protest was published in the *Daily News*, and the fact of its appearance was flashed by telegram to the remotest parts of the Kingdom. The local press largely reproduced it. Among the two thousand signatures which it obtained in a short time there were those of Florence Nightingale, Harriet Martineau, Mary Carpenter, the sisters and other relatives of the late Mr. John Bright, all the leading ladies of the Society of Friends, and many well-known in the literary and philanthropic world.

Josephine Butler,
Personal Reminiscences of a Great Crusade, 1898 edn

7.2.2 *Josephine Butler's Crusade*

... I never myself viewed this question as fundamentally any more a woman's question than it is a man's. The legislation we opposed secured the enslavement of women and the increased immorality of men; and history and experience alike teach us that these two results are never separated . . .

We arose—we women as well as men—in defence of the grand old principles . . . [which I believe] have their foundation in the Ethics of Christ . . .

It was much less of a simple woman's war against man's injustice, than it is often supposed to have been. It was wider than that. It was as a citizen of a free country first, and as a woman secondly, that I felt impelled to come forward in defence of the right. At the same time, the fact that this new legislation *directly* and shamefully attacked the dignity and liberties of women, became a powerful means in God's Providence of awakening a deeper sympathy amongst favoured women for their poorer and less fortunate sisters than had probably ever been felt before. It consolidated the women of our country, and gradually of the world, by the infliction on them of a double wrong, an outrage on free citizenship, and an outrage on the sacred rights of womanhood. It helped to conjure up also a great army of good and honourable men through the length and breadth of the land, who, in taking up the cause of the deeply injured class, soon became aware that they were fighting also for themselves, their own liberties, and their own honour.

Thus the peculiar horror and audacity of this legislative movement for the creation of slave class of women for the supposed benefit of licentious men forced women into a new position. Many, who were formerly timid or bound by conventional ideas to a prescribed sphere of action, faced right round upon the men whose materialism had been embodied in such a ghastly form, and upon the Government which had set its seal upon that iniquity; and so, long before we had approached near to attaining to any political equality with men, a new light was brought by the force of our righteous wrath and aroused sense of justice into the judgment of Society and the Councils of Nations, which encouraged us to hope that we should be able to hand down to our successors a regenerated public spirit concerning the most vital questions of human life, upon which alone, and not upon any expert or opportunist handling of them, the hopes of the future must rest.

loc. cit.

7.2.3 *Evidence to the Royal Commission on Contagious Diseases,* 1871

9152. You have spoken of the marked decrease in the number of brothels in the three towns; could you prove that decrease by putting your hand upon houses that were formerly houses of ill-fame and are now private dwelling-houses?—Yes, there is not the slightest difficulty in that. I could take you to Pembroke Street, Devonport, in which I think, in 1863, there were 22, but at any rate in 1865 there were 17 brothels, and at present there is only one ... In Mount Street, which runs parallel to that, there were several, but now there are none ...

9153. Now supposing the Acts did not exist, are you of opinion that the utmost vigilance and activity on the part of the police and the greatest desire on the part of the magistrates to repress disorderly houses would be effectual under the present state of the law?—I am quite sure it would not, for I find in Torquay, where the Acts do not reach, the prostitutes have increased, whilst at Stonehouse, with the Acts and the same [county police], they have decreased more than two-thirds.

Evidence of Inspector Anniss to the
Royal Commission on Contagious Diseases, 1871

12,897. .... You would not recommend the extension of these Acts to the civil community?—I do not understand that question, because they now apply only to the civil community.

12,898. The Acts operate only in certain specified districts?—I am perfectly aware of that.

12,899. And one question which has been referred to this

Commission, is, whether it is desirable to extend these Acts to the whole country?—I perfectly understand that, but those who are dealt with are women—not soldiers and sailors, but civilians.

12,921. You desired in your letter to the Secretary of the Commission to express the opinion which the working men entertained?—I did desire that, because I thought it was a point on which I had authority more than others. You were asking as to the kind of working men, what men they are. I should say the temperance men almost always lead in this matter,—abstainers, steady men, and to a great extent members of chapels and churches, and many of them are men who have been engaged in the anti-slavery movement and the abolition of the corn-law movement. They are the leaders in good social movements, men who had had to do with political reforms in times past, and who have taken up our cause ... They are secretaries of trades' councils, and presidents of working men's clubs, etc. ... Now the one thing on which they are strongest in every town in the north, is the fact of these Acts being an outrageous piece of sex legislation; that they apply to women only, not to men. They think this unmanly, cowardly, mean; there is such indignation in the working classes in this matter of its being sex legislation, that I am sometimes afraid of touching upon that topic, because it raises such a commotion in the meeting that we can scarcely quell it . . .

12,932 . . .—I desire to speak with all respect of you, gentlemen, as individuals ... We have the Word of God in our hands—the law of God in our consciences. We know that to protect vice in men is not according to the Word of God. We hold that the practical working of an Act, which is vicious in principle, is no fit subject for an inquiry, and therefore we do not require your verdict any more than if it were to tell us if there is a God or not. You may be sure that our action in this matter will continue to be exactly the same, even if the Commission pronounce the Acts highly moral. This legislation is abhorred by the country as a tyranny of the upper classes against the lower classes, as an injustice practised by men on women, and as an insult to the moral sense of the people . . .

12,951. . . . A certain number of these women are reclaimed through the agency of others ... or from a change of character apparently without outward influence, drift out of their mode of life?—Just so; they marry or get a little trade ... They have got enough money together to buy a sewing machine, and from that time they have been honest girls.

13,109. Because you have made a statement with regard to persons who voluntarily incur the disease, and you do not see that they ought to be protected, but as regards those who have contracted the disease involuntarily, do you think there is any distinction in the argument?— It is the law of nature that children should suffer for the sins of their parents, and I do not think that we can venture by legislative measures to interfere with that law, but that we may very much prevent the sufferings of infants by moral influences exercised on those who transmit to them this evil.

Evidence of Josephine Butler to the
Royal Commission on Contagious Diseases, 1871

7.2.4   *The working of the Acts*

A gigantic insult to the female sex is being offered by legislators to us, and *legislators must remove it* ... The question is whether the two sexes are entitled to equal rights, or whether one is created for the use of the other. This once settled, the rest follows easily. Granting medical assistance for stamping out a disease, then *any law to effect this must affect both sexes equally.*

J. E. Carpenter, *The Life and Work of Mary Carpenter,* 1879, p. 428

As for the sanitary question, that I leave to the medical profession. As Christian men and women we are bound to regard the moral effects of such legislation. If the body is to be saved from disease, and Satan to have their souls by such Acts, the sooner they are repealed the better.

Letter from the Rev. C. Bosanquet, *Shield,* 18 April 1870

A girl who was committed to prison by the Bench at ... said, 'It did seem hard, ma'am, that the Magistrate on the bench who gave the casting vote for my imprisonment had paid me several shillings, a day or two before, in the street, to go with him'.

Mrs Butler's second letter, *Shield,* 2 March 1870

I recall the bitter complaint of one of these poor women: 'It is *men, men, only men,* from the first to the last, that we have to do with! To please a man I did wrong at first, then I was flung about from man to man. Men police lay hands on us. By men we are examined, handled, doctored, and messed on with. In the hospital it is a man again who makes prayers and reads the Bible for us. We are had up before magistrates who are men, and we never get out of the hands of men till we die!' And as she spoke I thought, 'And it was a Parliament of men only who made this law which treats you as an outlaw. Men alone met in committee over it. Men alone are the executives. When men, of all ranks, thus band themselves together for an end deeply concerning women, and place themselves like a thick impenetrable wall between women and women, and forbid the one class of women entrance into the presence of the other, the weak, the outraged class, it is time that women should arise and demand their most sacred rights in regard to their sisters.

Mrs Butler's third letter, from Kent, *Shield,* 9 March 1870

... Will this stop the contagion? May it not be spread by the men who it is not proposed should be examined? Every medical man admits that it may ... Dr. Balfour, deputy-inspector of military hospitals, who is at the head of this statistical branch of the medical board, is asked—'The old practice which use to prevail of periodical examinations among the men is given up—is it not?—Yes. Do you think that periodical examinations would be very unpopular among the men?—I think that they would be very unpopular, and I should myself be very sorry to see them again introduced, because I think that they would tend to destroy the men's self-respect. The object of all our recent legislation for the army has been to raise the *morale* of the soldier: We have been endeavouring to 'level up', to use a current phrase, and I think that the reintroduction of those inspections would have the effect of destroying his self-respect, and in that way would be very injurious and directly antagonistic to the legislation which you have been carrying out of late years.' But if men are ashamed to submit to such an ordeal, shall we be so lost to our own self-respect as to make light of a woman's shame and insist that she shall be examined? (Applause.) The truth is, my lord, that this kind of regulation of the trade is not fitted to stamp out the disease. It is fitted for another purpose however, for which it almost seems to be intended. It is fitted to enable men to gratify their passions at less risk to their persons. (Loud applause.)

Mr James Balfour, at a public meeting in Edinburgh,
Shield, 9 March 1870

It appears to have been a common thing at Plymouth for a woman to be 'run in', as it is there called, on information often of the most malicious and groundless character. Let me give an actual case. A young woman, an orphan, had creditably filled a situation in domestic service for upwards of a year. She 'had a young man'. Wanting her to leave her situation, to go and live with him, on her refusal he denounced her to the secret police. These fellows went to the house, found the girl at her dinner, her mistress (a respectable tradesman's wife) being out, and ordered her to go to the hospital at once to see the doctor. She informed her mistress of the fact on her return, who, feeling perfectly assured of her good behaviour, told her not to go. The police came again, insisted on her going up, and threatened her with imprisonment if she did not appear. The mistress said she had better go and see the doctor, as she could not have the police continuing to come there, neither of them apprehending the consequences which would follow. The girl went, saw the doctor, and, not being in a condition to be examined by him, was detained the specified time authorised by the Act. Her mistress, finding she was detained in the hospital, began to believe that the police had been correct in their imputations, and her own credit and convenience being alike involved, at once procured another servant to fill the girl's place. When the girl was released from the hospital she went straight to her mistress, but finding her situation filled, took lodgings, with the hope of shortly finding another, but failing, and stung with shame and despair at the examination, and at being herded with prostitutes, and treated as one, she took the desperate resolve of plunging into vice. 'And so', said the poor girl to me, with tears in her eyes, 'I owe my ruin in life to those bad men.'

Letter from N. B. Williams, *Shield,* 17 September 1870

7.2.5 *The Colchester by-election, 1870*

Mrs. Hampson and I slipped into the Hall in the guise of some of the humbler women going to the meeting. I had no bonnet or gloves—only an old shawl over my head—and looked quite a poor woman. We passed safely through crowded lines of scoundrel faces and clenched fists, and were unrecognised. It was a solemn meeting. The women listened most attentively while we spoke to them. Every now and then a movement of horror went through the room when the threats and groans outside became very bad. At the close of the meeting some friend said to me, in a low voice, 'You best plan is to go quietly out by a back window which is not high from the ground, while the mob is waiting for you at the front'. The Mallesons and two friendly constables managed admirably. They made the mob believe I was always coming, though I never came. Mrs. Hampson and I then walked off at a deliberate pace from the back of the Hall, down a narrow, quiet, star-lit street: about thirty or forty kind, sympathising women followed us, but had the tact to disperse quickly, leaving us alone. Neither of us knew the town, and we emerged again upon a main street, where the angry cries of the mob seemed again very near. I could not walk any further, being very tired, and asked Mrs. Hampson to leave me and try to find a cab. She pushed me into a dark, unused warehouse, filled with empty soda-water bottles and broken glass, and closed the gates of it. I stood there in the darkness and alone, hearing some of the violent men tramping past, never guessing that I was so near. Presently one of the gates opened slightly, and I could just see in the dim light the poorly-clad, slight figure of a forlorn woman of the city. She pushed her way in, and said in a low voice, 'Are you the lady the mob are after? Oh, what a shame to treat a lady so! I was not at the meeting, but I heard of you and have been watching you.' The kindness of this poor miserable woman cheered me ... We overheard women going past in groups, who had been at the meeting, and their conversation was mostly of the following description:—'Ah, she's right; depend upon it she's right. Well, what a thing! Well, to be sure! I'm sure I'll vote for her whenever I have a vote!' . . .

The Pontefract by-election, 1872

At last we found a large hay-loft over an empty room on the outskirts of the town. We could only ascend to it by means of a kind of ladder, leading through a trap-door in the floor. However, the place was large enough to hold a good meeting, and was soon filled. Mr. Stuart had run on in advance and paid for the room in his own name, and had again looked in to see that all was right. He found the floor strewn with cayenne pepper in order to make it impossible for us to speak, and there were some bundles of straw in the empty room below. He got a poor woman to help him, and with bucket of water they managed to drench the floor and sweep together the cayenne pepper. Still, when we arrived, it was very unpleasant for eyes and throat. We began our meeting with prayer, and the women were listening to our words with increasing determination never to forsake the good cause, when a smell of burning was perceived, smoke began to curl up through the floor, and a threatening noise was heard below at the door. The bundles of straw beneath had been set on fire, and the smoke much annoyed us. Then, to our horror, looking down the room to the trap-door entrance, we saw appearing head after head of men with countenances full of fury; man after man came in, until they crowded the place. There was no possible exit for us, the windows being too high above the ground, and we women were gathered into one end of the room like a flock of sheep surrounded by wolves . . .

Mrs. Wilson and I stood in front of the company of women, side by side. She whispered in my ear, 'Now is the time to trust in God; do not let us fear'; and a comforting sense of the Divine presence came to us both. It was not personal violence that we feared so much as the mental pain inflicted by the rage, profanity and obscenity of the men, of their words and their threats. Their language was hideous. They shook their fists in our faces, with volleys of oaths. This continued for some time, and we had no defence or means of escape. Their chief rage was directed against Mrs. Wilson and me. We understood by their language that certain among them had a personal and vested interest in the evil thing we were opposing. It was clear that they understood that 'their craft was in danger'. The new teaching and revolt of women had stirred up the very depths of hell. We said nothing, for our voices could not have been heard. We simply stood shoulder to shoulder—Mrs. Wilson and I—and waited and endured.

Josephine Butler,
An Autobiographical Memoir, pp. 107-8, 121-3 (1911 edn)

7.3 Petition of the Moral Reform Union against the Double Standard

That having before them the fact that women are constantly annoyed and imperilled by the solicitation of profligate men in the streets and elsewhere, your Petitioners humbly pray that your Honourable House will, in justice, make the male offender in this matter of solicitation equally punishable with the female offender, against whom laws now exist; and that in all future legislation the same principle of equality between the sexes shall be observed.

Petition of the Moral Reform Union,
quoted in *Englishwoman's Review,* March 1884

7.4   The Sale of Children

This very night in London, and every night, year in and year out, not seven maidens only, but many times seven, selected almost as much by chance as those who in the Athenian market-place drew lots as to which should be flung into the Cretan labyrinth, will be offered up as the Maiden Tribute of Modern Babylon ... nightly levied in London by the vices of the rich upon the necessities of the poor ... If we must cast maidens nightly into the jaws of vice, let us at least see to it that they assent to their own immolation, and are not unwilling sacrifices procured by force and fraud ...

[In the words of a former madam:]

'Every woman who has an eye to business is constantly on the look out for likely girls. Pretty girls who are poor, and who have either no parents or are away from home, are easiest picked up. How is it done? You or your decoy find a likely girl, and then you track her down. I remember I once went a hundred miles and more to pick up a girl. I took a lodging close to the board school, where I could see the girls go backwards and forwards every day. I soon saw one that suited my fancy. She was a girl of about thirteen, tall and forward for her age, pretty and likely to bring business. I found out she lived with her mother. I engaged her to be my little maid at the lodgings where I was staying. The very next day I took her off with me to London and her mother never saw me again. What became of her? A gentleman paid me £13 for the first of her, soon after she came to town. She was asleep when he did it—sound asleep. To tell the truth, she was drugged. It is often done ... with laudanum ... Next morning she cries a great deal from pain, but she is 'mazed, and hardly knows what has happened except that she can hardly move from pain. Of course we tell her it is all right; all girls have to go through it some time, that she is through it now without knowing it, and that it is no use crying. It will never be undone for all the crying in the world. She must now do as the others do. She can live like a lady, do as she pleases, have the best of all that is going, and enjoy herself all day. If she objects, I scold her and tell her she has lost her character, no one will take her in; I will have to turn her out on the streets as a bad and ungrateful girl ... In a week she is one of the attractions of the house.'

The moment a child is thirteen and is a woman in the eye of the law, with absolute right to dispose of her person to anyone who by force or fraud can bully or cajole her into parting with her virtue ... While the law forbids her absolutely to dispose of any other valuables until she is sixteen, it insists upon investing her with unfettered freedom to sell her person at thirteen ...

[An interview with Mesdames X and Z:]

'Do you do anything in the foreign trade?' I asked.

'Oh, no', she said, 'Our business is in maidenheads, not in maids ... We deal only with first seductions, a girl passes only once through our hands, and she is done with. Our gentlemen want maids, not damaged articles, and as a rule they only see them once.'

'What comes of the damaged articles?' 'They all go back to their situations or their places. But', said the procuress reflectively, 'they all go back to the streets after a time . . .'

'Do the maids ever repent and object to be seduced when the time comes?'

'Oh yes', said Miss X, 'sometimes we have no end of trouble with the little fools. You see they often have no idea in the world as to what being seduced is. We do not take much trouble to explain, and it is enough for us if the girl willingly consents to see or to meet or to have a game with a rich gentleman ... If a girl makes too much trouble she loses her maidenhead for nothing instead of losing it for money. The right way to deal with these silly girls is to convince them that now they have come they have got to be seduced, willing or unwilling, and that if they are unwilling, they will be first seduced and then turned into the streets without a penny. Even then they sometimes kick and scream and make no end of a row ... We had fearful trouble with that girl, Janie. She wrapped herself up in the bed-curtains and screamed and fought and made such a rumpus, that I and my friend had to hold her down by main force in bed while she was being seduced.' . . .

'But how do you manage to pick up so many?'

The senior partner replied with conscious pride, 'It takes time, patience and experience. Many girls need months before they can be brought in. You need to proceed very cautiously at first. Every morning at this time of the year my friend and I are up at seven, and after breakfast we put a shawl around our shoulders and off we go to scour the park. Hyde Park and the Green Park are the best in the morning; Regent's Park in the afternoon. As we go coasting along, we keep a sharp look out for any likely girl [nurse-girls], and having spotted one we make up to her; and week after week we see her as often as possible, until we are sufficiently in her confidence to suggest how easy it is to earn a few pounds by meeting a man ... Thus we always have a crop of maids ripening, and at any time we can undertake to deliver a maid if we get due notice.'

'Come', said I, in a vein of bravado, 'what do you say to delivering me five on Saturday next ... for me to distribute among my friends, after having them duly certificated?'

'... We will try, although I have never before delivered more than two, or at the most three, at one place. It will look like a boarding-school going to the midwife.'

[The bargain was struck and the girls were delivered.]

W. T. Stead, 'The maiden tribute to modern Babylon.

Pall Mall Gazette, 6 July 1885

Part Eight

Public Service

Introduction

Philanthropy, as Hannah More made clear at the beginning of the nineteenth century, was peculiarly the profession of a lady (8.1.1). It became one of the tools by which 'organic' village values, of a 'face-to-face' society, were to be imported into the new mass cities, in an attempt to bind rich and poor together in an 'invisible chain of sympathy', to use Kay-Shuttleworth's phrase, mitigating distress, softening class hostility.

Philanthropy was never simple almsgiving; the donor must be concerned with the true well-being of the recipient, and must never merely confirm the idle and the dissolute in their anti-social ways. Julia Wedgwood and John Stuart Mill both (8.1.2) feared that women would be a soft touch, because charity offered easy pleasures and women, dependent themselves, were unable to appreciate the value of self-dependence. The *English Woman's Journal* (8.1.3) felt that the teaching of political economy (which located pauperism in the irresponsibility of the pauper) was too harsh. But few would have disagreed with Canon Barnett, founder of Toynbee Hall, that the poor needed friends as much as funds, counsel as much as cash.

This was a task for which women were well suited, with their ready sympathy, tact, delicacy and discernment, leisure, and taste for detail. They could offer their domestic skills, caring for the young, old and sick, to the families they visited. Such a concern was to propel some women into public service on local government boards, and others into pressure group activity. But, as Mrs Butler pointed out (8.2.1), though it was acceptable for men to help poorer men, for women to help other women was regarded with distaste by such as Mrs Lynn Linton (8.2.2), who assumed that public agitation by women was pathological rather than highly principled, and stemmed from their sickness rather than from their sympathies.

Utilitarianism and political economy both encouraged a 'scientific' approach to voluntary work. From the early 1830s, cities like Manchester had their own Statistical Societies which collected information about local conditions to feed into the educational movements of the 1830s and the public health movements of the 1840s. In 1857 was established the National Association for the Promotion of Social Science, its president Lord Brougham, its members including Shaftesbury, Kingsley, and women, who contributed to its proceedings from the very first (8.3). The Association brought together members of the Law Amendment Society (who were petitioning for a Married Women's Property Act in

1856); the Reformatory and Ragged School Union, in which Shaftesbury and Mary Carpenter were prominent (8.4); and was in turn to espouse women's employment (3.11.2), sanitary reform (8.5), workhouse visiting (8.6) and ultimately the Charity Organization Society (8.9.1).

Mary Carpenter's concern for 'moral orphans' developed out of her ragged school teaching in Bristol in the 1840s; she devised a network of agencies for the children of 'the perishing and dangerous classes'— ragged schools for the destitute children of the slums, industrial schools for the vagrant children of the streets, and reformatories for the delinquent children of the courts. She swept them up, extracted them from the adult penal system, and by respecting their right to childhood, tried to re-create for them the family life they had been denied (8.4.1). The Acts of 1854 and 1856, grant-aiding her work, meant that by 1866 there were sixty-five reformatory schools with 5,000 children, and fifty industrial schools with 2,000 children in them. As with children, so with adult women: they must be enlisted in their own salvation (8.4.2) and without the care and concern of other Christian women they failed and fell. Louisa Twining, writing twenty-five years later, was saddened that so few women had come forward to work in this field.

Sanitary reform (8.5) was another major concern of the Social Science Association. Under Chadwick's influence, public health had since the 1840s been treated mainly as an engineering matter of sewage disposal and clean water. The Association argued that public health was more than sanitary streets; it was also sanitary homes and sanitary families. This 'domestic' version naturally fell to women (8.5.1) whose Ladies' Sanitary Association circulated 140,000 tracts in four years on housing, dress, vaccination and child care, lectured teachers and lady visitors, and financed itinerant lady missionaries (8.5.2). But in the field of health, much that was local, voluntary and permissive in its initiative and powers in the 1830s, was, by the 1870s, a compulsory responsibility imposed by central government on local authorities. With this shift, women were drawn into local government work as lay members and as professional employees (8.5.3).

The Workhouse Visiting Society (8.6.1) was also sponsored by the Social Science Association. Louisa Twining, the daughter of a wealthy tea merchant, had on visiting a former servant in the local workhouse been appalled to discover the mixed wards of sick and well, idle and aged, the unwashed, the ill-fed, the infected and the verminous found in 'unreformed' workhouses. Children in particular failed to thrive and became second-generation paupers and prostitutes. She established committees of lady visitors and 'one abuse after another was disclosed, discussed, condemned and finally, in most cases, abolished' (Frances Power Cobbe, *Life by Herself*, Vol. I, p. 318). In

1871 the Local Government Board was established and two years later Mrs Nassau Senior was appointed as the first woman Poor Law Inspector. In 1875 Miss Martha Merrington was the first woman to be elected to a poor law board, in South Kensington. By the end of the century there were to be nearly a thousand women guardians sitting on over half the country's boards. Louisa Twining's *Suggestions for Women Guardians* (8.6.2) is telling in its very detail and in its dependence on voluntary organisations. The suitability of women for poor law work was a regular theme in the *Reviews* (8.6.3).

Frances Power Cobbe, friend of Mary Carpenter, had found in Bristol that some of the worst aspects of the poor law lay in its neglect of its sick poor (8.7.1). In 1869, of 158,000 workhouse inmates, over a third were sick poor, a far larger number than the 20,000 being nursed in voluntary hospitals. Their nurses were usually fellow inmates, too illiterate to read the medicine labels and often too drunk and infected to follow the simplest instructions in hygiene. William Rathbone, Liberal MP, and merchant prince of Liverpool, sought Florence Nightingale's aid to establish nurses for the sick poor (8.7.2). In 1865 Agnes Jones, a Nightingale nurse, arrived with a band of fellow nurses to supervise his workhouse infirmary of 1,300 patients. She died of typhoid in three years; but Florence Nightingale obtained in the 1867 Metropolitan Poor Law Act the provision that the sick poor should be nursed in infirmaries by trained nurses (8.7.3). But given the niggardliness of Guardians and the shortage of qualified nurses, it was an uphill struggle. In 1879 Miss Twining's ladies formed the Association for Promoting Trained Nursing in Workhouse Infirmaries, and they trained and placed some 800 women in twenty years. Not until 1897 were inmates forbidden to act as nurses, and by then there were over 5,000 trained and probationer nurses within the poor law. But most of the sick were still being nursed in the workhouse rather than in an infirmary, and the custodial flavour remained.

The other way was to nurse the sick poor in their homes which, Rathbone expected, would reduce mortality and class hostility simultaneously (8.7.2). Other cities quickly followed, and in 1874 Rathbone and Miss Nightingale founded their Metropolitan and National Association for Providing Trained Nurses for the Sick Poor which trained hospital nurses for district work. Their success was ensured when the Queen's Golden Jubilee Fund in 1889 was devoted to it (for hospital nurses, see 3.9 above).

Part of public health was the eradication of slum housing. But given that the urban poor were tied to the inner city in their search for casual employment, they faced a combination of high rents and erratic earnings. Slum clearance merely intensified the overcrowding that created slums in adjacent streets. Some of the many Evangelical missions of the mid-century turned from ragged schools to ragged homes (8.8.1). This was 'professionalised' by Octavia Hill. The grand-daughter of Dr Southwood Smith, she was encouraged by Ruskin in the late 1860s to manage some Marylebone courts, in which tenants and property alike were in need of attention (8.8.2). Rather than disperse the tenants, she sought to moralise them into habits of regularity and self-reliance through the visits of her lady rent-collectors. Philanthropy could produce a 5 per cent return on capital. Her methods were widely copied, her training was sought by many women, one of the first being Emma Cons, later the LCC's first woman alderman; and became the basis of modern housing manage-ment (8.8.3). But not until many London trades moved out of the inner city at the end of the century was there a decline in casual labour and the consequent overcrowding, that was at the heart of the housing problem.

Octavia Hill was part of a highly influential and able circle, which included the Samuel Barnetts, the Charles Booths, and Beatrice Potter (later Beatrice Webb). With Charles Loch, and colleagues from the Social Science Association, Miss Hill founded the Charity Organiza-tion Society in 1869, which sought to apply the methods of business and the principles of political economy to philanthropy, in the belief that 'the mass misery of the great cities arose from spasmodic, indiscriminate and unconditional doles' (Beatrice Webb, *My Apprenticeship*, ch. 4). In Samuel Barnett's phrase, 'the poor starve because of the alms they receive'. The COS therefore tried to eradicate casual almsgiving, to insist on the responsibility of personal service from the donor, and to rationalise the relation of charities to each other and to the poor law. Its vehicle was the 'lady visitor' whose case work and counselling of the poor into industry and self-reliance fore-shadows much later social work (8.9.1). Helen Bosanquet became one of their most active members, editing their journal, the *Charity Organization Review*. But ultimately the COS was to be defeated by its sheer financial inability to aid the deserving, especially the sick and the elderly—a task that was to fall on state insurance and state pensions (8.9.2).

The 'befriending' function of philanthropy continued. In 1893 Baroness Burdett-Coutts, a very rich philanthropist, surveyed the range of English philanthropy in a collection of papers she edited for the Chicago International Exhibition. One of her contributors, Louisa Hubbard, estimated that 20,000 women were paid officials of charitable societies, and a further half-million women were voluntary workers (*Woman's Mission*, p. 364). One major field was child care—orphanages, feeding clubs, holidays; another, the protection of girls; highly popular were missions to service men; nursing was important as was the provision of articles ranging from scrapbooks to surgical instruments. The energy was awesome; the scale, as with 'Aggie' Weston's early NAAFIs, involving capital of £150,000, impressive (8.9.4); and the sustained sympathy with the derelict and the down-and-out inspiring. Baroness Burdett-Coutts reported that when she referred to fallen women, she was corrected by one of the workers: 'Call them knocked down women, if you will, but not fallen' (loc. cit., p. 157). The extract on women's work for girls (8.9.5) indicates both the scale and the service that women brought to philanthropy, offering country girls in the city a surrogate family of sisters and mothers.

Much philanthropic work was religious in inspiration and conservative in intention. Since Bishop Blomfield's efforts at Church extension in the 1830s (building churches in the inner cities and attaching a network of welfare agencies, from maternity to bootblacking clubs, to tempt the poor to use them), the Church had become a heavy user of women's voluntary services (8.10.1)—to raise funds and to serve as parish and district visitors; although the response of the Women's Co-operative Guild to the Mothers' Union suggests that their efforts were not always gratefully received (see below, 8.13.2). Southey in 1829 had asked why the Church did not possess Sisters of Charity on the continental model, devoting their lives to service; and under the influence of the Oxford Movement and the example of Florence Nightingale in the Crimea (8.10.2), a handful of Sisterhoods developed in the late 1840s, led by Elizabeth Sellon of Plymouth. By the end of the century, perhaps a thousand Sisters were nursing, teaching and working in refuges and reformatories, but they remained distrusted because of their 'popish' propensities.

Within Evangelical and dissenting circles, women had always been permitted to preach. In the 1860s, the Sankey and Moody revivalist atmosphere produced some outstanding women preachers, the Anglican Geraldine Hooper, Jessie Macfarlane, and the most remarkable, and most reluctant, of them all, Catherine Booth. With her husband, she resigned from the Methodist New Connexion in order to retain their itinerant Christian Mission. In 1877 this became the Salvation Army. Having insisted from her youth that there was 'no male or female in Christ', she ensured that all ranks in the army were open to women (8.10.3). It was calculated that 40 per cent of Army officers were women (though not on equal pay); and their Hallelujah Lasses were their most effective workers, tackling drunkenness, vice and sin, in the roughest of working-class streets and courts.

Like nursing, education was a traditional female task (8.11.2), requiring high moral and religious sensibility, patience, and a skill with children. But the reliance on voluntary societies to provide and staff elementary schools meant that those areas with the greatest educational needs remained often the most neglected. So the great Education Act of 1870 established elected school boards to provide rate-funded non-denominational elementary schools where the voluntary societies had failed to do so. The previous year women had obtained the municipal vote; now they were permitted not only to vote but also to stand for the new boards. Four women were immediately successful in their elections—Elizabeth Garrett came top of the poll in Marylebone (8.11.1), Emily Davies was returned in Greenwich, both joining the London School Board; Lydia Becker was returned in Manchester and Miss Flora Stevenson in Edinburgh. Their work was real and substantial (8.11.3). Over 200 women were on school boards by the 1890s; though when school boards were absorbed by the county councils in 1902, women were squeezed out of the management of education until in 1907 they were permitted to serve on county councils in their own right.

Education, poor law and sanitary work drew many women who had begun as charitable workers into public service on local government boards. Lydia Becker, the organising brain behind women's suffrage, pointed out that local government was a vital step towards Westminster (8.12.1). Women had obtained the municipal vote in 1860, and in the 1870s joined school and poor law boards. The 1888 reform of local government created county councils for which women could vote but on which they could not sit. Jane Cobden and Lady Sandhurst were actually elected to the LCC in 1889 but were unseated on appeal by Beresford Hope (a staunch Tory opponent to women's rights, see 9.2.5 below). So in 1888 the Society for Women as County Councillors was formed, which was to become the Women's Local Government Society, publishing numerous tracts which argued both that women had special skills to offer and that women local government employees needed the care of women members (8.12.2). The Local Government Act of 1894 completed the local government structure by constructing parish, rural and district councils for which women could vote and on which, suitably propertied, they could serve. In 1907 county councils and borough councils were opened to women candidates, and Elizabeth Garrett Anderson became the first woman mayor in her home town of Aldeburgh. Local government was becoming a significant employer of women (8.12.3). By 1898 the *Westminster Review* calculated that 812 women were guardians on 359 of the country's 641 poor law unions; over 200 women were on school boards, another 200 were serving as parish councillors and 150 as district councillors. What their job entailed is described by Mrs M'Ilquham and Mrs Barker (8.12.4) and the appropriate 'professional' attitude in section 8.12.5.

The Liberal Party brought forward many women into public service. The organisation which encouraged working-class women in particular was the Women's Co-operative Guild. Founded in 1883 as a women's adjunct to the Co-operative Movement, by the end of the century under Margaret Llewelyn Davies (niece of Emily Davies) it had over 350 branches and 18,000 members, mainly wives of working men (8.13.3). From being a women's social club around the local store, the Guild quickly undertook to educate women as consumers and to appreciate their 'basket power'; and from that, to encourage women to enter public life by training them in public speaking, backing them for school and poor law boards and vestries. In 1894 the Guild estimated that forty-five of their candidates stood, of whom twenty-two were successful. They met and overcame some early opposition from men (8.13.4); but not until the property rate-paying basis of the local franchise was removed could working-class married women have full access to local government.

Suggestions for further reading:
On philanthropy, M. G. Jones, *Hannah More,* 1948; D. Owen, *English Philanthropy, 1660-1960,* 1962; M. Simey, *Charitable Effort in Liverpool,* 1951; K. Heasman, *Evangelicals in Action,* 1962; C. L. Mowat, *The Charity Organization Society,* 1961; B. H. Harrison, 'The Girls' Friendly Society', *Past and Present,* 1961. And on the growth of the State, D. Roberts, *Victorian Origins of the British Welfare State,* 1959, and on health, S. Finer, *Edwin Chadwick,* 1951.

More specifically, J. Manton, *Mary Carpenter,* 1974; L. Holcombe, *Victorian Ladies at Work,* 1973; G. Stedman Jones, *Outcast London,* 1971, on the housing problem; O. Anderson, 'Women preachers in mid-Victorian England', *Historical Journal,* 1969; M. Hill, *The Religious Order,* 1973; J. Gaffin, 'Women and co-operation', in L. Middleton (ed.), *Women and Labour,* 1977.

8.1 Philanthropy, a Woman's Profession

8.1.1 *Philanthropy, the profession of a lady*

Mrs. Stanley said, 'I have often heard it regretted that ladies have no stated employment, no profession. It is a mistake: charity is the calling of a lady; the care of the poor is her profession. Men have little time or taste for details. Women of fortune have abundant leisure, which can in no way be so properly or pleasantly filled up, as in making themselves intimately acquainted with the worth and the wants of all within reach. With their wants, because it is their bounden duty to administer to them; with their worth, because without this knowledge, they cannot administer prudently or properly . . . We are far from thinking that charity should be limited to our own immediate neighbourhood. We are of opinion that it should not be left undone anywhere, but that *there* it should be done indispensably. We consider our parishes our more appropriate field of action, where Providence, by 'fixing the bound of our habitation', seems to have made us peculiarly responsible for the comfort of those whom he has doubtless placed around us for that purpose. It is thus that the Almighty vindicates his justice, or rather calls on us to vindicate it. It is thus he explains why he admits natural evil into the world, by making the wants of one part of the community an exercise for the compassion of the other . . .'

Hannah More, *Coelebs in Search of a Wife,* 1809

8.1.2 *The irresponsibility of charity*

When we see the patent harm done by rich benevolent ladies, when we watch their influence in extinguishing all idea of independence and encouraging a number of people to leave off all exertion, and bring into the world large families to whom the idea of working for their living is actually never presented,—when we are awakened to the enormous evil which results from women's habit of looking at the great facts of life as exceptions, instead of as coming under a general law,—we may be inclined to think that legislation is required rather to shut off the influence of women on the poor than to give a larger scope to that influence . . . What we want is to give women a sense of *responsibility* in dealing with the poor. It is so painful to see squalid misery, however well deserved; it is so pleasant to hear words of gratitude, however shallow, and watch a gleam of relief, however temporary . . . It needs the sense of a national life to bring this home to us; no sense of individual justice will support us under what we have to witness of suffering and degradation. Nothing but the sense of a common life, to be purified through individual suffering from the

evils which those individuals have not always brought upon
themselves, will strengthen us to confront our duty in regard to those
evils.

> Julia Wedgwood, 'Female suffrage, considered chiefly with
> regard to its indirect results', in Josephine Butler (ed.),
> *Woman's Work and Woman's Culture,* 1869

The education given to women—an education of the sentiments rather
than of the understanding—and the habit inculcated by their whole
life, of looking to immediate effects on persons, and not to remote
effects on classes of persons—make them both unable to see, and
unwilling to admit, the ultimate evil tendency of any form of charity
or philanthropy which commends itself to their sympathetic feelings
... A woman born to the present lot of women, and content with it,
how should she appreciate the value of self-dependence? She is not
self-dependent; she is not taught self-dependence; her destiny is to
receive everything from others, and why should what is good enough
for her be bad for the poor? Her familiar notions of good are of
blessings descending from a superior. She forgets that she is not free,
and that the poor are; that if what they need is given to them
unearned, they cannot be compelled to earn it: that everybody cannot
be taken care of by everybody, but there must be some motive to
induce people to take care of themselves; and that to be helped to help
themselves, if they are physically capable of it, is the only charity
which proves to be charity in the end.

> J. S. Mill, *On the Subjection of Women*, 1869, ch. 4

8.1.3   *The need for philanthropy*
While listening to the political economist who warns us that charity is
often only another name for self-indulgence in feeling, sowing the
seeds of greater misery than it professes to alleviate ... yet it is our
plainest duty to feed the hungry and clothe the naked, and to afford
shelter to the aged, while striving that benefit to the individual shall
not result in injury and degradation to the class.

   For, be it observed, life is no such smooth and easy matter that we can
say of any one who has fallen into misfortune that it is their fault, or
that of any one now living. It has pleased Providence to place us in a
moral atmosphere of so many mingled elements that we cannot assign
in many cases the particular causes of a particular poverty. There are
such things as hereditary diseases and hereditary incapacity;—banks
will break and swallow up the fortunes of helpless hundreds, and a
commercial crisis drags into its vortex houses which were guiltless of
speculation or expense ... While certain general laws can be
discovered which form the moral scheme of Providence, there come
up individual questions every day which cannot be settled by reference

to any such laws. We know, as a matter of certainty, that the drunken workman will bring his children to hunger and cold;—yet we cannot therefore let the children die ... remembering the story of the good Samaritan who, when he saw that the stranger was wounded, did not stop to speculate on the best way of rendering roads secure from thieves, but *went up to him and bound his wounds.*

'The profession of the teacher',
English Woman's Journal, March 1858

8.2 Public Work for Women

[handwritten marginalia: "class great gender"]*

8.2.1 *Women for Women*

I wish it were felt that women who are labouring especially for women are not one-sided or selfish. We are human first; women secondarily. We care for the evils affecting women most of all because they react upon the whole of society, and abstract from the common good ... When men nobly born and possessing advantages of wealth and education have fought the battles of poor men, and claimed and wrung from Parliaments an extension of privileges enjoyed by a few to classes of their brother-men who are toiling and suffering, I do not remember ever to have heard them charged with self-seeking; on the contrary, the regard that such men have had for the rights of men has been praised, and deservedly so, as noble and unselfish. And why should the matter be judged otherwise when the eyes of educated and thoughtful women of the better classes are opened to the terrible truth regarding the millions of their less favoured countrywomen, and they ask on *their* behalf for the redress of wrongs, and for liberty to work and to live in honesty and self-reliance? ...

It is sometimes supposed that the most fervent advocates of woman's cause are persons who have been pinched and starved in the matter of affection, disappointed in life, embittered by isolation, and therefore glad to exchange the exclusiveness of the domestic hearth for a communism in which they would not feel themselves left out, starved and solitary ... Many of those who are toiling, praying and arguing for the promotion of this cause, are among the happiest ladies in the land ... Not but that the happiest among us have not observed and pondered with amazement, from our very childhood, on certain customs, laws, and maxims prevalent among us, which seem only to recognise the existence of one half of the human family ... To be very patient under the miseries of *others*, appeared to us, as we grew up to years of discretion, to be an easy virtue: we desired to practise some sterner virtue than this, and we saw that our own happiness was the very reason why we should speak out boldly for the unhappy; and it continues to be a reason determining us to labour on in the same course, through evil report, and good report. It is from the heart of my beloved home, with my children around me, that I speak; wherefore I trust I shall be believed to be free from indifference to the fear that our homes may be revolutionized or destroyed ...

Josephine Butler, *Woman's Work and Woman's Culture,* 1869

8.2.2   *Modern Man-Haters*

With the advanced class of women, the modern man-haters, one of the articles or their creed is to regard men as their natural enemies from whom they must both protect themselves and be protected . . .

If she has a husband she holds him as her enemy *ex officio*, and undertakes home-life as a state of declared warfare, where she must be in antagonism if she would not be in slavery. Has she money? It must be tied up safe from his control; not as a joint precaution against future misfortune, but as a personal protection against his malice; for the modern theory is that a husband will, if he can get it, squander his wife's money simply for cruelty and to spite her, though in so doing he may ruin himself as well . . . If it would please her to rush into public life as the noisy advocate of any nasty subject that may be on hand—his refusal to have his name dragged through the mire at the instance of her folly is coercion in its worst form—the coercion of her conscience, of her mental liberty; and she complains bitterly to her friends among the shrieking sisterhood of the harsh restrictions he places on her freedom of action . . .

As for the man, no hard words are too hard for him. It is only enmity which animates him, only tyranny, and oppression which govern him. There is no intention of friendly guidance in his determination to prevent his wife from making a gigantic blunder—feeling of kindly protection in the authority which he uses to keep her from offering herself as a mark for public ridicule and damaging discussion, wherein the bloom of her name and nature would be swept away for ever. It is all the base exercise of an unrighteous power; and the first crusade to be undertaken in these latter days is the woman's crusade against masculine supremacy.

This sect of modern man-haters is recruited from three classes mainly—those who have been cruelly treated by men, and whose faith in one half of the human race cannot survive their own one sad experience; those restless and ambitious persons who are less than women, greedy of notoriety, indifferent to home life, holding home duties in disdain, with strong passions rather than warm affections, with perverted instincts in one direction and none worthy of the name in another; and those who are the born vestals of nature, whose organization fails in the sweeter sympathies of womanhood, and who are unsexed by the atrophy of their instincts as the other class are by the perversion and coarsening of theirs. By all these men are held to be enemies and oppressors; and even love is ranked as a mere matter of the senses, whereby women are first subjugated and then betrayed.

Eliza Lynn Linton,
'Modern man-haters', in *The Girl of the Period,* 1883

8.3   Social Science Association

Can woman's influence ever come to us otherwise than in private conversation—in her visible work—and in her written books? ... Whether by public reading or by merely writing on philanthropic subjects, the extreme usefulness of women has been demonstrated beyond dispute by the Social Science Association ... The secretary publicly concedes no small share of the credit to the aid of his assistant, Miss Isa Craig, whose business talents excite the admiration of all connected with the Society. Lord Brougham announced in 1859 that the most important papers hitherto presented had been those of Florence Nightingale, of which the Council thought it well to send copies to all the hospitals in the kingdom. It were idle to talk of the share which Mary Carpenter has had in one of the noblest departments of Social Science—the reformation of juvenile criminals ... Each of the three affiliated societies is worked almost exclusively by women [the Ladies Sanitary Association; the Society for the Employment of Women; the Workhouse Visiting Society]. Lord Shaftesbury said, in his opening address to the Association at Bradford, 'Not a little is due to the share which women have taken, and most beneficially taken, in the business of the Society. I insist especially on the value and peculiar nature of the assistance. Men may do what must be done on a large scale; but, the instant the work becomes individual, and personal, the instant it requires tact and feeling, from that instant it passes into the hands of women. It is essentially their province, in which may be exercised all their moral powers, and all their intellectual faculties. It will give them their full share in the vast operations the world is yet to see.'

Frances Power Cobbe, 'Social science congresses, and women's part in them', *MacMillan's Magazine,* December 1861

The Association was of immense use to the women's movement in giving us a platform from which we could bring our views before the sort of people who were likely to be disposed to help in carrying them out.

Emily Davies, *Family Chronicle,* quoted in Barbara Stephen, *Emily Davies and Girton College*, 1927, p. 75

8.4 The Delinquent

8.4.1 *Reformatories*

We call, then, on Christian women, who are not bound by their pecuniary circumstances to work for their own living ... to some earnest work for the good of others ... and those who are mothers in heart, though not by God's gift on earth, will be able to bestow their maternal love on those who are more to be pitied than orphans made so by the Lord, those most wretched moral orphans whose natural sweetness of filial love has been mingled with deadly poison ...

Nor let women fear the difficulties to be contended within this work, the apparent publicity to which it may expose them, or the unwillingness of the other sex to allow them to work. A true woman will surmount all obstacles by the God-sent strength of her very weakness;—while *apparently* placed in a public position, she will know how to keep the privacy of her individual nature guarded by an invisible but impenetrable shield ...

What, in the first place, is a Reformatory School? It is, under one aspect, a place of detention for juvenile delinquents, more merciful of course than prisons, but by compulsory confinement partaking of its character; under another, it is a moral hospital for the young; under a third, it is an asylum for worse than orphans, where they are to be nurtured and prepared to go forth into the world alone ...

The Christian woman who devotes herself to this work must endeavour to combine these elements ... The children are brought to her by the hand of the law ... she gives it a mother's love, and devotes herself to save it. Though she desires to bind the children by cords of love, yet in the wild and undisciplined condition of many of the children there must be an admixture of the prison element of compulsory power wisely and lovingly administered. There must be a deep study of human nature, practical experience and a strong religious element, to heal the diseases of the spirit; and finally, all the household arrangements must be so made as to secure health of body and mind, intellectual education, and training to useful work, which will properly prepare the child to go forth, after due time, a good and useful member of society ... Women of education and independence are needed to work in Reformatories with the paid officials [i.e. matron, industrial teacher, etc.], sustaining them in their work, bearing the brunt of extra difficulties, and infusing a high spirit into the establishment. Such ladies should besides be prepared to enter into business details, and even if they have the aid of gentlemen in the more public and official work, yet they should themselves understand it, and be able to do it on emergency ...

Many reformatories for girls have been recently established ... but the great difficulty is to find paid workers, and still more to meet with ladies who are not only willing, but *able*, by their previous training and business habits, to conduct the management and superintendence of such institutions.

Mary Carpenter, 'Women's work in the
reformatory movement', *English Woman's Journal,* July 1858

8.4.2 *Prisons*

Among the hundreds of girls sent to our reformatories ... there are failures ... most of them we fear will find their way, ere long, to the Female Convict Prisons ...

[The Rev. T. Carter, Chaplain of Liverpool gaol, has stated] 'The number of adult females who were committed there last year exceeded the number of males ... viz. 4,440 females against 4,419 males ... Of 207 female convicts released (between May 1856 and June 1859), 97 cannot be traced ... 73 have been recommitted, 17 are known to be living disorderly lives and maintaining themselves by crime; 7 have been pardoned on medical grounds, dead or lunatics; 4 have migrated ... 1 is in a refuge in London, whilst only 8 are known to be so far doing well.' The system adopted must be completely wrong ... Why not enlist in the work the voluntary efforts of true-hearted women, as has been done in Mountjoy, Ireland, and in our reformatories? Thus only do I believe that these women can be rescued from their evil ways and be restored to society.

Mary Carpenter, 'Female convicts', *Transactions of the National
Association for the Promotion of Social Science,* 1864

It is a great pain to me to be brought into any degree of notoriety, but yet I *must speak* ... It was intense conviction on my part that determined me to write in spite of obstacles and cold water, to speak the truth without fear ...

Mary Carpenter, quoted in J. E. Carpenter,
The Life and Work of Mary Carpenter, 1879, pp. 116-17

Amongst the most degraded and hardened class of men and women in prisons the pure and the high minded are called for, and yet but little has been done in this direction, since the efforts made by Elizabeth Fry more than seventy years ago. There are at present 318 women employed as prison officers, of these only three come under the description of Lady Superintendents (with salaries of £400 and £500 a year); thirteen are matrons ... the rest is made up of Warders of different grades. What an enormous field of work and influence is here open to women of power and character, yet we are told, 'Gentle-women do not often apply'. It is strange that no 'Sisterhood' had yet

taken up this sphere of work where self-denial, order and discipline
are so urgently demanded. Still more surprising is it that women have
as yet been allowed but little share in the management of
reformatories for boys and girls, where the motherly and the sisterly
influence would naturally exert so strong a power ... Yet more
astonishing is it that even on committees of management in
penitentiaries for women and girls, men should, as at present, act
alone. In five of the principal societies in London for the reclamation
of women, there is not one person of their own sex acting on the
committee . . .

Louisa Twining, 'Women's work, official and unofficial',
National Review, July 1887

8.5　Sanitary Reform

8.5.1　*Household sanitation*

Woman's systematic co-operation is essential to the success of Sanitary Reform ... 'The Health of Towns Act' may ensure good drainage and water-supply, pure air, and other important external sanitary requisites; but till every woman frames a Health of *Homes* Act, and becomes a domestic 'officer of health', none can ensure that the pure air shall ever be breathed, the good water ever be sufficiently used, or other sanitary conditions ever be fulfilled in-doors. The Government may, by appointing public analysts and inspectors of markets, check adulteration and the sale of diseased meat; it may, by a wise foreign policy and abolition of needless imposts, empty the world's cornucopia at our feet; but only woman can ensure that wise selection of diet, and that scientific cookery without which even plenty may lead to disease ... Architects may build houses which in point of structure shall be very temples of Hygeia; but while woman who dwells there ignorantly violates household sanitary law, she will ever make them nurseries of disease and death ... Fathers may work, and legislate, and struggle all their days to secure the moral and material blesssings of Christian civilization to their children; but while woman is too ignorant rightly to fulfil even her first great duty of mother, thousands of those children must, as now, die ere they see the Light, and thousands more, ere they can enjoy their heritage: though they be not offered to Moloch, as of old, they must, as now, be sacrificed to ignorance ...

The great field of sanitary labour may be considered as divided into parts:—the amelioration of injurious external circumstances and the reform of injurious habits and customs. Of these parts, the former may be considered as belonging principally to man, the latter principally to woman. It is for man's comprehensive mind to devise schemes for draining and cleansing our towns, for improving dwellings, and for placing the necessaries of life within the reach of all; and it is for his strong hand to execute these schemes. It is for him to discover the laws of health, and to teach and apply them in his special sphere. It is for woman, in her functions of mother, housewife, and teacher, to effect those urgently-needed changes in infant management, domestic economy, education, and the general habits of her own sex, without which humanity could never even approximate to bodily perfection, though all injurious external circumstances were changed. It is for her to teach and apply the laws of health in her own sphere, where man cannot act ...

After studying sanitary science, and applying it personally, woman will be prepared to commence her work for the physical elevation of others. This, like all her ministrations, should begin in her own home. That sphere, narrow though it seems, presents scope for an amount of sanitary labour which could not be fully indicated in many volumes ... Prominently among them, may be placed the use of unsuitable and badly-cooked food ... In the nursery, woman's ignorant violations of the laws of health are still more frequent and mischievous. The present high rate of infant mortality among us and other civilized communities, is something unparalled in all creation. After the home-work, should come efforts for the improvement of health among our poor neighbours; though a very large number of the sore physical evils that afflict them are undoubtedly the natural results of their low moral and spiritual condition, and consequent wilful wrongdoing, probably most charitable workers attribute too much to this score. Nothing is more certain than that many physical evils befall men irrespectively of their moral and spiritual condition or deserts.

Much good may be done by the distribution of simple, interesting tracts containing expositions of the laws of health ... There seems, indeed, no reason why sanitary tract distribution should not be quite as efficient in the work of physical elevation as religious tracts have been in that of spiritual improvement.

Those who hold maternal meetings, have in them excellent opportunities for imparting knowledge. The following remarks on this point, are from the pen of a lady who has worked long and successfully for the elevation of her poor neighbours, and has introduced sanitary teaching at the maternal meetings conducted by her:—

'Maternal meetings are just the opportunities for imparting sanitary knowledge to poor mothers. I find it necessary to vary the mode of instruction. Sometimes I have read one of the sanitary tracts, and conversed a little upon its subject, concluding the strictly religious part of the exercises a little sooner for the purpose. Again, it may happen that the [religious] subject on which I may be speaking leads to sanitary topics. For instance when speaking of bereavement, and the consolation which mothers may derive from religion in the death of their little ones, the remarks in the tract on infant management come in very naturally, and then at some length the causes of infant mortality may with great propriety be stated, parts of the tract read, and at the conclusion copies of it given to those who have been led to take an interest in the subject ...'

Women engaged in writing for the press may do much towards the diffusion of a knowledge of the laws of health, not only among the poor, but among all classes. The numerous works of fiction, magazine articles, and tracts written by women could easily be made a medium for the diffusion of this kind of information ... Let us have a sanitary 'Jane Eyre', 'Adam Bede', and 'John Halifax'.

In many schools for girls of the poorer classes, also, the health of the pupils is much injured through bodily inaction and other preventable causes. The lady-visitors and supporters of such schools may do very much to remedy these evils.

The visitor should observe whether the children are comfortably seated. It is common to find little children perched on a high form, with their feet hanging in mid-air, several inches from the floor; others will be found tightly packed together, herring fashion, in various uncomfortable postures. These and other physical discomforts are often the great cause of the children's irritability and so-called 'naughtiness', which are generally attributed to something very different ... if therefore, we wish to make them 'good', we must first make them comfortable. The visitor should ascertain how much time is allotted to out-door exercises in the playground. Half an hour, both in the morning and the afternoon, should be thus spent when the weather is suitable ...

Besides their own direct sanitary work, women may do much indirectly, through their influence over men. The best and most useful men in sanitary and all other labours are, other things being equal, invariably those whose wives, mothers, daughters, and sisters, aid and encourage them in their good work. Men engaged in public sanitary labours have almost invariably to encounter most depressing opposition and difficulty in the prosecution of them; and for want of woman's sympathy, have often to endure discouragement by their own firesides. This must not be; for, from the leading member of parliament, endeavouring to introduce legislative sanitary measures, and the rich landowner, anxious to improve his cottage property, to the obscure author, and the poor medical man, spending their leisure in diffusing sanitary knowledge, all need woman's intelligent appreciation, encouragement, and sympathy; and it is part of her divine mission to bestow them largely.

English Woman's Journal, April 1859,
S.R.P. [Miss S. R. Powers]

8.5.2. *Public health missionaries*

A member of the Committee, Mrs. William Fison, has devoted the principal part of her time to the promotion of sanitary improvement in various parts of the kingdom. Mrs. Fison has visited Manchester and ... organized a Ladies' Auxiliary, delivered addresses to the town missionaries, to the pupils of the Ladies' College, and to several meetings of the working classes. Mrs. Fison afterwards delivered addresses at a series of meetings and conversazioni held for the discussion of the means of effecting improvements among the poor in

Andover, Bradford, Brighton, Brompton, Chertsey, Darlington, Highbury, Maidenhead, Middlesboro', Oxford, Reading, Stainton, Watlington and Wilton. Some of these meetings were attended by district visitors and other ladies working among the poor, others by the poor themselves.

Fourth Report of the Ladies' Sanitary Association, 1861

8.5.3.   *Public health inspectors*

At the present time only four out of the twenty-nine London Vestries, viz., Kensington, Islington, St. Pancras, and Southwark, have appointed women as Sanitary Inspectors ...

In 1893, the Kensington Vestry led the way ... Two women inspectors [were appointed] for a period of six months, to assist in enforcing the sanitary provisions of the Factory and Workshop Acts, and the Public Health (London) Act, 1891, in the several factories, workshops, workplaces and laundries in the parish, where women were employed ... To Dr. Dudfield, Medical Officer of Health for Kensington, a great debt is due. It may fairly be surmised that, without effort on his part, the women inspectors would not have been appointed ...

In Kensington, where the workshops employing women have been registered, and are shown, in March 1895, to have numbered 567, containing a total of 1,168 workrooms, the number of inspections in that year was 1,302, and of re-inspections 522. The number of workrooms found to be overcrowded was 50, insufficiently ventilated 48, and dirty 136. The number of nuisances reported was 277, and the works carried out under supervision are thus enumerated: additional means of ventilation provided 10; rooms cleansed and whitewashed 153; yards, floors, roofs, etc., repaired 49; and sanitary conveniences constructed 18. Workroom cards distributed, showing number of persons permitted in each room, 218; and statutory notices and written intimations issued, 161.

Mary Stewart Kilgour, *Women as Sanitary Inspectors,* 1896

8.6 Poor Law

8.6.1. *Workhouse Visiting Society*
This Society has been established to promote the moral and spiritual improvement of workhouse inmates, of whom there are upwards of 600,000 in England and Wales alone, and will provide a centre of communication and information for all persons interested in that object.

Acknowledging the importance of moral influence over all classes of inmates, the chief object at which the Society aims is the introduction of a voluntary system of visiting, especially by ladies, under the sanction of the guardians and chaplains, for the following purposes:—

1. For befriending the destitute and orphan children while in the schools, and after they are placed in situations.
2. For the instruction and comfort of the sick and afflicted.
3. For the benefit of the ignorant and depraved, by assisting the officers of the establishment in forming classes for instruction; in the encouragement of useful occupation during the hours of leisure; or in any other work that may seem to the guardians to be useful and beneficial.

The co-operation of guardians is earnestly desired in furthering these objects. Similar plans have been adopted in prisons for many years with considerable success ...

'The Workhouse Visiting Society',
English Woman's Journal, July 1858

8.6.2. *Work of Women Guardians*
It is well known that a large proportion of our pauper population consists of women and children, and of the other, the male portion, the greater number are the sick or aged ... Nearly all the details of the vast institutions which come under the care and supervision of Guardians are such as women would naturally control in their own households, and which men do not concern themselves about ...

Amongst the defects which may, I fear, be very generally discovered, I may name the stiffness and hardness of the stays, the ill-fitting of boots or shoes, the absence of pocket-handkerchiefs as well as of nightgowns, a matter of even greater importance, causing day-chemises to be worn continuously for a week, and also the absence of drawers; omissions which continue even when the girls leave the schools for service and have outfits provided ... That each child should have a seperate towel, and brush and comb is most important in view of the great prevalence of opthalmia, ring-worm, etc., to be found in almost all pauper schools. I fear we shall hardly be supported in the suggestion that tooth-brushes would help to prevent much of the sad trouble and misery experienced in after life by the lower classes from their defective teeth. It is important to ascertain that the water, whether for daily washing or for baths, is changed for each child. The clothes taken off at night should be either hung on pegs to air, or laid lightly folded in baskets, not placed on or under the beds, as is sometimes the case where no provision is made.

The dietary, being suggested, or at least approved, by the Central Board, hardly comes within the control of Guardians, except as regards the cooking and the quality of the food; but of course suggestions of changes are always possible should serious deficiencies in quantity or character be found to exist (especially as regards vegetables) . . . Had not experience shown that the hint is needed, I should hardly have thought it necessary to remind Guardians to look to the supply of toys and amusement for the children, there being too often an entire absence of all these important elements of child life. No expense need be incurred, as it can be only 'want of thought' that keeps families of the upper classes from occasionally sending their children's toys to the forlorn little ones of the workhouse.

In the case of the separation of the children from the school, owing to ring-worm or other causes, sometimes of months' or years' duration, it has been left to women to suggest that their education should not wholly cease, with the result that on recovery they must be placed at a sad disadvantage with other children, and a teacher has been provided for a short period daily.

As the examination of the beds and bedding is an important part of a woman's duties, I need hardly say that it is so more especially for the children, where neglect of cleanliness and frequent changing is essential for health. There is also the matter of blinds for the sleeping rooms; often in large wards and dormitories there have been none, and the children, so liable to weak eyes, sleep in broad sunshine.

I hope that there are few women who will not endeavour to look after the moral as well as the physical condition of the children, whose guardians they are; and especially as regards their welfare after they leave the school, this matter being too often left to the Relieving Officers, even if attended to at all. It can hardly be necessary to name the 'Association for Befriending Young Servants' to which all girls in the Metropolitan districts are admissible, and for the country, beyond this sphere, the 'Girls' Friendly Society', of which there is now a special branch, with its own rules, for workhouse girls . . . I would earnestly advise all Guardians to promote a branch in their unions.

If ladies can be found who will take the girls first into their own households on leaving the schools, giving them a few months' training under their own servants, an incalculable advantage will be secured. And, wherever Industrial Training Homes exist within reach, a year in one will be well spent in enlightening the ignorance and helplessness which can hardly fail to result from the life of the workhouse school. The subject of boarding-out pauper children, both boys and girls, is now so well known, having been begun in 1870, that its plans are probably familiar to Women Guardians ... The advantage of providing a home and family life for orphan and deserted children can hardly be over-estimated, but the later development of an Association for Promoting Cottage Homes for Children (now connected with the former Society) is less known and understood. Women are earnestly requested to ascertain if there are any, either boys or girls, in the schools, who can be drafted into such Homes; they need not be orphans or deserted, and can be taken at any age for industrial or other training ...

Why Sunday school teaching should not be adopted for pauper children I have never been able to understand, for they need the change and the variety of teachers even more than others. Some ladies must live within reach of every union who could surely undertake this work of love and duty, were permission obtained through a Guardian.

One very important matter, too often overlooked, is the supervision of children out of school hours, when they are sent out to the national schools, as is now often the case. Then, if they are under the care of pauper inmates on their return and for the rest of the day, their fate is worse than if they were kept altogether in the workhouse with a schoolmistress and master ...

Before I leave the subject of the schools, I would ask that the question of temperance should not be forgotten ... No more important field for Bands of Hope can exist than amongst our pauper children, if they are to be saved from joining the ranks of their parents, and, too, probably, of many former generations of pauperism ...

Amongst the matters requiring inspection amongst the sick and adults, I have already named the beds and bedding. Pillows are often made of horsehair, which are much too hard, and require frequent picking, too often neglected; even flock is less objectionable than this. There is generally a deficiency of pillows, and bed-rests should always be supplied. Chairs and seats with backs, arms, and cushions, are now more generally to be found than some years ago, but I fear there are still many country workhouses where there are tiled floors, with no bits of carpet or mats, even for the infirm wards, wholly insufficient arrangements for ablution, and no pictures, flowers, or books, to brighten the monotony of the lives, not only of the inmates, but of the nurses also.

There is one matter to which I reluctantly refer, but which demands the attention of women, viz., suitable provision for decency and cleanliness in the closets. Strange to say, although the subject of official order in prisons, no notice is taken of this neglect in workhouses. Pocket-handkerchiefs are also very generally lacking for the adults, as well as for the children, and in some cases this has been one of the first successful suggestions of a lady Guardian.

I would ask Guardians to remember that their duties and their guardianship are not limited to the poor alone, but are equally required for the officers, for whose welfare they are also responsible. Their care as well as sympathy is needed for all, more especially for the nurses, on whom so much depends and whose work and trials are often heavy and monotonous ... As regards the moral and spiritual welfare of the nurses, I would ask that women should use their influence to procure for them in all cases a recreation room for the hours when they are off duty, with a library, a piano, and all the innocent amusements of games, which may satisfy and cheer the mind and the tired body, without the craving for unhealthy excitement ... Allow afternoon and not evening hours for out of door exercise and recreation.

I have referred to temperance work as a part of the important duties of a woman, and more so as regards the nurses than any other class. A branch of the Women's Union of the Church of England Temperance Society has been successfully started in, at least, one infirmary for the nurses, who have their own meetings in their recreation room at hours convenient to them; and meetings are also arranged for the workhouse, both men and women being invited to become members.

In all unions with sick wards, generally in a separate building in the country, there should be at least one nurse who has been trained in a hospital or large infirmary, but we fear there are still many where this is not the case, and where incompetent, or even pauper, women are employed. I would remind Guardians of the existence of the 'Association for Promoting Trained Nursing in Workhouse Infirmaries, . . .

A special help for the lying-in wards, so clearly a prominent sphere of women's work, will be found in the formation of 'Workhouse Girls' Aid Societies', for helping girls with their first children to make a fresh start in the world ... The separation of such persons from the more hardened offenders should be carefully attended to, as well as a distinction between married women and all others. Indeed I may say that the whole subject of classification, with some regard to character, is one of the most urgent and important of a Guardian's duties, the neglect of which contributes so materially to demoralisation and an increase of pauperism ...

As women Guardians are frequent visitors, it may well form part of their work to see that the nurses do not neglect the reading of prayers in their wards, night and morning, if such an arrangement is made, as is desirable in all Infirmaries for the sick, where either books of prayers are used, or cards printed for the purpose.

Let me say, in conclusion, how earnestly I would ask women Guardians to consider the importance of their work and of their continuance at their posts as long as it is possible after a short term of service, and it helps to strengthen the impression that women's work is not lasting nor to be depended upon ... Let us well consider the importance of the service we undertake for the benefit of the social life of our country, by carrying out its laws, and helping to interpret them in the most just and merciful manner, in the interests of all classes, both rich and poor, who are affected by the wide-reaching operations of our Poor-laws.

Louisa Twining, *Suggestions for Women Guardians,* 1885

8.6.3. *Women and the poor law*

Poor Law work is specially fitted for women; for it is only domestic economy on a larger scale. Accustomed to regulate her own house, a lady has had precisely the training necessary to fit her for a Poor Law Guardian; she has had the management of children, and looked after their health, their clothing, and education; she has ordered in the household supplies, and is accustomed to examine into their prices and quality; she has supervised her servants and allotted to them their employments; and finally, she knows something of the requirements of the sick room. Enlarge a household and it becomes a workhouse; multiply the servants by tens and the children by hundreds, and you have a workhouse school; increase the sick room, and it becomes an infirmary; so that every woman who has managed her own household with wisdom and economy possesses the qualities chiefly necessary in a guardian of the poor.

... Last year 31 ladies were officiating as Poor Law Guardians, fourteen of these being in London, five in Birmingham, four in Bristol and eight in Edinburgh ... Why do not a greater number of ladies undertake the work? ... The novelty of the employment, the publicity of the election, the real wearisomeness of the work, and the exaggerated unpleasantnesses have all caused women to shrink from offering themselves as candidates. The ladies already engaged in visiting among the poor or in relief committees are hard worked as it is, and do not yet realize how much more effective their work would be if they occupied the responsible position of guardians. They also hesitate, doubting if they have business training enough ... But there is another restriction, the qualification which compels all persons desirous of being guardians to be qualified householders, whose names are on the rate-book. The rating is in some unions as high as

£40 ... Not only is the actual number of women householders only about one-sixth in proportion to the men householders, but the women who are householders are not as a rule those with most time to spare for the work. They have businesses of their own or families depending upon their care and exertions ... It is obvious that in the most crowded portions of our cities—in the East End of London for instance—few ladies of leisure are residing as ratepayers, though many would gladly go and do the needful work on the Boards if this qualification were removed.

'The work of women as poor law guardians',
Westminster Review, vol. 123, 1885

8.7 Nursing of the Poor

8.7.1. *Workhouse nurses*

In the male wards they are usually old men... in the women's... the most depraved and abandoned... The ways in which a hard unfeeling nurse may torment her wretched patient are beyond enumeration. She moves her roughly when every touch is agony, she neglects every little precaution which might make her bed more comfortable, she gives her food cold, she speaks brutally so as to shake her nerves to misery, she monopolizes for herself, or refuses to use for the patient, the easy chairs, cushions or bed rests any kind visitor may have provided. And when the wretched sufferer has reached the last stage... she refuses... to give her the cold Workhouse tea she craves for her in her agony, to save herself the trouble of the needful arrangements.

Frances Power Cobbe, *The Workhouse as an Hospital,* 1861

8.7.2. *District nursing in Liverpool*

Prospectus: The Liverpool Training School and Home for Nurses is intended to supply a want universally felt by medical men, and now generally acknowledged by the public.

The work which the new Institution is designed to effect divides itself into three heads, viz.:

1. To provide thoroughly educated Professional Nurses for the Infirmary.
2. To provide District or Missionary Nurses for the poor.
3. To provide Sick Nurses for private families.

1. To provide thoroughly educated Professional Nurses for the Infirmary.—There are in the Infirmary, Nurses of whose efficiency and kindness we cannot speak too highly, but the supply of good Hospital Nurses is quite inadequate to the requirements. And the misconduct of the unsuitable ones, who from necessity are employed, discredits a profession which is in its nature most honourable, and would otherwise attract many whose ability and character would peculiarly fit them for its duties.

2. To provide District or Missionary Nurses for the Poor.—In cases which are not suitable for and cannot be reached by Hospitals, to do in nursing what the Dispensaries do for them in medical aid. We propose to furnish Nurses to those districts which will, by means of local committees or individuals, find the necessary medical comforts

and superintendence. The results of district nursing, though only tried on a small scale, and with an imperfect organization, have been invariably satisfactory. It relieves an amount of suffering most intense in its character, and capable of alleviation to a great extent, by a proportionately small expenditure. It does more than this; it teaches the people to nurse their own sick, and by introducing a knowledge of sanitary laws among the working classes, tends to prevent illness and strengthen health.

In a merely economical point of view, by restoring parents to their work and place, it often prevents whole families from steadily sinking into hopeless poverty, misery and vice, the consequences of which, in the end, take vengeance on society for its neglected duties.

In a moral and political point of view, aid thus given to the suffering poor does away with an irritation against God and man, the extent of which is not suspected by those who have not been in a position to see it ... Assistance thus bestowed would open the hearts of the sufferers and of their families to all benevolent persons in their attempts to benefit the working classes, physically, morally and religiously ... Much has been said and written of the duty and importance of more sympathy and intercourse between rich and poor ... but to do any good, such connection and intercourse must be natural and unenforced. Now, in sickness and death, rich and poor are on common ground. In this work the sympathy between them is natural, the results are apparent, immediate and satisfactory ...

The Organization of Nursing in a Large Town, 1862

Florence Nightingale on the proposals, to Mr William Rathbone. I quite agree with you that missionary nurses are the end aim of all our work; hospitals are, after all, but an intermediate state of civilization. While devoting my life to hospital work, to this conclusion I have always come, *viz.*, that hospitals were not the best place for the sick poor, except for severe surgical cases.

loc. cit.

An example of district nursing. Afflicted with asthma, and other diseases. Found lying on the floor, covered with bed sores, and so thin that she had to be lifted on a sheet; her husband is a porter, with two children, unable to pay for nursing; she was attended by the Dispensary Doctor, but in other respects was left to the mercy of the world in a low neighbourhood, in dirt and bad air, wretched in body and mind, causing her husband to feel wretched also on coming home and finding his house in such a condition; to use the expression, he thought he was forsaken by God and by man. Our Nurse comes in, washes her, and lends bedstead and bedding; and shows her how to use an air cushion, changes her linen, etc., cleans the house, persuades the husband to whitewash the apartments; suitable nourishment is sent, and she and the household are now in comparative comfort; she is able to get up. The man is now helpful and hopeful, and has added by his own exertions and savings to the comfort of his home.

loc. cit.

Nursing the room. The district nurse must be trained. She must do the nursing work under Doctor's orders ... but next to this she must 'nurse the room' i.e. put it into nursing order so that it shall not hinder the patient's recovery . . . She should be the friend not the law giver of the family . . . For this purpose she must never say, e.g. 'I hope when I come again all this rubbish will be cleared out from under the bed' (where probably there will be old boots, dirty linen, potatoes, etc.). But she must just do many things herself, such as clean a disorderly grate, dirty windows, etc., and so *show* them how to do it. She must also know—about nuisances which she cannot remedy herself—what is the province of the Sanitary authorities and give notice at their office. She must know if meat, brandy, etc. is required, where to apply for it (whether Poor Law or Charity), also where, in a very poor place, for blankets.

Florence Nightingale, 1884,
quoted in C. Woodham-Smith, *Florence Nightingale*, 1950, p. 568

8.7.3. *Sick poor nursing*
A. To insist on the great principle of separating the Sick, Insane, 'Incurable', and, above all, Children, from the usual population of the Metropolis.

B. To advocate a single Central Administration . . . So long as a sick man, woman, or child is considered *administratively* to be a pauper to be repressed, and not a fellow-creature to be nursed into health, so long will these most shameful disclosures have to be made. The care and government of the *sick* poor is a thing totally different from the government of paupers. Why do we have Hospitals in order to cure, and Workhouse Infirmaries in order *not* to cure? . . . The past system of mixing up all kinds of poor in workhouses will never be submitted to in future.

Uniformity of system is absolutely necessary, both for efficiency and for economy.

For the purpose of providing suitable establishments for the care and treatment of the Sick, Insane, etc. consolidation and a General Rate are essential.

Memorandum of Florence Nightingale, Mr Farnall,
Poor Law Inspector, and Dr John Sutherland, 1865,
quoted in E. Cook, *The Life of Florence Nightingale,* 1913,
Vol. 2, p. 133

8.8 Housing

8.8.1. *Ragged homes*

About seven or eight women assembled who looked at her with curiosity. She read to them a few verses of scripture and then explained that the purpose of the meeting was to help them to manage their homes better. She started by teaching them needlework, providing material for them to buy at a reduction of 2d. in the 1s. to be paid for a few pence at a time, with a pattern thrown in. During the winter they made several garments for themselves and their children. The following year the meetings took a more definite form. Experiments in simple cookery were introduced, and ways of looking after children were discussed. Clothing and savings clubs were formed, and whitewash brushes and saucepans hired out. They were taught how to whitewash the walls of their dwellings and given instructions in the cheapest way of making nourishing soup. Thus she hoped to improve the homes of poor women living in the potteries and piggeries of Notting Hill.

Mrs Bayley, *Ragged Homes and How To Mend Them*, 1859, p. 116

8.8.2. *The principles of Housing Management*

I feel most deeply that the disciplining of our immense poor population must be effected by individual influence; and that this power can change it from a mob of paupers and semi-paupers into a body of self-dependent workers...

About four years ago, I was put in possession of three houses in one of the worst courts in Marylebone... The houses were in a most deplorable condition—the plaster was dropping from the walls; on one staircase a pail was placed to catch the rain that fell through the roof. All the staircases were perfectly dark; the banisters were gone, having been burnt as firewood by tenants. The grates, with large holes in them, were falling forward into the rooms... The pavement of the back yard was all broken up, and great puddles stood in it, so that the damp crept up the outer walls. One large but dirty water-butt received the water laid on for the houses; it leaked, and for such as did not fill their jugs when the water came in, or who had no jugs to fill, there was no water... Six, seven, or eight weeks' rent was due from most tenants...

As soon as I entered into possession, each family had an opportunity of doing better: those who would not pay, or who led clearly immoral lives, were ejected. The rooms they vacated were cleansed; the tenants who showed signs of improvement moved into them, and thus, in turn, an opportunity was obtained for having each room distempered and painted. The drains were put in order, a large slate cistern was fixed, the wash-house was cleared of its lumber, and thrown open on stated days to each tenant in turn. The roof, the plaster, the woodwork were repaired; the stair-case walls were distempered; new grates were fixed; the layers of paper and rag (black with age) were torn from the windows, and glass was put in; out of 192 panes, only 8 were unbroken. The yard and footpath were paved.

The rooms as a rule were relet at the same prices at which they had been let before; but tenants with large families were counselled to take two rooms, and for these much less was charged than if let singly ... The elder girls are employed three times a week in scrubbing the passages in the house ...

The pecuniary result has been very satisfactory. Five per cent interest has been paid on all the capital invested ... The sum allowed yearly for repairs is fixed for each house, and if it has not all been spent in restoring and replacing, the surplus is used to provide such additional appliances as the tenants may themselves desire. It is therefore to their interest to keep the expenditure for repairs as low as possible ...

Week by week when the rents are collected, an opportunity of seeing each family separately occurs. There are a multitude of matters to attend to. First there is the mere outside business—rent to be received, requests from the tenants respecting repairs to be considered; sometimes decisions touching the behaviour of other tenants to be made, sometimes rebukes for untidiness to be administered. Then come the sad or joyful remarks about health or work, the little histories of the week. Sometimes grave questions arise about important changes in the life of the family - shall a daughter go to service? or shall the sick child be sent to a hospital? etc. Sometimes violent quarrels must be allayed ...

It will be readily understood that in such a crisis as that which periodically occurs in the East-End of London, instead of being unprepared I feel myself somewhat like an officer at the head of a well-controlled little regiment, or, more accurately, like a country proprietor with a moderate number of well-ordered tenants. For firstly, my people are numbered; not merely counted, but known, man woman and child. I have seen their self-denying efforts to pay rent in time of trouble, or their reckless extravagence in seasons of abundance ... Even among this very lowest class of people, I had found individuals whom I could draft from my lodging-houses into resident situations (transplanting them at once into a higher grade) simply because I was able to say, 'I know them to be honest, I know them to be clean'. Think of what this mere fact of *being known* is to the poor ...

Whoever will limit his gaze to a few persons, and try to solve the problems of their lives—planning, for instance, definitely, how he, even with superior advantages of education, self-control, and knowledge, could bring up a given family on given wages, allowing the smallest amount conceivably sufficient for food, rent, clothes, fuel and the rest—he may find it in most cases a much more difficult thing than he had ever thought, and sometimes, maybe, an impossibility. It may lead to strange self-questioning about wages. Again, if people will watch carefully the different effects of self-help and of alms, how the latter, like the outdoor relief system under the old Poor Law, tends to lower wages, and undermines the providence of the poor, it may make them put some searching questions to themselves about the wisdom of backing up wages with gifts . . .

You cannot deal with the people and their houses separately. The principle upon which the whole work rests is, that the inhabitants and their surroundings must be improved together. It has never yet failed to succeed.

> Octavia Hill, 'Management of a London court',
> *Homes of the London Poor,* 1875

8.8.3.　*Housing management, a profession*

I realized that my best plan would be not only to train such volunteers as offered, and the professional workers whom we required, but to train more professional workers than we ourselves can use, and as occasion offers, to introduce them to owners wishing to retain small tenements in their own hands, and to be represented in them by a kind of Manager not hitherto existing . . . If there existed a body of ladies, trained to more thorough work, qualified to supervise more minutely, likely to enter into such details as bear on the comfort of home life, they might be entrusted by owners with their houses. We all can remember how the training of nurses and of teachers has raised the standard of work required in both professions. The same change might be hoped for in the character of the management of dwellings let to the poor. Whether or no volunteers co-operated with them would settle itself. At any rate owners could have, as I have often told them they should have, beside their lawyer to advise them as to law, their architect as to large questions of building, their auditor to supervise their accounts, also a representative to see to their people, and to those details of repair and management on which the conduct of courts and blocks inhabited by working people depends.

> Octavia Hill, 1902(?),
> quoted in E. Moberley Bell, *Octavia Hill,* 1942, p. 249

8.9 Professional Philanthropy

8.9.1 *Scientific philanthropy*

A little sick child must be sent away into the country. The father of a family must go to a Convalescent Hospital. The large and expensive room must be given up by the old couple whose wages are falling lower and lower. The kitchen, the dampness of which is sapping the children's strength, must be left; the idle son must be made to work. [The advice of the Charity Organization Society's] committee is generally refused, but they need not despair. They know that in a day or two the visitor will call—she will tell the mother how kind are those who care for sick children, and will gradually persuade her to send her little one out of the hot, close air which is killing it. She will tell the man how much better it would be to get thoroughly strong than to work on in his weak state; she will stir him up by thoughts of the bright grounds which surround the Convalescent Hospital; and soon she will come to the committee for the offered letter. Going day by day she will break down the apathy and carelessness which has allowed a high rent or an unhealthy situation so long to cripple the strength of the family. She will tell of better and cheaper rooms, she will appeal to both love and prudence, and by kind words today, and by stern refusals tomorrow, give help till they so far help themselves to move... Perhaps she will find and talk to the truants, or the idler, and them she will induce to go with some of their playmates to school; him she will stir up to apply for the work of which the committee told him. Thus the visitor in her visits will persuade and rouse the people to the action that the committee saw to be good, but were powerless to enforce... She is not only a channel through which useful information reaches the committee, but is, in almost every instance, their actual agent in carrying out the plans of help adopted...

Each visitor had to keep a book, in which the name of every applicant was entered, together with the information obtained about him through the local branch of the Charity Organization Society. An account of all money given to him by any charitable agency, and a short notice from month to month of the events in his family were also entered... The result of this system was to train a body of visitors in judicious and organized modes of work... When this system had been in operation two or three years, it became clear that these volunteer visitors might be valuable to the relieving officer... I was asked to fill this position [of liasion worker] with relation to the Guardians... The connection with the Poor Law system is calculated to be of great advantage to the visitors. They will learn something of its working;

they will be enabled to use with much greater effect, and with much greater frequency, the lever which distaste for the 'house' puts into their hands; and knowing that while the workhouse exists even the idle and improvident and reckless need not starve, they will be encouraged to refuse to such persons the pauperising doles of a merely impulsive charity, in the belief that such refusal will probably benefit the individual, and will certainly in the long run benefit the class.

Octavia Hill, 'The work of volunteers',
'Volunteers and poor law officials', in
Homes of the London Poor, 1875

8.9.2   *Principles of the Charity Organization Society*

Charity is in a better position than the Poor Law for drawing distinctions between the worthiness and unworthiness of the applicants...The qualification for charitable relief may be considered to be temporary and unavoidable distress (whether amounting to destitution or not) with evidence of thrift and good character...

Report of the Council of the Charity Organization Society,
1878, quoted in Helen Bosanquet, *Social Work in London,*
1869-1912, 1914, p. 309

How can we bring it about that they [the very poor] shall have a permanently greater command over the necessaries and luxuries of life? The superficial remedy is that of gifts...The less obvious, but more effective, remedy is to approach the problem by striking at its roots in the minds of the people themselves; to stimulate their energies; to insist upon their responsibilities; to train their faculties. In short, to make them efficient.

Helen Bosanquet, *The Strength of the People,* 1902, p. 114

They stuck to the theory of individual independence and of the danger of State interference in a world where man-made laws were enabling the rich to grind the faces of the poor...The efficacy of charity for the redress of social grievances was at an end, and the time had come when the community as a whole must shoulder its responsibilities...

Another arbitrary assumption of the charity organizers is that for any man to enjoy any benefits which he has not definitely worked for and earned is injurious to his character...One begins to wonder how those of us whose income is derived from dividends have any independence of character left...Is it true or not true that a man's personal character determines the comfort and wellbeing of himself, his wife and family? If so, the agricultural labourer at twelve shillings a week, whose family cannot have clean skins, clean clothes, and enough to eat, must be a worse man morally than the fox-hunting squire who is his landlord...Is it true or is it not true? If not, then not character, but the accident of birth is the condition of conditions, together with the laws and customs of the time and country into which a man is born.

Mrs Townshend, 'The case against the
Charity Organization Society', *Fabian Tract No. 158,* 1911

8.9.3 *The professionalisation of philanthropy*
The World has need of the ministrations of women. As long as it lasts, children must be taught, sick people nursed, the poor visited and relieved, dull lives made bright, the better life made possible, and this comes strictly within their province ... A woman worker, whether paid agent or volunteer, will be wise if she train in some definite and specialized way ... She must study causes before she attempts to deal with effects. She must 'fence the precipice at the top before she provides an ambulance at the bottom'. She must inspire reverence for womanhood and shield the unprotected before she tries to rescue the fallen ...

Women have followed the lead of Miss Octavia Hill as rent-collectors; they join local committees of the Charity Organization Society, they look after boarded-out children, they start girls' clubs, they become Poor Law Guardians. Hardly a girl leaves some of our women's colleges—e.g. Cheltenham and Westfield—without interesting herself in some aspect of philanthropy. There are settlements of women-students under able guidance in Southwark, at Mayfield House, Bethnal Green, and at Victoria Park ... In some of our large cities, in Liverpool, Birmingham, Sheffield, Glasgow, Aberdeen, a Union of Women Workers has established itself which brings them together periodically for consultation. In Liverpool, for example, these quarterly meetings are attended by ladies on some forty to fifty committees, and their deliberations have already affected public opinion to a marked extent. The way has been smoothed for the appointment of women Poor Law Guardians, the excessive hours of work exacted from female pupil-teachers have been lessened, the younger ladies have been impressed with the importance of whole-heartedness in work, the public has learnt a new respect for the capacity of women.

Emily Janes, 'On the associated work of women in religion
and philanthropy', in A. Burdett-Coutts (ed.),
Women's Mission, 1893

8.9.4 *Mission to sailors*
We determined to do something in Plymouth close to her Majesty's Dockyard, and in 1876 started a Sailors' Rest, the first of its name and kind ... The number sleeping at our premises last year, at the

Plymouth Sailors' Rest was 72,822, and at Portsmouth 42,875 . . .
When the Sailors' Rest was first opened, naturally, as now the
publicans looked upon us with no little disfavour; for was not their
trade in danger? It was a fair fight and no favour, beer *versus*
coffee . . . The publicans loudly proclaimed the Sailors' Rest 'a
disgraceful innovation, a place that ought to be crushed by all
right-thinking men'. 'If there is anyone on earth that I hate, it is that
Miss Weston of yours . . . she brings a blight upon all honest trade'.
This was sad but encouraging. The seamen crowded the Sailors' Rest
and we did all we could to make them happy; and as to the publicans,
we advised them to change their trade to a better one, and insured our
plate glass windows, which they had threatened to break . . . We held
our own, enlarging the Sailors' Rest, building a high block of
dormitories, and then a hall on a large scale . . . The large sum needed
for the purchase of the [adjacent] public houses and their sites was
raised . . . we all rejoiced that the temptations adjoining the gates of
H.M. Dockyard had been destroyed . . .

Bright meetings, Gospel, temperance, and social classes, naval clubs
and benefit societies, and much else make Jack's home bright and
happy. A staff of devoted workers, ladies and others assist Miss Wintz
and myself. We are not in debt, and we make the places more than
self-supporting. The buildings are vested in trustees for continuity of
work, and well they may be; as the sum of something like £150,000 has
been spent upon them. They are the headquarters of the 'Royal Naval
Temperance Society', and the 'Royal Naval Christian Union'. Nor are
the wives and little ones, Jack's best bower anchors, forgotten. Large
meetings of sailors' wives and sailors' children are held regularly,
winter clubs, savings banks, etc. I roughly estimate the attendance
during the year at our meetings of 150,000 seamen, their wives and
children, naval pensioners, and others, and 50,000 at our Saturday
night temperance entertainments.

Agnes Weston, 'Work among sailors', in loc. cit.

8.9.5 *Women's work for girls*

The warding-off of evil is the chief aim of our most important
benevolent undertakings, especially of those organized for securing
the welfare of young girls . . .

Some twenty years ago, our London Poor Law Guardians were
brought face to face with an unpleasant fact. The majority of the girls
for whose training they were responsible turned our worse than the
veriest little street wanderers . . . they appealed to Mrs. Nassau Senior
for advice. 'It is mothering the girls want', she told them
emphatically . . . Having secured the co-operation of a number of
ladies, she organized the *Metropolitan Association for Befriending
Young Servants*, every member of which undertakes to act as friend,

adviser, mother, in fact, to girls trained in workhouses. During the last twenty years the association has extended its operations in the most marvellous fashion; and it now acts as general protector to all the servants in London between the ages of thirteen and twenty. It consists of a central committee, thirty two district committees, and visitors; in all some eleven hundred ladies. The central committee has under its surveillance thirty-two free registries, seven training homes, a convalescent home, and thirteen servants' lodging-homes... The office of a visitor is no sinecure... No matter how often a girl loses her place, a fresh one must be found for her... some visitors make a point of going with their charges when on shopping bent. The uninitiated can form no idea of the value of the service they thus render. The souls of servant-maids hanker sorely after feathers and flowers, and their love of gorgeous colour is quite Oriental... The most difficult of all the duties that fall to her lot is dealing with the 'followers' of her charges... Then a little friendly interest, the expression of a wish to see the chosen one, a few cautiously worded inquiries as to his character and means, may make all the difference in life to a young woman's future... In 1891, its working expenses amounted to £7,484; and the number of girls whom it befriended to 13,398. Already it has wrought a wonderful change amongst servants of the poorer class. When in 1873 the guardians appealed to Mrs. Senior for help, not 16% of workhouse girls could be reported later in life as doing well. At the present time, 90% of them turn out satisfactory. And of the 10% who prove failures the majority are feeble-minded, a class most difficult to deal with...

The work of the *Young Women's Christian Association* lies amongst a class of girls who, though socially better placed than servants, often stand as sorely in need of a helping hand. Year by year hundreds of girls drift up to London to serve in shops, or engage in some kind of business. As often as not they have no friends in town, no place to go to, when their work is done, but their one poor little room, a most comfortless and expensive refuge. The late Lady Kinnaird was so touched by the loneliness and the joylessness of the lives many of these girls lead, that in 1856 she opened a home for them near Fitzroy Square... The London branch of this society now has some 17,000 members on its rolls. It owns 142 institutions of one sort or another, including nineteen lodging-homes for girls. No country member accepts a situation in London until its character has been inquired into by the society... All the members are invited to pass their leisure time at one of the society's institutes... If their taste incline towards self-improvement, there are classes of all sorts, at nominal fees, which they may join... If a girl be ill, she is nursed in one of the society's homes; if she needs rest, a holiday is arranged for her...

The Girls' Friendly Society was founded in 1875 by Mrs. Townshend, for the purpose of uniting in one great fellowship women and girls of all ranks ... It has now 1,126 branches ... The work is divided into ten departments—the first devotes itself to promoting the interests of the better educated of the members, such as teachers, the second takes charge of those who work in factories; the third, of those who are servants; the fourth, of those who have been brought up in workhouses. Then there are departments which manage the free registries ... the lodging homes, and gives aid to those who wish to emigrate. The eighth is responsible for the schools and homes in which the members may receive industrial training; the ninth undertakes to provide, by means of circulating libraries and magazines, all classes with cheap and wholesome literature. The department however which takes charge of members when they are ill is the one doing perhaps, the best work of all ...

The Ladies' Association for the Care of Friendless Girls differs from these; whilst they insist upon unblemished reputations ... it devotes itself with special zeal ... to the friendless ... There are now one hundred and twenty of these associations ... some devote themselves to temperance work; others to educational; others again to warding off starvation from their charges. They all unite, however, in trying to remove girls from dangerous surroundings, and putting them in the way of earning an honest livelihood. The members regularly visit workshops, lodging houses of the worst kind, police-courts, all the places in fact where there is a chance of coming across young lives in danger of shipwreck. The ladies have proved themselves doughty champions, and have waged ruthless warfare against unjust employers and drunken vicious parents. Many are the girls they have rescued from 'sweating dens'; many too from home surroundings just as degrading.

Edith Sellers,
'Women's work for the welfare of girls', in loc. cit.

8.10   Religion

8.10.1   *Church extension*

The work of English Church-women is almost limitless ... Of Foreign and Home Missions, the Church Missionary Society has no fewer than 850 associations worked by women, who yearly raise the large sum of £31,000 for carrying on the work abroad. Similarly, the Society for the Propagation of the Gospel is enabled by the help of women in England to educate upwards of 5,000 of their less fortunate sisters in foreign parts; whilst at home the women's branches of the two societies which support additional clergy for evangelization in the denser and more difficult parishes of our own land, are doing equally good work. There is hardly a diocese without a ladies' branch of the Additional Curates, or the Church Pastoral Aid, Societies ... The main object for which these societies enlist the help of women is to gain funds, obtain volunteers for carrying on their work, and to stimulate and spread an interest in it ...

'Waifs and Strays Society' not only [employs] women as collectors, they enter into its actual management of the homes ... Three other agencies must be mentioned here as specially availing themselves of the help of Church organization in their endeavour to spread throughout the land ... The Women's Help Society ... seeks to band the women of the parish, young and old, married and single, in one common endeavour after a higher life, one society embracing all. The Mothers' Union seeks to enlist those who have the care of children in a determination to shelter them from evil of all sorts, and lead and guide them in right ways ... The Girls' Friendly Society works solely amongst the young and unmarried, and has one clearly defined object, the maintenance of purity ... The Church Penitentiary Association (found in thirty dioceses) devotes itself chiefly to the maintenance of houses of mercy and refuge; the Church Mission to the Fallen is engaged in combating vice in its strongholds, in holding mission services, and in direct mission work ... The penitentiaries and refuges alone contain accomodation for upwards of 7,000 women ...

Then there are the sisterhoods and deaconesses' institutions, the object of both being to train for and employ in, parish and mission work women who can devote their lives to such a purpose ... It includes visiting the poor, nursing the sick, establishing dispensaries, convalescent homes, cottage hospitals, homes of rest, schools, orphanages, industrial homes, nurseries, night shelters, laundries, workrooms, class work, cheap dinners and teas in time of distress, beside mission work and ordinary parochial work ... Except in the actual ministry of the sanctuary there is hardly a department in which women cannot take their part . . . A parish is mapped into districts, and to each is assigned a lady as district visitor; her office entitling her to call at every home . . . persuading the parents to come to church, to send their children to school . . . She will notice their material needs and encourage wise thrift by the establishment of blanket, coal and maternity clubs . . . She will also notice their moral needs. There is hardly a parish in which a mothers' meeting is not held, presided over by a lady who reads some helpful book, whilst the women sew garments, which they can afterwards buy for the cost of the material . . . Sickness may enter the home . . . The district visitor first learns of the trouble, she carries the news to the clergyman, and obtains such relief as the Church can afford, either gifts of money, coal, beef tea, blankets, or the assistance of a trained nurse . . . many of whom fulfil the double office of Bible woman or Evangelist . . . If in the parish there are large factories and mills . . . the dinner hour can be used for reading to the mill-hands . . . In cases where women can only earn very low wages for piece-work, the Church has not thought it outside her province to provide for them a common work-room, to organize them, and in the person of some lady worker undertake on their behalf large Government contracts for work at a better price then they could command individually . . . In almost every parish of England—and there are between fourteen and fifteen thousand parishes—there are to found ladies, or paid agents, or both, engaged in one or other of the good works we have touched upon. A noble army . . .

Mrs Boyd Carpenter, 'Women's work in connection with the Church of England', in loc. cit.

8.10.2 *Sisters of Charity*

[In the public applause of Florence Nightingale] . . . there has been something to sadden and humiliate a thinking and feeling mind. There has been perpetual reiteration of *astonishment* at their magnanimity . . . as if to assuage suffering and to prefer a sacred and sublime duty to the temptations of leisure or pleasure, were not the woman's province and privilege as well as the man's . . . Send such a woman to her piano, her books, her cross-stitch; she answers you with *despair*!—But send her on some mission of mercy, send her where she may perhaps die by inches in achieving good for others, and the whole spirit rises up strong and rejoicing.

One of the ladies at Scutari, rich, well-born, and accomplished, on being informed that she had been selected as one of those who were to be sent to a post where additional difficulty, suffering, and even danger awaited her, clasped her hands and uttered a fervant 'Thank God!'

I remember a Sister of Charity who had been sent off at half an hour's notice to a district where the cholera was raging among the most squalid and miserable poor, and I never shall forget the look of radiant happiness and thankfulness on that face... [Such women need training] for hundreds of women will fall into the common error of mistaking an impulse for a vocation. But I do believe that there are also hundreds who are fitted, or would gladly, at any self-sacrifice, fit themselves, for the work, if the means of doing so were allowed to them... They might be trained as hospital and village nurses, visitors of the poor, and teachers in the elementary and reformatory schools; so that a certain number of women should always be found ready and competent to undertake such work in our public charitable and educational institutions as should be fitted for them... We have works of love and mercy for the best of our women to do, in our prisons and hospitals, our reformatory schools, and I will add our workhouses; but then we must have them such as we want them,—not impelled by transient feelings, but by deep abiding motives,—not amateur *ladies* of charity, but brave women, whose vocation is fixed and whose faculties of every kind have been trained and disciplined to their work under competent instruction for men, and tested by a long probation.

Anna Jameson, *Sisters of Charity,* 1855, pp. 92-119

8.10.3   *The Salvation Army*

As the Army refuses to make any difference between men and women as to rank, authority and duties, but opens the highest positions to women as well as to men, the words 'woman, she, and her' are scarcely ever used in orders, 'man, he, his' being always understood to mean a person of either sex unless it is obviously impossible.

Regulations of the Salvation Army

Mrs Booth at Birmingham, 1863. The women left their work and in all sorts of odd costumes flocked to the meetings... When the invitation was given, what a scene ensued... Crowding, weeping, rushing to the communion rail came convicted sinners and repentant backsliders. When the rail was filled the penitents dropped upon their knees in the aisles or in their seats, so that it was difficult to move about.

Many a time did dear Mrs Booth appear to be completely exhausted... Her pose was perfectly modest and refined, her delivery was often wonderfully impassioned, eloquent and fervid. My education and associations had made me very much opposed to female ministry, so that I went to hear her with a mind full of prejudice and prepared to criticize. But her first words disarmed me...

F. de L. Booth-Tucker,
The Short Life of Catherine Booth, 1893, p. 165

In Scotland, 1868. The spirit of conviction worked irresistibly in their hearts. The people fell in every part of the building. In the pews, in the gallery, round the pulpit, in the dingy little vestry with its break-neck approach there were men and women sobbing and crying aloud for salvation.

loc. cit., p. 206

The Hallelujah Lasses. We have changed the name of the Mission into the Salvation Army . . . I see no bounds to our extension; if God will own and use such simple men and women (we have over thirty women in the field) as we are sending out now, we can compass the whole country in a very short time. And it is truly wonderful what is being done by the instrumentality of quite young girls . . . In one small town where we have two girls labouring, a man, quite an outsider, told another that if they went on much longer all the publics would have to shut up, for he went to every one in the town the other night and he only found four men in them all! The whole population, he said, had gone to the 'Hallelujah Lasses'!

Letter of Catherine Booth,
23 October 1878, quoted in loc. cit., p. 251

8.11 Elementary Education

8.11.1 *Standing for a school board*

After Mr. Hill's visit I had a deputation from working men...They think there must be meetings to teach people to be interested...I suppose it is part of the whole thing and ought not to be refused, tho' I am sorry it is so. I dare say when it has to be done I can do it, and it is no use asking for women to be taken into public work and yet to wish them to avoid publicity. We must be ready to go into the thing as men do if we go at all, and in time there will be no more awkwardness on our side than there is on theirs. Still I am very sorry it is necessary, especially as I can't think of anything to say for four speeches! and after Huxley too, who speaks in epigrams!

Elizabeth Garrett to Emily Davies, 24 October 1870,
quoted in Barbara Stephen, *Emily Davies and Girton College,*
1927, pp. 120-1

8.11.2 *Lady school managers*

A recognised lady member, if not two, upon the managing committee of every girls' mixed and infant school in the country, would be of the greatest advantage to the schools, to the teacher, and to the Department...Women are slow to see their duty in these matters, and sometimes seem to think it more feminine to shrink from a definite position, preferring the greater, and, as it seems to them, less fettered liberty of desultory action.

The duties which fall to the share of school managers are simple, and require common sense and a real sympathy with the teacher and the children more than any special gifts. A lady can probably enter into the difficulties of the locality and of the home associations of the children, their social and family circumstances, and be on terms of greater intimacy with the teachers, than is possible for any man, or, at any rate of the busy men of whom such committees are generally composed...If our schools are to be places of *education*, if they are to be schools of morality as well as places of instruction, questions arise which require wise and delicate handling, and need the united efforts and the fullest mutual confidence between the managers and teachers to deal properly with them...

There are two departments of school-work in which teachers, almost without exception, will warmly welcome assistance; and this would therefore seem naturally to fall to the share of the lady manager—help in teaching the needlework, and some extra instruction afforded to the pupil-teachers...Visitors may do great good by taking classes in needlework and cutting out, provided they do so *regularly* and in *subordination* to the time table. Much valuable assistance may also be given out of school hours in helping the teachers to prepare the work etc. A lady may also give useful help by taking the reading lesson, both as to pronunciation and intelligence. She may also look up absentees, and provide for proper precautions when infectious illness is discovered among the children. But the help which a kindly and judicious lady manager may render to her head teachers and to the school generally by befriending the pupil-teachers, is almost as great as the advantage which her instructions will prove to them.

But it is with respect to the moral conditions of the school and its influences upon the children for good or for evil that the lady manager may be of most service.

Louisa Hubbard, 'Duties of women as school managers', *Transactions of the National Association for the Promotion of Social Science,* 1878

8.11.3 *The work of women on school boards*

Two-thirds of School Board teachers are women, while more than half the pupils are girls; added to this are the infant boys, who as much as the girls need a woman's influence in legislating for them ...

The work of the London school board committees. The committee on School Accommodation and Attendance has to enforce the bye-laws dealing with attendance at school of all the children, including the blind, deaf, difficult and crippled children; it watches the growth and shifting of population, decides on the districts in which additional School provision is needed, and decides where a new site should be acquired or an old one disposed of; it also watches all Bills in Parliament which affect the Board's work, and conducts most of the Board's correspondence with the Education Department.

Miss Davenport Hill and Mrs Homan were on this Committee.

The works committee ... selects contractors to build all the schools and to carry out enlargements; to see to all repairs, either to building or apparatus; to attend to the sanitary and warming arrangements of all schools ...

Mrs Maitland served on it.

The school management committee, on which sat Miss Eve and Mrs Maitland, and until 1896 Miss Davenport Hill and Mrs Homan: Its sub-committees [on which women members sat]: Evening Continuation schools; Domestic Subjects; Pupil Teachers; Requisitions and Stocktaking; Royal Normal College for the Blind; Special

Instruction, the deaf, the dumb, the blind; Special Subjects of Instruction, manual training, hand and eye training, physical education, kindergarten, and music; Teaching Staff, appointments and complaints.

The committee on Industrial Schools [affecting] about 2,000 children yearly, all under magistrates' orders.

Attendances	1895/6	
	possible	actual
Miss Eve	238	202
Miss Davenport Hill	268	250
Mrs. Homan	262	248
Mrs. Maitland	250	235

The above record shows a considerable amount of work as the share of 4 members of the London school board out of a total of 55 . . .

Florence Davenport Hill, *Women on School Boards, 1896*

8.12 Local Government

8.12.1 *The local franchise and the parliamentary franchise*
Men in this country obtained parliamentary representation in and
through local government. They used the power they had, and they
obtained more extended power. We urge women to follow their
example—to take an interest in the local affairs in which they have a
legal right to be represented, to make their votes felt as a power which
must be recognized by all who would govern such affairs, and to be
ready personally to fill such offices as they are liable to be nominated
for, and to seek those positions to which they are eligible for
election . . . Political freedom begins for women, as it began for men,
with freedom in local government. It rests with women to pursue the
advantage that has been won, and to advance from the position that
has been conceded to them in local representation to that which is the
goal of our efforts—the concession of the right to a share in the
representation of our common country.

Lydia Becker,
The Rights and Duties of Women in Local Government, 1879

8.12.2 *The need for women on county councils*
I.—To County Councils is committed the management and control of
    Lunatic Asylums in which men and women are received.
In Asylums controlled by County Councils there were living, as we
find by the Census returns in 1894—31,960 female lunatics. No kindly
female visitor ever comes to cheer the lives of these poor women; no
ray of womanly sympathy lightens the dullness of their gloomy
seclusion, except in the case of patients sent on from Union
Workhouses. Yet in our Workhouse Infirmaries, where about 900
women are to be found, the watchful care and occasional visitations
of some female Guardian are considered indispensable . . . In these
Institutions there are also female attendants and many female
servants, amounting in all to many thousands of women under the
jurisdiction of County Councils in England and Wales. On all
questions concerned with the health, the clothing, the cleanliness, the
sanitary arrangements for these persons; on all questions of
house-cleaning and household details—in all matters culinary and
domestic—County Councils are the only ultimate court of appeal. Yet
on these bodies no woman finds a place, nor is there an opportunity of
appeal to any woman outside the Asylum.

II.—County Councils are directly responsible for the management of
    boys as well as of a few girls in the Reformatories and Industrial
    Schools.

Countless instances from the experiences of the first female Guardians of the Poor could be adduced of blunders, omissions, and neglect in dealing with pauper children, leading to results disastrous for the health and well-being of these little ones ... These blunders were the natural and direct consequence partly of the lack of knowledge on the part of male Guardians, partly of the absolute impossibility of their exercising a close and intimate supervision over the minutiae of the Dormitory, the Wash-house, and the Wardrobe ... [for Industrial Schools and Reformatories]. There is no woman sitting on County Councils to whom an appeal on all such domestic matters can be addressed.

III.—Infant Life Protection Act.
But the fatuity of the framers of the Local Government Act is pushed farther still. It is the duty of male Councillors to appoint Inspectors to visit Baby Farms. It is their business to ensure that hapless infants, whose presence in the world may have been considered undesirable, should be protected from the imminent risk of being hustled away out of existence, or worse still kept in a condition of slow torture and starvation in the out-of-the-way holes and hidden corners of our great cities, or in lonely country cottages. Is not a woman's assistance and judgement especially indispensable in such work as this? is not female inspection imperatively called for here? and is this sufficiently provided for through the appointment by the London County Council of one woman who has to make her report to a Sanitary Committee composed entirely of men? Perhaps the supreme triumph of legislative inconsistency is to be found in the fact that women who by the Acts of 1894 may be elected to serve on Urban District Councils are called upon to administer this very Act for the Protection of Infant Life, which in the case of County Councils is relegated entirely to the hands of male Councillors.

IV.—To County Councils belong the control and supervision of Theatres and Music Halls—the power of granting or withholding licences from these places.
In these so many young girls are employed; their only security for protection against the risk of fire and other dangers—and their only guarantee for the morality and decency of the performances in which they have to take part—lies in the wise regulations and the close supervision of the County Councillors.

To give only one concrete instance: during Miss Cons' short tenure of office on the L.C.C. she discovered in a Theatre a dressing room in which the girls nightly ran imminent risk of catching fire from the quality and position of the lights used, many of which were brought in by the girls themselves. What male Councillor could have penetrated during dressing time to this hidden woman's region of the establishment, and have discovered this serious danger? To the various classes of women already mentioned in various institutions may be added also a large number of charwomen and caretakers...

V.—The Housing of the Poor and the administration of the Artizans' Dwellings Act.

Now the first serious attempt to deal with the lowest and poorest homes in the slums of London was made, long before County Councils existed, by a woman—Miss Octavia Hill—about the year 1865. No sooner was Miss Cons once her co-worker, elected an Alderman of the London County Council than she was put by her colleagues on the Housing Committee of the Council.

VI.—The Providing of Open Spaces.

To the same woman the citizens of London are indebted for the founding of a Society for the Protection of Open Spaces which has made many dull and dreary acres of wilderness in this great city 'to rejoice and blossom as the rose'. The work of laying out the Metropolitan Gardens is now superintended by a woman.

VII.—The Protection of Wild Birds Act...

VIII.—The Regulation of Slaughter Houses.

Very much remains still to be done in the prevention of cruelty . . .

IX.—The Rivers Pollution Act.

This is an Act of Parliament on the due administration of which the health of great cities largely depends, and the prevention of those epidemics of fever and diptheria which are so fatal to young children.

X.—The Act for Regulating Cow-houses and Dairies.

By which a supply of pure milk from healthy sources is ensured. Can you exclude the matters which these two last-mentioned Acts are concerned from the purview of women? It has been well said that County Councils have taken in hand the house-keeping of the nation. Does it need exhaustive logic to prove that the domestic matters treated of above are scarcely likely to be better understood by the country squire, the busy merchant, the man engrossed with the fluctuations of the Exchange or the Market, than by those persons who, alike by nature, by tradition, and by practice of many centuries, have become experts in matters of domestic management? And is not the State—in its character of Guardian of the Community—bound to summon to its councils the best knowledge, the most trained experience, which is at the service of the community?

Technical Education. Our contention, however does not end here. In view of the great and ever-growing importance of the question of Technical Education in our Counties, it is absolutely essential that women should sit on County Councils; not merely that they may assist in the carrying out of this work, but especially in order to secure to women and girls their full share in the benefits of those Classes and Lectures from which now they are too frequently excluded.

There is work of supreme importance waiting which may soon double the labours of County Councillors. The Secondary Education of the Country will most certainly be put under their jurisdiction. Are we to suppose that the Educational Board or Committee which must be created to carry out this scheme, will exclude trained experts, if they happen to be women? . . .

It is almost impossible to enumerate all the different ways in which women on County Councils could be of service, or to catalogue all that County Councils may in the future be called upon to undertake. That the tendency exists to throw more and more work into their hands may be gathered from the recommendations made in 1893 by the Select Committee appointed to consider the compulsory registration of midwives, which advised that 'the duty of carrying out locally the Act which will be required should be placed in the hands of the County Councils'.

In conclusion: That which we urge as a beneficial measure has stood the test of actual experience. For nearly four months Lady Sandhurst and Miss Jane Cobden—both elected by majorities of about 270 over the next candidate—served on the largest of all County Councils—the London County Council—of 1889, consisting of 118 members. Miss Cons was afterwards elected on it as Alderman. During their very short tenure of office—independently of other duties—Lady Sandhurst undertook the supervision of 23 Baby Farms, Miss Cobden the visitation of the Cane Hill Lunatic Asylum, and membership of the Parks Committee, while the services of Miss Cons on the Committees concerned with the Housing of the Poor were felt by her colleagues to be so valuable that in her absence from London she was elected on six Committees and eleven Sub-committees, and after she had been obliged to resign her seat on the Council was invited still to attend the Sanitary and Housing Committees as a Visitor.

On May 20th, and on June 18th, 1889, the L.C.C. voted by a large majority in favour of presenting to Parliament a Petition in support of the Bill for enabling women to sit as County Councillors.

The experience of the L.C.C. has established beyond dispute that neither the Electorate nor those members of a County Council who have had practical experience of women's capability of work as citizens, consider their presence on County Councils as either inappropriate or superfluous.

And we would urge upon all women that they should make the most strenuous efforts, both as private individuals, and as members of Political Associations, to obtain the redress of that inequality, the amendment of those anomalous laws which, while granting to women the right to sit on (nearly) every other Municipal Body, forbids their presence on Town and County Councils.

Mrs Charles Mallet, *Shall Women Be Eligible To Serve on County Councils?*, 1896

8.12.3　*Women employed in local government*

There are now women overseers in many unions ... As Inspectors under the Infant Life Protection Act they are doing admirable work. There are at least two women relieving officers. The number of women medical officers in the workhouse infirmaries and county asylums is slowly but constantly growing. In some places there are women vaccination officers. There are several women registrars of births and deaths, and a large number of women deputy registrars. There are at least four women in England employed as rate collectors. Women are also employed as school attendance officers by some of our union school attendance committees and by various school boards. The school board of one of our large northern cities employs no fewer than twenty-eight women in this capacity. Many women are now engaged as sanitary inspectors—these, however, mainly by municipal corporations and London vestries.

'Women in local administration', *Westminster Review,* vol. 150, 1898

8.12.4　*Women on parish, rural district and urban district councils*

(In the words of Mrs. M'Ilquham, since 1881 a member of a rural sanitary authority, and then chairman of the Staverton Parish Council.)

'As rural district councillors, women are guardians of the sanitary condition of the whole union outside boroughs and urban districts, of which the parish for which they were elected is but one unit. They deal with questions affecting the welfare, comfort and morality of the people, and it is their duty to endeavour to secure the best possible conditions of health for the inhabitants of rural parishes. The rural district councils receive all complaints of nuisance and overcrowding, and it is their business to remedy these. It is their duty also to certify that any newly erected house is fit for habitation unless they are satisfied that it has a sufficient water supply, which it is also their duty to endeavour to secure for every habitation within their area. All new buildings within that area must be submitted for their approval, and by their orders all houses unfit for habitation ought to be closed. It is the duty of their inspectors to disinfect houses in which there has been an infectious disease, and the councils are also responsible with regard to baby farms and canal boats. They have to provide and superintend hospitals for reception of patients suffering from infectious diseases, and all schemes for the drainage and water supply... They have further the charge of all minor highways...'

Mrs. Barker on the work of parish councils. 1896 I was unanimously elected to the chair. The other five members were a butcher, a carrier, a builder, a market gardener, and the village shopkeeper... the majority Nonconformists, and Radicals as to politics. From the very outset I earnestly deprecated any sectarian or political cleavage, and in my first address to them I took my stand on the broad Christian basis of doing our best for 'our neighbour' in the largest sense of the word... The first concern was to place the charities of the parish on a new footing... These matters settled, we took the footpaths in hand... and allotments...

It has been objected that parish council business has no opening for definitely feminine work. Well I grant that there is none that a woman can do *better* than a man, as there is in workhouse management, and school boards and committees; but for all that I must strongly urge all women who have the good of their fellows at heart not to shrink from standing for their parish councils. Beyond the softening effect which I found so valuable, women are so much more earnest about small things than men, and parish council work deals with matters of seemingly small import. A polluted well, an overcrowded cottage, a barrier across a footpath, are too trivial for men to make a stir about, and perhaps offend the wage-giver into the bargain; but an independent woman... will be earnest for frequent meetings...

Motherly thought and influence are needed everywhere, and not simply in the individual home. It is to enlarge their sphere of duty, to carry the homelike qualities out into the world, and to help thus in the great regeneration of humanity which is to come, that women are now summoned by the recent legislation.

loc. cit.

8.12.5 *Women as councillors*
Women who wish to serve on Local Governing Bodies should submit themselves to a severe training before becoming candidates for election. Useful experience can be gained on some well-ordered committee, such as a children's care committee. Charity organization work also gives an excellent training, while, for those who can arrange it, six months or a year in a Woman's Settlement is invaluable. Special subjects must be 'got up' as if for examination and kept up to date; for social questions are continually developing and Local Government frequently altering in detail. For about a year a prospective candidate

ought to attend every open meeting of the authority to which she desires election ... At the same time she should do her best to become personally known to the electors and acquainted with their special needs, but always taking care to make no promises as to what she will do if elected, and confining herself to such remarks as 'the matter shall have my consideration'.

If possible a woman should stand as an independent candidate. The work she is going to do is not to advance any political party, but to benefit the community, with special regard to the needs of women, children and those who are helpless ...

The woman who takes up any form of public service literally gives herself, her time, her powers and sympathies to help uplift the nation. She must be guarded in word and deed, for she is subject to public criticism; humble ... and dignified because she represents woman-hood; judicial, because there are two sides to every question ... kind, for it is woman's task to help the desolate and oppressed.

J. M. E. Brownlow,
Women's Work in Local Government, 1911

8.13 Women's Co-operative Guild

8.13.1 *Guild women*

The members who form the Guild are almost entirely married women belonging to the artisan class, and are associated, through their husbands and relatives, with all the prevailing trades of the localities in which Guild branches are situated. We find husbands of Guild members among weavers, mechanics of every kind, miners, railwaymen, Co-operative employees, dock labourers, country labourers, bricksetters, printers, joiners . . . The Guild stands for the organized purchasing or consuming power of the working-class community of the country.

As regards the Guild women themselves, a certain proportion, especially in Lancashire, work in the mills, while others go out to nurse, wash, clean, and some are teachers and dressmakers. But for the greatest number, their homes are their workshops . . .

Among the subjects which have been taken up the following may be mentioned:— Anti-credit Campaign, Investigation into the Hours of Co-operative Women Employees, Co-operative and Trade Union Alliance Campaign, Investigations into Conditions of Women Workers, Public Health, Co-operation and the Poor, Housing, Land, and Free Trade Campaigns.

Margaret Llewelyn Davies,
Women's Co-operative Guild, 1883-1904, 1904, pp. 57, 148

WHY BUY SWEATED GOODS AND SUPPORT SWEATING FIRMS?

All TRADE UNIONISTS and their Wives should lay out their money at the

CO-OPERATIVE UNIONIST STORES,

436, COMMERCIAL ROAD,
227, BOW ROAD,
70, BRUNSWICK ROAD, POPLAR.

WHY?

1 Because the articles are good, and **made under fair conditions.** Let women boycott bad employers by refusing to buy their goods.

2. Because women can thus raise their husbands' wages. The Stores are managed by working people, who all share in the profits. **For every £1 spent there, each Member gets 1s. as his or her share in the profits.**

3. Because at the Stores you have a Free Library, Free Classes, Free Entertainments, etc.

Women's help is wanted in the Labour Movement.

Women must rally together and help on the good time coming by joining the Women's Co-operative Guild.

Women are the purchasers. They must be Co-operators.

Women also want help themselves. They need less work, more change, more to spend, more to read, more interests.

Come and give a hand, and see how the Guild can help you, at any or all of the following Meetings:

THURSDAY, FEB 18th, at 8 o'clock, in the CO-OPERATIVE HALL, Johnson Street, Commercial Road, **Joint Social Evening** for Tower Hamlets, Bow, and Poplar Branches. Music and Singing. ADDRESS by Miss LLEWELYN DAVIES (General Secretary, Women's Co-operative Guild) DIALOGUE between Mrs. STORE and Mrs. SHOPPER.

TOWER HAMLETS MEETINGS, at Toynbee Hall, Commercial Street, at 8 p.m.

MONDAY, MAR. 7 — DALOGUE between Mrs. STORE and Mrs SHOPPER.

MONDAY, MAR 21 — ARGUMENT : " Must Women always be Household Drudges " ?

BOW MEETINGS, at the Stores, 227, Bow Road, at 8 p.m

WEDNESDAY, FEB. 24. — DIALOGUE : "Must Women always be Household Drudges ";

WEDNESDAY, MAR. 9. — ADDRESS by Miss TOURNIER (Vice-President of the Women's Co-operative Guild), on " How Women can help in the Labour Movement " ?

WEDNESDAY, MAR. 23 — DISCUSSION : " Is it worth while to join the Women's Guild " ?

POPLAR MEETINGS, at the Stores, 70, Brunswick Road, Poplar, at 2 30

MONDAY, FEB. 22. — DISCUSSION : " For and Against the Women's Guild."

MONDAY, MAR 7 — ADDRESS by Mrs. JONES (President of the Women's Co-operative Guild).

MONDAY, MAR 21. — DIALOGUE " Must Women always be Household Drudges " ?

Reproduced in Margaret Llewelyn Davies, *Women's Co-operative Guild, 1883-1904,* 1904 (n.d., but c. 1891/2), p. 123

8.13.2   *The Guild versus the Mothers' Union*

I joined the Guild and found the benefit my neighbour had predicted. It meant a long walk to the meeting and back, something fresh to listen to while there, and something to think about all the week. I was not used to working-women managing their meetings. I had attended

Mothers' Meetings, where ladies came and lectured on the domestic affairs in the workers' homes that it was impossible for them to understand. I have boiled over many times at some of the things I have been obliged to listen to, without the chance of asking a question. In the Guild we always had the chance of discussing a subject. The Guild was more to my mind than the Mothers' Meeting, so I gave up the Mothers' Meeting and attended the Guild.

Another Guildswoman wrote: 'I used for a short time to attend a Mothers' Meeting, and did so more from a point of duty than anything, but after joining the Guild I did not feel to have patience to listen to the simple childish tales that were read at the former, and did not like to feel we had no voice in its control. There is such a different feeling in speaking of trials and troubles to Guilders (where they are real) than to speak to the ladies of the Mothers' Meeting. You know that they have a fellow-feeling being all on an equality, but there is the feeling in speaking to the ladies that after consulting this one, that one and somebody else, a little charity might be given—the tradesman perhaps who has always had your custom in better circumstances, he knows all about your business when you present your charity ticket. This sort of thing to honest working people hurts their feelings of independence, but when co-operators help them it is done in a different way.'

Mrs Layton, 'Memories of seventy years',
Life As We Have Known It
by Co-operative Working Women, 1930

8.13.3 *Men's response to the Guild*

I had put the mortgage in my name. This caused a little friction between my husband and myself. He thought that although I had earned and saved the money, the house should certainly be bought in his name. He said it did not look respectful for a woman's name to be put on the deeds when she had a husband alive. I thought different, and so the house is mine.

Sometimes my husband rather resented the teachings of the Guild... The Guild, he said, was making women think too much of themselves... The Guild's training altered the whole course of my life... From a shy, nervous woman, the Guild made me a fighter. I was always willing to go on a Deputation if there was a wrong to be righted, or for any good cause, local or national.

loc. cit.

Men bitterly resented this advent of women [as poor law guardians] in their special preserves. This has been lived down, and expressions such as 'I don't know what we should do without our women Guardians' are often heard. At a ward meeting, called to choose candidates, an

Alderman said he was in favour of putting another woman in, for he was convinced in his own mind that they made the best Guardians. One of the Guardians is rather deaf, and in describing his difficulty in following the business through this defect he said, 'I watch the women and see how they do, and I'm never far wrong'. This is all the greater compliment as he holds political views opposite to our own ...

Mrs Bury, Vice-President of the Women's Co-operative
Guild, quoted in Margaret Llewelyn Davies,
Women's Co-operative Guild, 1883-1904, 1904, p. 57

8.13.4   *The Guild and public health*

In 1897 we took up the subject of Public Health Laws ... The attendances were excellent, and Miss Ravenhill had the power of holding her audiences. As one of the hearers said, she 'brought in no three-and-sixpenny words', and she made each feel that public health was a matter of personal interest. Interest in the lectures was increased by a series of coloured diagrams. One of these was a large tree showing the machinery for making and carrying out the Health Laws; others gave statistics about vaccination and death rates; another was a picture of a notoriously unhealthy village, in which the churchyard was placed above the village at the top of a hill, thus polluting the water supply, where the houses were hovels, against which heaps of refuse were piled, while the tattered children showed the demoralising effect of the surroundings. 'I was not going to stand any more smells when I knew how to get rid of them', said a Guild woman after one meeting so she went to the Sanitary Inspector. The next morning all the dust-bins in her row of cottages were cleared, and by three o'clock the inspector had visited all the tenants to say what was and what was not, to be thrown in. On one branch sending up a list of questions to the local Health Committee the Mayor said—'If we give in to this kind of thing we may have to answer questions from Timbuctoo and Tasmania'. Nevertheless the Town Clerk was directed to obtain the required information ...

Such work was naturally followed up by similar campaigns on the Housing Question in [1898 and 1899], and the Land Question in 1901.

Margaret Llewelyn Davies, loc. cit., pp. 137-9

Part Nine

Politics

Introduction

Women had played a supportive role in many Victorian pressure groups and political agitations, particularly 'moral' causes—drink, cruelty to animals and children, the suppression of vice—areas which reinforced their philanthropic work. Predictably, perhaps they were not visible in the free trade and administrative reform lobbies; nor, more surprisingly, in religious pressure groups such as the Liberation Society. Two crusades in particular had brought women to the fore: anti-slavery, and the controversy of 1840 when the American delegation to London were denied seats for their women; and the Anti-Corn Law League (9.1.1). Their women not only raised funds but campaigned to impress on working men that cheap bread was a family issue on which masters and men were united. Croker professed himself appalled, Cobden asked his ladies to buy county votes for their men.

Working-class women were similarly supportive. In the 1830s, women had sold the unstamped press and organised the Victim Fund for those imprisoned; it was to women that Oastler and Stephens denounced the evils of the factory system from 1837 on, developing a Tory radical vocabulary to be employed by Charlotte Tonna (9.1.2—see also 3.5.1 above) in her fictionalised biographies of working girls. Political unions had their female branches in the 1830s and 1840s, and Chartism itself called for universal suffrage, though later retreated into manhood suffrage. Chartist women wanted the vote that they might more adequately fulfil their domestic role. The temperance movement and the campaign against the Contagious Diseases Acts (7.2) brought women on to the public platform.

At the heart of the women's movement was the demand for the vote. The anonymous woman author of *Women's Rights and Duties* (9.2.1) spelled out the objections—women were unfit for the vote; women, being virtually represented, did not need the vote; and the possession of the vote would unfit them as women. Those arguing for women's suffrage made three broad assertions: the vote was a natural right; the vote was a necessary protection; and that it was the vehicle for women's social contribution.

The natural rights argument had been staked out in 1792 by Mary Wollstonecraft: if women have souls, and the gift of reason to perfect those souls, then woman 'was not created merely to be the solace of man, and the sexual should not destroy the human character' (*Vindication of the Rights of Women,* ch. 4). Mrs Hugo Reid restated the arguments in her splendid book *A Plea for Women* in 1843, and her phrases were to recur in the following decades. She was followed by Harriet Taylor, whose article in the *Westminster Review* foreshadows her husband's *Subjection of Women* (9.2.2); by Frances Power Cobbe, and by Helen Taylor, Harriet's daughter. 'The right to belong to herself' was to represent advanced feminist thinking, unlike the more decorous and domestic campaign fought by Mrs Fawcett.

The second set of arguments for the vote was that women needed to protect their interests, especially at law, at work and in education (see above, Parts 3, 4 and 6). The third set was that women had a separate contribution to make, and that the political community would be improved and enriched by their presence. The vote, said Barbara Leigh Smith Bodichon, would create public responsibility in women (9.2.3) which itself would be educational—and the need for such a political education was acidly observed by Emily Davies and Florence Nightingale.

It was with John Stuart Mill's speech to the House of Commons in May 1867 that the possibility of women's suffrage came out of the fringes of politics (9.2.4). Until now, the feminist circle around Barbara Bodichon (Bessie Parkes, Emily Davies, Elizabeth Garrett, Helen Taylor, Maria Rye and Jessie Boucherett, Miss Buss and Miss Beale) had devoted their energies to legal and educational reform. On 23 May 1865 they formed the Kensington Society, and in the context of pressure for parliamentary reform they asked the new MP for Westminster, Mill, to present a petition to the House to enfranchise suitably qualified women. They obtained 1,500 signatures, including those of Florence Nightingale and Harriet Martineau. His speech in 1867 moved even firm anti-suffragists, like Mr John Bright, to cast their vote for women's suffrage; and the impression it made on contemporaries is reflected in the continuing parliamentary reference that was made to it in subsequent years. In 1870, since Mill was no longer in the House, Jacob Bright (brother of John) led the parliamentary campaign, but his bill was lost in committee. From 1871 to 1883, annual bills for women's suffrage were introduced but lost.

The speeches of Tory (9.2.5) and Liberal (9.2.6) opponents make it clear why. The Tory objections of Beresford Hope and Bouverie lay in the distaste of men and inconvenience to men that would follow even a limited women's franchise (9.2.5), though Tory leaders, such as Disraeli, professed sympathy. On the Liberal side, however, while many backbenchers supported women's suffrage, Liberal leaders, headed by Gladstone, made their opposition known: the women's vote was likely to be a Tory vote, and as Captain Maxse argued, a clerical vote, and would thus be used against the interests of working men. Votes for ladies would impede social progress (9.2.6). Arabella Shore, one of the suffrage lecturers and later organising secretary of

Newnham's correspondence teaching, briskly dismissed the Tory and Liberal objections (9.2.7) as did a flood of other male and female pamphleteers.

Meanwhile, Barbara Bodichon's committee turned itself in 1866 into the London Committee for Women's Suffrage, which was to bring Mrs Fawcett to the fore. In Manchester, under the sponsorship of Jacob Bright, Lydia Becker became secretary; and a year later the Edinburgh Society was established. The three societies federated themselves into the National Society for Women's Suffrage in November 1867, and other provincial societies, at Birmingham, at Bristol, quickly joined them. The Manchester Society found that a Miss Lily Maxwell had managed to slip her name on to the electoral register and had voted in 1867; and Lydia Becker promptly obtained 5,346 women householders to ask for their registration. Their case (*Chorton* v. *Lings*) came to court in November 1868, and despite Dr Pankhurst's best oratory was rejected. The NSWS held its first public meeting in April of that year (9.3.1); and somewhat to their surprise obtained through the parliamentary efforts of Jacob Bright the municipal franchise (see above, 8.12). Lydia Becker calculated that over 14,000 women voted in the municipal elections in 1871 (9.3.2).

Already Lydia Becker had established a corresponding network across the country; and her position as organising secretary of the movement was secured when from 1870, with the help of Jessie Boucherett, she produced the *Women's Suffrage Journal* which for the next twenty years held the strands of the movement together. Meetings and petitions multiplied, and from 1871 systematic speaking tours were undertaken, requiring considerable courage from speakers for whom it was often their first public platform (see above, 1.1.2). Women such as Caroline Ashworth Briggs, Rhoda and Agnes Garrett, Helen Blackburn and Helen Taylor, Isabella Todd, Arabella Shore, Jessie Craigen, even Mrs Fawcett herself, became semi-professional itinerant lecturers travelling the length of the country.

In 1872, again on Jacob Bright's suggestion, the local branches of the National Society agreed to form a central committee of women's suffrage societies to co-ordinate their activity. Only London dissented (9.3.3) on the grounds that the connection of other branches with such controversial issues as the repeal of the Contagious Diseases Acts would damage the credibility of the suffrage campaign. But in 1877 when Josephine Butler's campaign had acquired a moral legitimacy, the Old London came in with the rest of the societies. Helen Blackburn served as their corresponding secretary, Lydia Becker as their parliamentary agent and editor.

Relations with other aspects of the women's movement remained a matter for debate. Emily Davies, for example, after 1869 held aloof from the suffrage movement lest it jeopardise the respectability of higher education; women anxious to open up the medical profession, Elizabeth Garrett, Sophia Jex-Blake, would not lend their names to other issues, particularly the Contagious Diseases campaigns. Mrs Fawcett refused to testify for Annie Besant in 1877.

The second issue dividing the women's suffrage movement was the question of votes for married women, particularly since after 1870 and 1882 married women might qualify by property, just as single women. Jacob Bright had lost his seat in 1874, and the parliamentary work was entrusted to Mr Forsyth, Conservative MP for Marylebone. His Bill of 1874 specifically excluded married women, to the distress of many suffragists (9.3.4) who believed that this would make marriage an explicit bar to political rights, and would suggest that the civil status of married women was to be inferior to that of single women. Gladstone was to use this argument (see 9.4 below) and Mrs Fawcett for one continued to argue that the vote for married women would introduce domestic disunion and set man against wife (see 9.5.2 below). The issue was reopened when Mr Woodall's bills of 1885 to 1889 again excluded women 'under coverture' and prompted Mrs M'Ilquham, Mrs Wolstenholme Elmy, Dr and Mrs Richard Pankhurst, Mrs Butler, Mrs Fenwick Miller, Mr and Mrs P. A. Taylor to form the Women's Franchise League in July 1889, to include all women suitably qualified.

The third issue which searched the Society's organisational conscience was its relation to other political parties, an argument that was in dispute until the First World War. The argument became acute when Chamberlain and Lord Randolph Churchill devised mass electoral machinery for their respective parties; and when with the Corrupt Practices Act of 1883 limiting electoral expenditure, the constituency parties had to rely increasingly on voluntary and female support. The Primrose League, founded in 1884, used women extensively (see 9.5.2 below) and the Liberal Party sponsored the Women's Liberal Federation in 1886 under the presidency of Mrs Gladstone 'to help our husbands', in Mrs Gladstone's words (9.3.5). Split over Home Rule, the Liberal Unionists under Mrs Fawcett promptly set up their own women's auxilliary. By 1892 the Women's Liberal Federation had been captured by suffragists, so the majority of 'official' ladies, wives of MPs, seceded to form the Women's Liberal Association which was anti-suffrage. Meanwhile the women's movement, faced with demands for affiliation, split in 1888 into the Central National Society for Women's Suffrage which welcomed the affiliation of women's Liberal societies; and the Central Committee of the National Society for Women's Suffrage, which remained politically neutral. But in 1897 the two wings of the movement came together in the National Union of Women's Suffrage Societies, the NUWSS, with Mrs Fawcett as its president.

Women's suffrage seemed most probable in conjunction with other major parliamentary reform, as in 1867, and as again in 1918. Women's hopes were therefore high that, after nearly twenty years of parliamentary agitation, some measure of women's suffrage might be carried as part of the 1884 Franchise Reform Act (which extended to rural areas the household franchise obtained by boroughs in 1867). The defeat of the women's bill the previous year in 1883 had been by the narrowest margin of defeat ever (130 votes to 114); the National Liberal Federation had in October 1883 declared itself for female suffrage; and the cause seemed to have an absolute majority of 'known friends' in the House when in June 1884 Mr Woodall moved his amendment on behalf of women. Gladstone who had ambiguously supported Bright's bill of 1871 now offered the amendment 'the strongest opposition in my power' (9.4) and 104 'known friends' voted against the amendment which was lost by 271 votes to 135. Gladstone's reasoning was spelled out more fully in his letter to Samuel Smith in April 1892: it was a novel measure (?), it disadvantaged married women, and other women were hostile to it. Sir Albert Rollit's bill was accordingly lost by 152 votes to 175. Mr Faithfull Begg's bill of 1897, the last of the century, was lost when it was talked out.

Some strength had been given to the women's opponents by the *Appeal against Female Suffrage,* organised in 1889 by Mrs Humphrey Ward (author of *Robert Elsmere* and active in the Settlement Movement). She went on in 1908 to found the Women's National Anti-Suffrage League (9.5.1). Lydia Becker and Mrs Fawcett were among the many who replied to it. *The Westminster Review* had anticipated the arguments of the *Appeal.* (9.5.2).

But it was clear by the 1880s that all the arguments had been made and nothing fresh was being said. It was no longer a question of whether women should enter political life—as they were already in it. The issue had become the much narrower one of the desirability of women's suffrage. The very success of the women's movement in other fields made this argument that much harder to substantiate. Women no longer needed to vote in order to contribute to wider social and community life, since they were already offering public service in the 'domestic' version of government, local government. Women had less cause to claim the vote in order to redress unfair and unjust laws as the most glaring of these had already been remedied without the vote. Increasingly the calculations were to be made, not on ethical nor on educational grounds, but on political expediency. The argument used by Captain Maxse (see above, 9.2.6) that the woman's vote was a Tory vote, was to have the longest run.

Suggestions for further reading:

D. Thompson, 'Women and nineteenth-century radical politics', in J. Mitchell and A. Oakley (eds), *The Rights and Wrongs of Women,* 1977; B. Harrison, 'State intervention and moral reform', in P. Hollis (ed.), *Pressure from Without,* 1974.

H. Blackburn, *Women's Suffrage,* 1902; R. Fulford, *Votes for Women,* 1957; R. Strachey, *The Cause,* 1928; C. Rover, *Women's Suffrage and Party Politics, 1866-1914,* 1967; A. Rosen, *Rise up Women,* 1974.

9.1 Political Training

9.1.1 *The Anti-Corn Law League*

Women had been made useful agents in the earlier stages of the French revolution; and it is probable that some idea of that sort suggested the frequent exhibition which these Anti-Corn Law Associations make of *female* countenance and co-operation—a practice in our opinion equally offensive to good taste and good feeling, and destructive of the most amiable and valuable qualities of the female character. We find that the Council of the Manchester Anti-Corn-Law Association had invited the inhabitants to 'an *anti-Corn-law tea-party,* to be held on the 20th of May, 1841—gentlemen's tickets, 2s.; ladies 1s. 6d.' ... ladies were advertised as *stewardesses* of this assembly. So now the names of about 300 Ladies were pompously advertised as the *Patroness* and *Committee* of the *National Bazaar.* We exceedingly wonder and regret that the members of the Association and League (the *Councils* of these two bodies organized the bazaar), and still more that anybody else, should have chosen to exhibit their wives and daughters in the character of political agitators; and we most regret that so many ladies—modest, excellent, and amiable persons we have no doubt in their domestic circles—should have been persuaded to allow their names to be *placarded* on such occasions—for be it remembered, this Bazaar and these *Tea-parties* did not even pretend to be for any *charitable* object, but entirely for the purposes of *political agitation.*

Of the Bazaar committee Mrs. Cobden was president, Mrs. Armitage, vice-president, Mrs. T. Woolley (the wife of a leading member of the Association and League), secretary ... We have before us a letter from Mrs. Secretary Woolley to one body of workmen ... She 'appeals to them to stand forth and denounce as *unholy,* unjust, and cruel all restrictions on the food of the people'. She acquaints them that 'the ladies are resolved to perform *their* arduous part in the attempt to *destroy a monopoly* which, for *selfishness* and its *deadly* effects, has no parallel in the history of the world'. 'We therefore', she adds, 'ask you for contributions ...' Now surely, if there were any truth in the statements of the Leaguers, or any charity in their hearts, not only should the *poorer classes* have been exempt from such unreasonable solicitations, but whatever subscriptions might be obtainable from the wealthier orders should have been applied, not to *political agitation* throughout England, but to charitable relief at home.

J. Croker,
'Anti-Corn Law agitation', *Quarterly Review,* December 1842

The women of Manchester have set a noble example to their sisters throughout the country. They have already obtained more than 50,000 signatures to the memorial adopted at the Corn Exchange. The ladies of Bolton, Wigan and Stockport are engaged in canvassing their respective towns.

Anti-Corn Law Circular, 30 December 1841

There are many ladies, I am happy to say, present; now, it is a very anomalous and singular fact, that they cannot vote themselves, and yet that they have a power of conferring votes upon other people. I wish they had the franchise, for they would often make a much better use of it than their husbands ... Now ladies who feel strongly on this question—who have the spirit to resent the injustice that is practised on their fellow-beings—cannot do better than make a donation of a county vote to their sons, nephews, grandsons, brothers, or any one on whom they can beneficially confer that privilege.

J. Bright and T. Rogers (eds), *Speeches of Richard Cobden,*
1878, speech delivered 15 January 1845, Covent Garden, London

9.1.2   *Chartism*

Fellow Countrywomen—

We call upon you to join us and help our fathers, husbands and brothers, to free themselves and us from political, physical and mental bondage . . .

We have been told that the province of woman is her home, and that the field of politics should be left to men; this we deny ... Is it not true that the interests of our fathers, husbands, and brothers, ought to be ours? If they are oppressed and impoverished, do we not share those evils with them? If so, ought we not to resent the infliction of those wrongs upon us? . . .

We have seen that because the husband's earnings could not support his family, the wife has been compelled to leave her home neglected and, with her infant children, work at a soul and body degrading toil . . . We have seen the poor robbed of their inheritance, and a law enacted to treat poverty as a crime . . .—this law was passed by men and supported by men, who avow the doctrine that the poor have no right to live . . .

For years we have struggled to maintain our homes in comfort, such as our hearts told us should greet our husbands after their fatiguing labour. Year after year has passed away, and even now our wishes have no prospect of being realised, our husbands are over-wrought, our houses half-furnished, our families ill-fed, and our children uneducated—the fear of want hangs over our heads; the scorn of the rich is pointed towards us; the brand of slavery is on our kindred, and we feel the degradation . . .

We have searched and found that the cause of these evils is the

Government of the country being in the hands of a few of the upper and middle classes, while the working men who form the millions, the strength and wealth of the country, are left without the pale of the Constitution, their wishes never consulted, and their interests sacrificed by the ruling factions ... For these evils there is no remedy but the just measure of allowing every citizen of the United Kingdom, the right of voting in the election of the members of Parliaments, who have to make the laws that he has to be governed by, and grant the taxes he has to pay; or, in other words, to pass the people's Charter into a law and emancipate the white slaves of England ...

We tell the wealthy, the high and mighty ones of the land, our kindred shall be free. We tell their lordly dames that we love our husbands as well as they love theirs, that our homes shall be no longer destitute of comfort ... we call on all persons to assist us in this good work, but especially those shopkeepers which the Reform bill enfranchised ... They ought to remember that our pennies make their pounds ...

> Address of the Female Political Union of Newcastle to their Fellow Countrywomen, *Northern Star,* 2 February 1839

We assert the unalienable right of woman to preside over her own home, and to promote the welfare of her own family; we cry out against the grievous wrong that drags her thence to minister to the coveting selfishness of men who will be rich, even in defiance of God's most plain, most stringent laws ... Let us bear in mind that it is class against class; that the possessor of wealth and power now avails himself of that possession to grind the faces of the poor ... We are organizing an army of ferocious, fearless women, inured to hardship, exercised in masculine labours—drinking, swearing, smoking Amazons ...

There ever has been, and ever will be, a spirit of restless discontent seeking to unsettle the minds of the lower orders ... but so long as England's wives and mothers ... made such lowly homes pleasant to the labouring men ... so long a great but most effective opposing force was found in continual operation against the pernicious effects of political incendiarism ... But now, through the atrocious system ... our women are changed into men, and our men into devils: and the fair inheritance of England's Queen is becoming but as a throne whose pillars rest on an awakening volcano.

> Charlotte Tonna, *The Wrongs of Women*, 1844, pp. 133, 140, 301

9.1.3 *Temperance*

Your committee have already indicated the pleasure with which they welcomed the assistance of the *ladies* in the late bazaar. It will be one of the chief objects followed by your committee next year, if supported by the council, to develop a more complete and extended system of organization among the women of England. The main feature of such an organization should be, it appears to your committee, a systematic plan of domestic visitation, especially among the middle and higher classes. Much has been eloquently said and written with reference to woman's social mission. Here is a sphere singularly appropriate—a work which must commend itself to every womanly sympathy. To enlist the influence of their sex on behalf of sorrow and suffering—to raise the degraded and fallen, and to stem the tide of misery and ruin—to emancipate their poorer sisters from tyranny which benumbs the heart and makes the conscience reckless—surely here is a motive . . .

United Kingdom Alliance 4th Report, 1856

From the earliest commencement of the temperance reformation, appeals, arguments and expostulations have been addressed by earnest reformers to women, because it was felt that on any great social question the power of women to help or hinder was all-important . . . How invaluable is the aid of an earnest and right-minded woman, whether by active effort among her neighbours, or by the silent but forcible testimony of her life in her home circle, by the instruction of the young—as founding or carrying on Bands of Hope—or by the consecration of talents in writing or speaking on the diversified good to be promoted, or the dreadful evils to be avoided by the temperance reformation; in all such efforts there has been signal success permitted.

Mrs Balfour's paper, in Mrs S. Hall (ed.),
Women's Work in the Temperance Reformation, 1868, p. 15

9.1.4   *Contagious Diseases Acts*

It has been said that women were going about agitating on this subject, the Contagious Diseases Act. In any case, they have a right to their opinions. But why do they go about? It is because they have no legitimate mode (cheers) of giving effect to their opinions, and therefore they are compelled to resort to itinerancy as the only means open to them. (Renewed cheers.) Supposing that female ratepayers were allowed to give their votes for the election of members of Parliament, I believe that that itinerant agitation would subside.

Mr Hunt, House of Commons, *Hansard,* 3 May 1871

9.1.5   *Women's public work*

The public work of women began appropriately with the Anti-slavery agitation, when William Wilberforce than prophesied that the step thus taken by them would lead to their own emancipation. The Temperance cause opened another avenue for their energies, and as both of these agitations were considered philanthropic rather than political, it was ultimately decided that women were usefully employed in them. The Anti-Corn law league next appealed to them, and though their help in it was largely in the direction of raising funds by means of bazaars etc., the amount of interest they felt in the work, and the assistance they rendered indirectly, were great. But it was not until two great questions arose, one of them certainly not of their own seeking, that women generally claimed admittance into public life, and took their place as advocates of what they felt to be just, and assailants of what they knew to be wrong. The struggle for the repeal of the C. D. Acts was an ordeal such as men have never been obliged to undergo. It involved not merely that women should speak at public meetings, which was a great innovation, but that they should discuss the most painful of all subjects, upon which up to that time even men had not dared to open their mouths . . .

Those who more especially devoted themselves to the other question of the Suffrage had a task only one degree less difficult. If the former were abused, the latter were ridiculed, and both were denounced as unwomanly. They survived each form of attack ... Is it then worthwhile contending any longer against the inevitable?

'The emancipation of women',
Westminster Review, vol. 128, 1887

9.2 The Right to the Vote

9.2.1 *Sex war the result*

A question has occasionally been raised ... Whether the right of voting be not unjustly withheld from women. But it seems an almost conclusive objection to giving them the franchise, that by the very principle upon which it is bestowed, women are unfit for it, being always under influence ... Further, women have no political interests apart from men. The public measures that are taken, the restrictions or taxes imposed on the community, do not affect them more than male subjects. In all such respects, the interests of the two sexes are identical. As citizens, therefore, they are sufficiently represented already. To give them the franchise would just double the number of voters, without introducing any new interest; and, far from improving society, few things would tend more to dissever and corrupt it.

But disabilities or oppressions, to which they are subject as *women*, could not be in any degree remedied by possessing the franchise. Interests of that description, being exclusively female, would come into collision, not, as in the other cases, with the interests of a class or party, but with those of the whole male sex, and one of two things would happen. Either one sex would be arrayed against another in a sort of general hostility, or they would be divided amongst themselves. Than the first, nothing could possibly be devised more disastrous to the condition of women. They would be utterly crushed; the old prejudices would be revived against their education, or their meddling with anything but household duties. Every man of mature age would probably stipulate, on marrying, that his wife should forswear the use of the franchise, and all ideas connected with political influence, or the coarse and degrading contentions of the elections.

If each sex were divided among themselves on particular questions, unprincipled men would endeavour to secure their elections by creating female parties ... If women had the franchise, men would address themselves to the worst part of the sex, the most clamorous, and those least restrained by female decorum ...

Conducted as elections now are, scenes of violence and tumult, women would be subject to every species of insult. It may be imagined that a remedy might be found for that; but what remedy could be found for the inflictions no law could reach or define, and which they would suffer at home for that exertion of their right, which was opposed to the interests or prejudices of their male relations? ... Intimidation and bribery ... would be far more dangerous to the timidity and comparative poverty of women, than they now are to men.

Anon., *Women's Rights and Duties*, 1840

9.2.2 *A natural right*

The ground on which equality is claimed for all men is of equal force for all women ... It is the possession of the noble faculties of reason and conscience which elevates man above the brutes, and invests him with this right of exercising supreme authority over himself ... He feels that he has a *right* to have all those duties exercised by others towards him, which his conscience tells him he ought to exercise towards others; hence the natural and equal rights of men ... without distinction of sex ...

The exercise of those rights would be useful in two ways: it would tend to enable and elevate the mind; and it would secure the temporal interest of those who exercise it. No doubt can be entertained of the debasing nature of slavery ... Likewise, it is found that when one class legislates for any other class, it attends first to the bearing of that legislation on its own class interests ... The many laws which have been obliged to be passed to protect women from their nearest male relatives are a sufficient answer [to the claim that women are virtually represented in Parliament] ... Those laws, then, are in themselves a convincing proof, first, that woman requires representation, and second, that she is not represented ...

We do not mean to assert that man and woman are strictly the same in their nature, or the character of their minds; but simply, that in the grand characteristics of their nature they are the same, and that where they differ, it is in the minor features; that they resemble far more than they differ from each other ... And by equality, we mean equal civil and legal rights; such an equality as will prevent the rich or wise man from having more power over his fellow-creatures than his riches and wisdom naturally gives him. And from this rule we can see no reason whatever for excluding the female half of the race. The weaker they are, the greater is their need of equal rights, that they may not fall under the tyranny of the stronger portion of their race.

Mrs Hugo Reid, *A Plea for Women*, 1843, pp. 49, 53, 64

Many persons think they have sufficiently justified the restrictions on women's field of action, when they have said that the pursuits from which women are excluded are *unfeminine*, and that the *proper sphere* of women is not politics or publicity, but private and domestic life.

We deny the right of any portion of the species to decide for another portion, or an individual for another individual, what is and what is not their 'proper sphere'. The proper sphere for all human beings is the largest and highest which they are able to attain to. What this is, cannot be ascertained, without complete liberty of choice.

Harriet Taylor,
'Enfranchisement of women', *Westminster Review,* vol. 55, 1851

Much time and more temper have been lost in debating the sterile problem of the 'equality' of men and women, without either party seeming to perceive that the solution either way has no bearing on the practical matters at issue; since civil rights have never yet been reserved for 'physical, moral and intellectual equals'. Even for political rights, among all the arguments eagerly cited last year against extending the franchise, no one thought it worthwhile to urge that the class proposed to be admitted to them was, or was not, physically, intellectually or morally inferior to the classes which already possessed it. As for civil rights—the right to hold property, to make contracts, to sue and be sued—no class, however humble, stupid, and even vicious, has ever been denied them since serfdom and slavery came to an end ... [We reply:] Granted let me be physically, intellectually and morally your inferior. So long as you allow I possess moral responsibility and sufficient intelligence to know right from wrong (a point I conclude you will concede, else why hang me for murder?) I am quite content. It is *only* as a moral and intelligent being I claim my civil rights.

> Frances Power Cobbe, 'Criminals, idiots, women, minors, is the classification sound?', *Fraser's Magazine,* vol. 78, 1868

In the beginning man and woman were created equals, made in the same divine image. God blessed them unitedly, and gave them conjoint dominion over the world. The distinctive characteristic differences that mark the sexes were intended to complement each other and blend in one harmonious and perfect unity, not to lead to the usurpation of power by the one over the other. But sin came and changed this natural order of things, by converting the precedence— necessarily taken by the protector—from a matter of expediency, into a sovereignty that increased with exercise, until mere physical power established a supremacy that has existed in a greater or lesser degree until now. Under this arbitrary rule woman has been more or less degraded to the position of a slave; been treated in many respects as a mere chattel, and she has rarely, if ever, been in a position fully to develop and freely to use the powers which God has gifted her. Political men have taken upon themselves the right of legislating for women, without any direct reference to their feelings and pains— without any direct acknowledgment of the truth that they are reasonable beings like themselves. So also socially. Men have arrogated to themselves in general the right to dictate to women what they should and should not be, and do, and learn; what is befitting for them, what unseemly, apparently quite unconscious that, in so doing, they treat them both unjustly and insultingly ...

But the very fact of such a protest being made, proves forcibly and conclusively, that neither in spirit nor in capacity is she a mere servile appendage to man ... She claims the right to belong to herself, as a self-contained individual existence—the right that every soul, stamped with the divine image, has of striving to perfect itself by the free exercise of its own faculties; the right to refuse submission to the sovereign rule of a fellow-creature, weak and erring as herself: the right to perfect liberty in fulfilling her duties to the world in accordance with nature's teachings and her own convictions: in short, her right to live up to the full measure of her capacities, to reach up to the highest and more useful standard she can attain ... As her interests are co-extensive with human interests, wherever they extend her voice should be heard. The widest political questions affect her well-being as much as that of men ...

> Helen Taylor, address to the third annual meeting of the
> Edinburgh branch of the National Society for Women's
> Suffrage, 1872

9.2.3 *The benefit from the vote*

Among all the reasons for giving women votes, the one which appears to me the strongest, is that of the influence it might be expected to have in increasing public spirit ... And I know no better means, at this present time, of counteracting the tendency to prefer narrow private ends to the public good, than this of giving to all women, duly qualified, a direct and conscious participation in political affairs. Give some women votes, and it will tend to make all women think seriously of the concerns of the nation at large, and their interest having once been fairly roused, they will take pains, by reading and by consultation with persons better informed than themselves, to form sound opinions. As it is, women of the middle class occupy themselves but little with anything beyond their own family circle. They do not consider it any concern of theirs, if poor men and women are ill-nursed in work house infirmaries, and poor children ill-taught in work house schools. If the roads are bad, the drains neglected, the water poisoned, they think it is all very wrong, but it does not occur to them that it is their duty to get it put right, they think it is men's business, not theirs, to look after such things. It is this belief—so narrowing and deadening in its influence—that the exercise of the franchise would tend to dissipate. The mere fact of being called upon to enforce an opinion by a vote, would have an immediate effect in awakening a healthy sense of responsibility. There is no reason why these women should not take an active interest in all the social questions— education, public health, prison discipline, the poor laws, and the rest—which occupy Parliament, and by bringing women into hearty co-operation with men, we gain the benefit not only of their work, but of their intelligent sympathy. Public spirit is like fire: a feeble spark of it may be fanned into a flame, or it may very easily be put out. And the result of teaching women that they have nothing to do with politics, is that their influence goes towards extinguishing the unselfish interest—never too strong—which men are disposed to take in public affairs.

Barbara Leigh Smith Bodichon,
Reasons For and Against the Enfranchisement of Women, 1866

Newspapers are scarcely supposed to be read by women at all. When the *Times* is offered to a lady, the sheet containing the advertisements, and the Births, Deaths, and Marriages, is considerately selected. This almost complete mental blankness being the ordinary condition of women, it is not to be wondered at that their opinions, when they happen to have any, are not much respected.

Emily Davies, *On Secondary Education as Related to Girls,*
a paper read to the National Association for the Promotion
of Social Science, 1864

It makes me mad, the Women's Rights talk about 'the want of a field' for them—when I know that I would gladly give £500 a year for a Woman Secretary. And two English Lady Superintendents have told me the same thing. And we can't get *one* ... They don't know the names of the Cabinet Ministers. They don't know the offices at the Horse Guards. They don't know who of the men of the day is dead and who is alive. They don't know which of the Churches has Bishops and which not. When I went to the Crimea I did not know a Colonel from a Corporal. But there are such things as Army Lists and Almanacs. Yet I never could find a woman who, out of sympathy, would consult one—for my work . . .

Florence Nightingale to M. Mohl, 13 December 1861, quoted in
E. Cook, *The Life of Florence Nightingale*, vol. 2, 1913, p. 14

9.2.4   *The speech of John Stuart Mill*

To lay a ground for refusing the suffrage to any one, it is necessary to allege either personal unfitness or public danger. Now can either of these be alleged in the present case? Can it be pretended that women who manage an estate or conduct a business—who pay rates and taxes, often to a large amount, and frequently from their own earnings—many of whom are responsible heads of families, and some of whom, in the capacity of schoolmistresses, teach much more than a great number of the male electors have ever learnt—are not capable of a function of which every male householder is capable? Or is it feared that if they were admitted to the suffrage they would revolutionize the State—would deprive us of any of our valued institutions, or that we should have worse laws, or be in any way whatever worse governed through the effect of their suffrages? No one, Sir, believes anything of the kind. And it is not only the general principles of justice that are infringed, or at least set aside, by the exclusion of women, merely as women, from any share in the representation; that exclusion is also repugnant to the particular principles of the British Constitution ... that taxation and representation should be co-extensive. Do not women pay taxes? Does not every woman who is *sui juris* contribute exactly as much to the revenue as a man who has the same electoral qualifications? If a stake in the country means anything, the owner of freehold or leasehold property has the same stake, whether it is owned by a man or a woman. There is evidence in our constitutional records that women have voted, in counties and in some boroughs, at former, though certainly distant periods of our history. The House, however will doubtless expect that I should not rest my case solely on the general principles either of justice or of the Constitution, but should produce what are called practical arguments. Now, there is one practical argument of great weight, which I frankly confess, is entirely wanting in the case of women; they do not hold great meetings in the Parks, or demonstrate in Islington ... As for novelty, the despotism of custom is on the wane; we are not now satisfied with knowing what a thing is, we ask whether it ought to be ...

[The reasons given are usually] such aphorisms as these:—Politics are not women's business and would distract them from their proper duties; women do not desire the suffrage, but would rather be without it; women are sufficiently represented by the representation of their male relatives and connections; women have power enough already. I shall probably be thought to have done enough in the way of answering, if I answer all this; and it may, perhaps, instigate any hon. Gentleman who takes the trouble of replying to me, to produce something more recondite. Politics, it is said, are not a woman's business. Well, Sir, I rather think that politics are not a man's business either; unless he is one of the few who are selected and paid to devote their time to the public service, or is a Member of this or of the other House. The vast majority of male electors have each their own business which absorbs nearly the whole of his time; but I have not heard that the few hours occupied, once in a few years, in attending at a polling-booth, even if we throw in the time spent in reading newspapers and political treatises, ever causes them to neglect their shops or their counting-houses. I have never understood that those who have votes are worse merchants, or worse lawyers, or worse physicians, or even worse clergymen than other people. One would almost suppose that the British Constitution denied a vote to every one who could not give the greater part of his time to politics; if this were the case we should have a very limited constituency. But allow me to ask, what is the meaning of political freedom? Is it anything but the control of those who do make their business of politics, by those who do not? Is it not the very essence of constitutional liberty, that men come from their looms and their forges to decide, and decide well, whether they are properly governed, and whom they will be governed by? And the nations which prize this privilege the most, and exercise it most fully, are invariably those who excel the most in the common concerns of life. The ordinary occupations of most women are, and are likely to remain, principally domestic; but the notion that these occupations are incompatible with the keenest interest in national affairs, and in all the great interests of humanity, is as utterly futile as the apprehension, once sincerely entertained, that artizans would desert their workshops and their factories if they were taught to read. I know there is an obscure feeling—a feeling which is ashamed to express itself openly—as if women had no right to care about anything, except how they may be the most useful and devoted servants of some man. But as I am convinced that there is not a single Member of this House, whose conscience accuses him of so mean a feeling, I may say without offence, that this claim to confiscate the whole existence of one half of the species for the supposed convenience of the other, appears to me, independently of its injustice, particularly silly. For who that has had ordinary experience of human affairs, and ordinary capacity of profiting by that experience, fancies that those do their own work best who understand nothing else? A man has lived to little purpose who has not learned that without general mental cultivation, no particular work that requires understanding is ever done in the best manner. It requires brains to use practical experience; and brains, even without practical experience, go further than any amount of practical experience without brains.

But perhaps it is thought that the ordinary occupations of women are more antagonistic than those of men are to the comprehension of public affairs. It is thought, perhaps, that those who are principally charged with the moral education of the future generations of men, cannot be fit to form an opinion about the moral and educational interests of a people; and that those whose chief daily business is the judicious laying-out of money, so as to produce the greatest results with the smallest means, cannot possibly give any lessons to right hon. Gentlemen on the other side of the House or on this, who contrive to produce such singularly small results with such vast means ... The notion of a hard and fast line of separation between women's occupations and men's—of forbidding women to take interest in the things which interest men—belongs to a gone-by state of society which is receding further and further into the past. We talk of political revolutions, but we do not sufficiently attend to the fact that there has taken place around us a silent domestic revolution; women and men are, for the first time in history, really each other's companions. Our traditions respecting the proper relations between them have descended from a time when their lives were apart—when they were separate in their thoughts, because they were separate equally in their amusements and in their serious occupations. In former days a man passed his life among men; all his friendships, all his real intimacies, were with men; with men alone did he consult on any serious business; the wife was either a plaything, or an upper servant. All this, among the educated classes, is now changed. The man no longer gives his spare hours to violent exercises and boisterous conviviality with male associates; the two sexes now pass their lives together; the women of a man's family are his habitual society; the wife is his chief associate, his most confidential friend, and often his most trusted adviser. Now, does a man wish to have for his nearest companion so closely linked with him, and whose wishes and preferences have so strong a claim on him, one whose thoughts are alien to those which occupy his own mind—one who can neither be a help, a comfort, nor a support, to his noblest feelings and purposes? Is this close and almost exclusive companionship compatible with women's being warned off all large subjects—being taught that they ought not to care for what it is men's duty to care for, and that to have any serious interests outside the household is stepping beyond their province? Is it good for a man to live in complete communion of thoughts and feelings with one who is studiously kept inferior to himself, whose earthly interests are forcibly confined within four walls, and who cultivates, as a grace of character, ignorance and indifference about the most inspiring subjects, those among which his highest duties are cast? Does any one suppose that this can happen without detriment to the man's own character? Sir, the time is now come when, unless women are raised to the level of men, men will be pulled down to theirs. The women of a man's family are either a stimulus and a support to his highest aspirations, or a drag upon them. You may keep them ignorant of politics, but you cannot prevent them from concerning themselves with the least respectable part of politics—its personalities; if they do not understand and cannot enter into the man's feelings of public duty, they do care about his personal interest, and that is the scale into which their weight will certainly be thrown. They will be an influence always at hand, co-operating with the man's selfish promptings, lying in wait for his moments of moral irresolution, and doubling the strength of every temptation. Even if they maintain a modest forbearance, the mere absence of their sympathy will hang a dead-weight on his moral energies, making him unwilling to make sacrifices which they will feel, and to forego social advantages and successes in which they would share, for objects which they cannot appreciate. Supposing him fortunate enough to escape any actual sacrifice of conscience, the indirect effect on the higher parts of his own character is still deplorable. Under an idle notion that the beauties of character of the two sexes are not incompatible, men are afraid of many women; but those who have considered the nature and power of social influence well know, that unless there are manly women, there will not much longer be manly men. When men and women are really companions, if women are frivolous, men will be frivolous; if women care for nothing but personal interest and idle vanities, men in general will care for little else; the two sexes must now rise or sink together. It may be said that women may take interest in great public questions without having votes; they may, certainly; but how many of them will? Education and society have exhausted their power in inculcating on women that their proper rule of conduct is what society expects from them; and the denial of the vote is a proclamation intelligible to every one, that whatever else society may expect, it does not expect that they should concern themselves with public interests. Why, the whole of a girl's thoughts and feelings are toned down by it from her schooldays; she does not take the interest even in national history which her brothers do, because it is to be no business of hers when she grows up. If there are women—and now happily there are many—who do interest themselves in these subjects, and do study them, it is because the force within is strong enough to bear up against the worst kind of discouragement, that which acts not by interposing obstacles, which may be struggled against, but by deadening the spirit which faces and conquers obstacles.

We are told, Sir, that women do not wish for the suffrage. If the fact were so, it would only prove that all women are still under this deadening influence; that the opiate still benumbs their mind and conscience. But great numbers of women do desire the suffrage, and have asked for it by petitions to this House. How do we know how many more thousands there may be who have not asked for what they do not hope to get; or for fear of what may be thought of them by men, or by other women; or from the feeling, so sedulously cultivated in them by their education—aversion to make themselves conspicuous? Men must have a rare power of self-delusion, if they suppose that leading questions put to the ladies of their family or of their acquaintance will elicit their real sentiments, or will be answered with complete sincerity by one woman in 10,000. No one is so well schooled as most women are in making a virtue of necessity; it costs little to disclaim caring for what is not offered; a frankness in the expression of sentiments which may be unpleasing and may be thought uncomplimentary to their nearest connections, is not one of the virtues which a woman's education tends to cultivate, and is, moreover, a virtue attended with sufficient risk, to induce prudent women usually to reserve its exercise for cases in which there is a nearer and a more personal interest at stake. However this may be, those who do not care for the suffrage will not use it; either they will not register, or if they do, they will vote—as their male relatives advise—by which, as the advantage will probably be about equally shared among all classes, no harm will be done. Those, be they few or many who do value the privilege, will exercise it, and will receive that stimulus to their faculties, and that widening and liberalizing influence over their feelings and sympathies, which the suffrage seldom fails to produce on those who are admitted to it. Meanwhile an unworthy stigma would be removed from the whole sex. The law would cease to declare them incapable of serious things; would cease to proclaim that their opinions and wishes are unworthy of regard, on things which concern them equally with men, and on many things which concern them much more than men. They would no longer be classed with children, idiots, and lunatics, as incapable of taking care of either themselves or others, and needing that everything should be done for them, without asking their consent. If only one woman in 20,000 used the suffrage, to be declared capable of it would be a boon to all women. Even that theoretical enfranchisement would remove a weight from the expansion of their faculties, the real mischief of which is much greater than the apparent.

Then it is said, that women do not need direct power, having so much indirect, through their influence over their male relatives and connections. I should like to carry this argument a little further. Rich people have a great deal of indirect influence. Is this a reason for refusing them votes? Does any one propose a rating qualification the wrong way, or bring in a Reform Bill to disfranchise all who live in a £500 house, or pay £100 a year indirect taxes? Unless this rule for distributing the franchise is to be reserved for the exclusive benefit of women, it would follow that persons of more than a certain fortune should be allowed to bribe, but should not be allowed to vote. Sir, it is true that women have great power. It is part of my case that they have great power; but they have it under the worst possible conditions because it is indirect, and therefore irresponsible. I want to make this great power a responsible power. I want to make the woman feel her conscience interested in its honest exercise. I want her to feel that it is not given to her as a mere means of personal ascendancy. I want to make her influence work by a manly interchange of opinion, and not by cajolery. I want to awaken in her the political point of honour. Many a woman already influences greatly the political conduct of the men connected with her, and sometimes by force of will, actually governs it; but she is never supposed to have anything to do with it; the man whom she influences, and perhaps misleads, is alone responsible; her power is like the back-stairs influence of a favourite. Sir, I demand that all who exercise the power should have the burden laid on them of knowing something about the things they have power over. With the acknowledged right to a voice, would come a sense of the corresponding duty. Women are not usually inferior in tenderness of conscience to men. Make the woman a moral agent in these matters; show that you expect from her a political conscience; and when she has learnt to understand the transcendent importance of these things, she will know why it is wrong to sacrifice political convictions to personal interest or vanity; she will understand that political integrity is not a foolish personal crotchet, which a man is bound, for the sake of his family to give up, but a solemn duty; and the men whom she can influence will be better men in all public matters, and not, as they often are now, worse men by the whole amount of her influence.

But at least, it will be said, women do not offer any practical inconvenience, as women, by not having a vote. The interests of all women are safe in the hands of their fathers, husbands, and brothers, who have the same interest with them, and not only know, far better than they do, what is good for them, but care much more for them than they care for themselves. Sir, this is exactly what is said of all unrepresented classes. The operatives for instance; are they not virtually represented by the representation of their employers? Are not the interest of the employers and that of the employed, when properly understood the same? to insinuate the contrary, is it not the horrible crime of setting class against class? ... And what is more, are not all employers good, kind, benevolent men, who love their workpeople, and always desire to do what is most for their good? All these assertions are as true, and as much to the purpose, as the corresponding assertions respecting men and women ... Workmen need other protection than that of their employers, and women other protection than that of their men. I should like to have a Return laid before this House of the number of women who are annually beaten to death, kicked to death, or trampled to death by their male protectors; and, in an opposite column, the amount of the sentences passed in those cases in which the dastardly criminals did not get off altogether. I should also like to have, in a third column, the amount of property, the unlawful taking of which was, at the same sessions or assizes by the same judge, thought worthy of the same amount of punishment. We should then have an arithmetical estimate of the value set by a male legislature and male tribunals on the murder of a woman, often, by torture continued through years, which, if there is any shame in us, would make us hang our heads. Sir, before it is affirmed that women do not suffer in their interests, as women, by the denial of a vote, it should be considered whether women have no grievances; whether the laws, and those practices which laws can reach, are in every way as favourable to women as to men.

Now, how stands the fact? In the matter of education, for instance. We continually hear that the most important part of national education is that of mothers, because they educate the future men. Is this importance really attached to it? Are there many fathers who care as much, or are willing to expend as much, for the education of their daughters as of their sons? Where are the Universities, where the high schools, or the schools of any description? If it be said that girls are better educated at home, where are the training-schools for governesses? What has become of the endowments which the bounty of our ancestors destined for the education, not of one sex only, but of both indiscriminately? I am told by one of the highest authorities on the subject, that in the majority of the endowments the provision made is not for boys, but for education generally; in one great endowment, Christ's Hospital, it is expressly for both; that institution now maintains and educates 1,100 boys, and exactly twenty-six girls. And when they attain womanhood, how does it fare with that great and increasing portion of the sex, who, sprung from the educated classes, have not inherited a provision, and not having obtained one by marriage, or disdaining to marry merely for a provision, depend on their exertions for subsistence? Hardly any decent educated occupation, save one, is open to them. They are either governesses or nothing ... No sooner do women (like Miss Garrett) show themselves capable of competing with men in any career, than that career, if it be lucrative or honourable, is closed to them. A short time ago women might be associates of the Royal Academy; but they were so distinguishing themselves, they were assuming so honourable a place in their art, that this privilege also has been withdrawn. This is the sort of care taken of women's interests by the men who so faithfully represent them. This is the way we treat unmarried women. And how is it with the married? They, it may be said, are not interested in this Motion; and they are not directly interested; but it interests, even directly, many who have been married, as well as others who will be. Now, by the common law of England, all that a wife has, belongs absolutely to the husband; he may tear it all from her, squander every penny of it in debauchery, leave her to support by her labour herself and her children, and if by heroic exertion and self-sacrifice she is able to put by something for their future wants, unless she is judicially separated from him he can pounce down upon her savings, and leave her penniless. And such cases are of quite common occurrence. Sir, if we were besotted enough to think these things right there would be more excuse for us; but we know better. The richer classes take care to exempt their own daughters from the consequences of this abominable state of the law. By the contrivance of marriage settlements, they are able in each case to make a private law for themselves, and they invariably do so. Why do we not provide that justice for the daughters of the poor, which we take care to provide for our own daughters? Why is not that which is done in every case that we personally care for, made the law of the land, so that a poor man's child whose parents could not afford the expense of a settlement, may retain a right to any little property that may devolve on her, and may have a voice in the disposal of her own earnings, which, in the case of many husbands, are the best and only reliable part of the incomings of the family? I am sometimes asked what practical grievances I propose to remedy by giving women a vote; I propose for one thing, to remedy this. I give these instances to prove that women are not the petted children of society which many people seem to think they are—that they have not the over-abundance, the superfluity of power that is ascribed to them, and are not sufficiently represented by the representation of the men who have not had the heart to do for them this simple and obvious piece of justice. Sir, grievances of less magnitude than the law of the property of married women, when suffered by parties less inured to passive submission, have provoked revolutions. We ought not to take advantage of the security we feel against any such consequence in the present case, to withold from a limited number of women that moderate amount of participation in the enactment and improvement of our laws, which this Motion solicits for them, and which would enable the general feelings of women to be heard in this House through a few male representatives. We ought not to deny to them, what we are conceding to everybody else—a right to be consulted; the ordinary chance of placing in the great Council of the nation a few organs of their sentiments—of having, what every petty trade or profession has, a few members who feel specially called on to attend to their interests, and to point out how those interests are affected by the law, or by any proposed changes in it. No more is asked by this Motion; and when the time comes, as it certainly will come, when this will be granted, I feel the firmest conviction that you will never repent of the concession.

Amendment proposed, to leave out the word 'man', in order to insert the word 'person'—(*Mr. Mill*)—instead thereof.

J. S. Mill, House of Commons, *Hansard,* 20 May 1867

(lost by 73 votes to 196)

9.2.5 *Tory Opposition*
Mr. Beresford Hope,
He was astonished to hear his noble friend allege as any argument that no women had petitioned against the Bill . . . Their not petitioning was indeed an argument against the change, for it proved that women shrank from thrusting themselves forward into the noisy turmoil of politics. No doubt women had sometimes petitioned Parliament— they had even crowded that table with petitions on a certain question which should have been the very last to attract their attention. So far from that fact being a reason for conferring this franchise upon

women, as showing that they took a deep interest in the proceedings of the House, he thought that the disgusting appearance of the petitions to which he alluded greatly strengthened the arguments of those who were conscientiously opposed to the principle contended for by the advocates of the present measure. He was opposed to the Bill, because he wished to protect women from being forced forward into the hurly-burly of party politics, and obliged to take part in all the disagreeable accompaniments of electioneering contests and their consequences. All who were familiar with contests knew that it was often as troublesome not to vote as to give a vote; and yet Parliament was asked to put the helpless female lodgers, seamstresses, and such persons, in this dilemma. The very nature of women called for sympathy and protection, and for the highest and most chivalrous treatment on the part of the men, but instead of this being accorded for the future, it was now proposed to thrust them into a position which they were by their sex, by their condition in life, and by their previous training totally unqualified to grapple with ... If this Bill should pass, and the number of emancipated women were found to produce no appreciable change in the quality of the representation in the House, then he would say that they had made a great disturbance to gain something very small indeed; but, on the other hand, if it were found to cause any serious alteration in the character of the representation, then, with all due respect to all the new constituencies, he believed that the alteration would be shown in the deterioration and not in the improvement of the quality of Parliament. On this head he desired to speak plainly. It was not a question whether the male or the female intellect were the superior one. He simply said that they were different, and that the difference made man more capable of direct government and woman more fitted for private influence. There were in the world women of a manlike-mind—a Mrs. Somerville or a Miss Martineau, and there were now and then men of feminine softness; but he reasoned from the generality and not from marked exceptions. Reason predominated in the man, emotion and sympathy in the woman ... though emotion and sentiment were admirable qualities in their way, he maintained distinctly that reason ought to govern emotion, and not emotion govern reason. If, indeed, our existing constituencies were exclusively composed of bachelors and widowers, it might be argued that the reason was not sufficiently tempered by sentiment. But with the large bulk which they contain of family men, he felt quite satisfied that the womanly nature had quite as much play in making up the national mind as could be healthfully desired. The character of the legislation of a woman-chosen Parliament would be the increased importance which would be given to questions of a *quasi* social or philanthropic character (viewed with regard to the supposed interests, or the partisan bias of special classes, rather than to broader considerations of the public weal) in excess of the great constitutional and international issues which the legislature was empanelled to try. We should have more wars for an idea, or hasty alliances with scheming neighbours, more class cries, permissive legislation, domestic perplexities, and sentimental grievances. Our legislation would develop hysterical and spasmodic features, partaking more of the French and American system than reproducing the tradition of the English Parliament. On these grounds he should vote against the second reading of the Bill.

Mr. Bouverie,
The happiness and interests of wife and daughter were far dearer to a head of a family than his own. (Hear.) His interests and theirs were entirely wrapped up together; and he maintained that this was the real protection of women against oppression and injury, and not the electoral power which his hon. friend proposed to confer on them. To his mind, his hon. friend struck at the very foundation of society— namely, the family. (Hear, hear.) Was the head of the family to be the master of the family or was he not? Was it nature's intention, and was it our Maker's intention, that when society was founded on the family, the man should be at the head of the family and should rule? ... The logical result ... were the socialistic views of those who asserted that the existing foundations of society were wrong ... Marriage was represented by these writers as a state of intolerable bondage and slavery ... There was a book far more esteemed by our countrywomen, if not by our countrymen, than the writings of Mr. Mill, and it said, 'Her desire shall be to her husband, and he shall rule over her'. (Cheers.)

Mr. James,
On the question of fitness to govern, was it not true that in all matters connected with the army, the navy, and matters commercial, diplomatic, and legal, women would have to judge on the basis of information obtained second-hand, and not from practical experience? ... The ballot was about to be adopted ... how enormous would be the power of the priest ... Surely it could not be expected that women would give an unbiassed vote, the result of political conviction? There was one other argument of which much had been made ... namely, that our Sovereign was a woman ... But when it pleased her to take beneath her roof one of her own age, a stranger and a foreigner, and one who had little knowledge and experience of the English people, Her Majesty chose to receive guidance and direction, the council and assistance of that foreigner, simply because she was a woman and he was a man. (Hear, hear.)

Women's Disabilities Bill, House of Commons,
Hansard, 3 May 1871

9.2.6 *Liberal opposition*

I have gradually formed the opinion that if women exercised direct political power, the effect would be most injurious to society . . .

I do not presume to justify the ways of nature, but it is clear that she has made women comparatively weak and obviously dependent upon men. Artificial circumstances should not blind us to a natural law. The physical dependence of women on men, combined with their difference of organization, is the justification of government by men. I hold it to be the duty of men to protect women, and to represent their interests in Parliament. We shall commit a fatal error if we set women up in political hostility to men . . . Of course the popular appeal in this case is to abstract right. 'If you may govern me why may I not govern you?' The question of the right of governing is entirely one of expediency . . . I defy women to base their refusal of the franchise to minors upon any other ground than that of expediency.

It is said, however, that men have not represented the interests of women in the legislature. But if women have been badly represented in Parliament hitherto—so have men! The highest interests of neither have yet been represented in the legislature: we have all suffered alike from the selfish class rule. The object of our present movement is to represent all classes and the women in them.

Sir, my concern in this question is the benefit of the entire community. What is likely to be the effect of Woman Suffrage? . . . It is my opinion that the collective thought of women—that is, the opinion of the majority of women—will be adverse to enlightenment and progress. I must decline to regard the ladies who demand Woman Suffrage as the mental representatives of their sex. They are entirely exceptional women . . . I welcome the presence of mental strength in women, all the more because it is so rare; and so far am I from sharing popular objections to Woman Suffrage that, while I would not give women the vote, I would most willingly remove their disability to sit in Parliament and assuredly remove all disabilities which now prevent their serving in many professions and trades—holding that Nature may be very well left to mark the limits of their work; but I appeal to these ladies not to compare themselves with men, but rather to compare their aspirations and ideas with those of the majority of their own sex.

They will find that the tendency of most women is favourable to arbitrary government and clerical supremacy. They seem to be incapable of sympathizing with great causes—they have a strong pre-dilection for personal Institutions. As a rule they are completely without interest in great national questions. Theirs is essentially the private life point of view. If I thought that their natural apathy concerning politics would lead them to abstain from voting, I should not so much dread their political power: but unfortunately they have a

vivid sense of the value of all property, and the vote would be
regarded as property intended for use; and subject as they are to
religious appeals it would be frequently used—as the woman vote is
now frequently used in School Board elections—under the influence
of the Clergy. Of course I am familiar with Mr. Mill's argument, that
if women do not interest themselves in great questions it is because we
have never encouraged them to do so—and that political responsibility
will educate them. I for my part doubt this. The conscience of women
towards the public is feeble, and when the conscience is feeble
responsibility is no educator ... It may take two or three generations
to awaken public spirit in the majority of women, and to educate them
out of their instinctive submission to *whatever is* and their dread of
ideas, which have not the sanction of custom; and in the mean time
what is to be our fate? The hands of the clock are to be put back that
women may pass through men's accomplished experiences, and we are
to be delivered over for a long period of uninterrupted Tory rule! ...
This proposal is not so much in favour of Woman Suffrage as it is in
favour of the extension of property representation. The effect of
embodying it in legislation will be that propertied widows and
spinsters will possess the franchise not on account of their sex, but on
account of their property, while marriage will stand out as a political
disqualification. The ladies say that they take the franchise as they
find it; but they are bound to recognize that the present electoral law
was constructed solely with a view to male suffrage, and that it cannot
be made, without some special wife qualification which they do not
propose, to include woman suffrage. It will on the contrary preclude
the possibility of a genuine woman suffrage being obtained, for when
the constitutional argument based upon property qualification has
been satisfied, it is probable that all agitation will cease ... Under a
delusive plea, it represents a class measure, for the propertied single
women exists mostly in the upper and middle classes: it will therefore
operate unfairly towards the working class and afford additional
means of class oppression. It is not surprising that the Conservatives
have taken charge of the measure proposed; they are always anxious
to increase property representation and would enfranchise boys if
boys held title deeds. But we consider that property is already over
represented. Upon these grounds I oppose the amendment and
earnestly entreat working class politicians, in the interest of the
working class especially, to offer it their uncompromising opposition.

Captain Maxse, Objections to Woman Suffrage,
speech delivered to the Electoral Reform Conference, 1874

9.2.7   *Opponents opposed: Arabella Shore's reply*

You are generally told that women are not fit to vote. To this perhaps
a few words furnish a conclusive answer—women are held fit to

possess property, and the possession of property is the only fitness required for the vote. But if we press for particulars, we are met by the great Nature-argument; we are told of the pecularities of our nature, our conditions, our duties, and our character; that is, in other words, our physical and mental inferiority, our home sphere, and our political tendencies . . .

First one would like to know when it is so glibly said that Nature is opposed to this or that, what is meant by Nature. Is it ancient usage or established convention, the law or custom of our country, training, social position, the speaker's own particular fancy or prejudice, or what? . . . It seems that for a woman to manage property, carry on large businesses, be a farmer, a merchant, a parish-overseer, a clerk in various capacities, a municipal elector, or member of a School Board, or even a Sovereign, is not against Nature, but to give a vote for a Member of Parliament is . . . We feel that politics means legislation, and that legislation enters into questions in which we have a right and a necessity to be interested. We cannot separate domestic politics from social conditions of life. If then we are told that we have nothing to do with politics, we can but answer that politics have a great deal to do with us.

As for that mental inferiority imputed to our sex—the mind hopelessly closed to logic, the incapability of taking large views, the want of a sense of justice, are these considered an inherent peculiarity belonging to sex or not? If they are, it would be idle to suppose that any woman ever did, or could do, political work, or any large general work at all . . . and all the women who have shone in various departments of thought, science, and action, must be dismissed as monstrosities . . .

The second argument drawn from our sex is that well-known one called by Mr. Jacob Bright, the 'spherical argument' . . .

With respect to the home as the woman's natural sphere . . . [it] is by no means her domain, for as wife and mother she has no legal power, hardly any legal rights. Nor am I aware that our 'women's sphere' friends mean anything more than that she is to be the chief working subordinate, by no means even an equal authority in it. So that this distinction seems to result in man's keeping the supremacy in every sphere to himself . . . Why should the giving of a vote every four or five years, or even taking an interest in politics as much, let us say, as men commonly do, take a woman out of her sphere, or prevent her fulfilling her duties? Moreover, since to a large and increasing number of women this sphere is denied, the restriction amounts for them to the exclusion from any . . .

No doubt, the home duties must be, and always will be, performed, but it is a misfortune, not a glory, if a woman finds it necessary to bound all her thoughts and cares to it; that is, to a very narrow range of personal interests. But every argument founded on the home importance of woman, as the educator of men, and her moral and social influence as man's companion, points to the necessity of her having a sense of wider responsibilities. She cannot educate men who are to be citizens without some knowledge of what citizenship is, or some feeling of citizenship herself.

I come now to the third class of alleged disqualifications of woman, her moral character, and her political tendencies ... Granting the favourite charge that she is more emotional and impulsive than man, what then? Can the more or less of qualities common to the race make the one half of a nation fit to be represented, the other not? Is the Irishman disqualified for a vote because he is more impulsive than the Englishman? And may not this variety in the proportion of qualities be an advantage rather than otherwise? May there not be a danger from the exclusive preponderance of a certain set of tendencies, and may not the infusion of a new moral element sometimes strengthen the higher considerations which might be in danger of being postponed to merely commercial, or other self-regarding interests? ...

But then there are the political tendencies of women, and here again our antagonists contradict each other; for some allege our political apathy and want of public spirit, and others our furious reactionary fanaticism ... The language of these theorists implies that man is, properly speaking, all human nature, with all his faculties perfectly balanced, and woman an imperfect anomalous accessory, a bundle of instincts always foolish, and mostly mischievous ... Women vary as men vary, they are moulded and modified by the same diversified influences as affect men, birth, education, family-belongings, social atmosphere; and these variations apart, Englishwomen are of the same race as Englishmen, and partake of the same strong national character. So that, on the whole, Magna Carta is not likely to be repealed by the female descendants of those who won it for us.

Others of our opponents dwell on our incapability of sympathising with great causes, our natural apathy about politics, and, at the same time, our stagnant Toryism. This, one might say, is adding insult to injury. We are excluded from all practical share in politics, we are taught that they are not our concern, our 'sphere' as it is called, we are brought up in perfect ignorance of them, and then we are reproached for our indifference to them! I might rather wonder that we care as much for politics as we do ...

As for the indictment of universal Toryism, if it be true that there are more Conservatives among women than among men, this cannot to the true Liberal be a just reason for their exclusion. What business have we to make or maintain laws to exclude the political party whose views we dislike? Try and educate them rather to a better view of things is what we should say about an excluded class of men; and if our Bill pass, I dare say my liberal friends will look to this in future in their own families ... It would be more fair to say that in politics women ordinarily adopt the opinion of the men around them than that all women have but one opinion amongst them. If this leads generally to Toryism, we can only say that on Constitutional principles the party that has a majority in the nation has a right to a majority in the House. But conversation, books, journals, joined to all the quickening influences of varied society, are rapidly giving women the power of forming their own opinions; and it is a certain fact that for the most part the highly-gifted and enlightened women who, in their own spheres, lead public opinion, are thorough Liberals ...

There is one more argument that I must notice—that the basis of government is physical force, that is, personal strength, and therefore women being physically the weaker are unfitted for the franchise. This is alarming, for physical weakness, combined with legal inequality, seems to ensure not so much protection as oppression. But what is meant by physical force being the basis of government? I have always thought that government was designed to *supersede* physical force, that civilization meant the reign of law instead of that of brute-strength. Public opinion, moral restrictions, mental power and organisation, make up now the forces on which government rests, compared to which bodily force is simply nothing. This would be going back to savagedom, indeed. Doubtless, before communities were formed, the man who could knock the other down would have most power. But as soon as people began to live in an orderly way together, it was the strongest headed, not the strongest handed, man who became chief of the tribe ... Our Cabinet ministers are not chosen from the men who can knock each other down. Depend upon it, it is something more than muscle that keeps society together, or we are living on the brink of a convulsion. If all the muscle of the nation were pitted against the brain, no doubt the women would go down, but so too would all the men of intellect ...

And, after all, what connexion has this theory of physical force with Women's Suffrage? ... Does it mean only that none are to be represented but those who can take by force what they want, or defend by force what others attack? This would exclude from the suffrage all sickly men, and most men above 60. But the embodiment of physical force, soldiers, sailors, and police, have no vote. It would be just as fair to say that women ought not to have property, because, if men wanted to take it from them, they could not defend it by force ...

Mr. John Bright ... [argues] that this demand is based on hostility to men, and will cause still more hostility; secondly, that electioneering is too vile a business for women to have anything to do with. As to the charge of hostility, it amazes me. We ask that we may help in the choice of men to maintain a masculine Government. We are not demanding the vote that we may elect women instead of, and in opposition to men ...

If such grossness, violence, and corruption are, as Mr. Bright says, inherent in the present political system, it becomes a question whether Representative Government is a thing that ought to continue, or whether *men* are fit to conduct it . . . Since the ballot the election day no longer presents the objectionable scenes that it once did . . .

One of these speakers, indeed, said that, when the majority of women wished for the vote it could not be refused them. But how are honourable gentlemen to discover that majority? The almost impossible task is set before women of *letting it be known* that the vote is wished for, without *showing* that they wish for it. No such paradoxical test was applied to *men* when it was decided that it was fit and just that the great majority of them should have the suffrage, whether they wish for it or no. But, in our case, petitions are scouted as no test; all agitation is regarded as the work of a few restless women, meetings and speeches are ridiculed; the many women of culture, thought and feeling, of social energy and devoted benevolence, who desire it, are passed over as unknown, or put aside as exceptional, or branded as masculine . . . If to have a warm interest in great national and public concerns, and to wish to help in them with our best work, is to be masculine, then let us be masculine, and be proud of being so. No virtue ought to be monopolised by either sex.

Lastly we are, it is said, not educated enough for the franchise. But what is the standard for a man? Not to be able to write his name, or even to read it when written, but to understand the mark made for it. That is all the education required for a male elector. Compared with this, the female standard will be that of high cultivation. No doubt women might be better educated (as well as men) but if in truth we are less fit than the humblest artisan, whose doing is it but that of the political and social legislation which has fixed our status for us, just as formerly the want of education of the lower orders who had undertaken to manage everything for them? . . . But women are not content with this, and are trying their best to improve it. They are struggling with immense difficulties—difficulties from that trades' unionism which shuts them out from established general institutions, from the means of special training, from the use of endowments lavishly applied for the other sex, difficulties from the indifference of the State, and still more from the indifference of the public. Yet, unhelped, at least at first, save by the private exertions of some good and wise men, women have struggled on . . .

And now to draw to a close. We have been told of women's indifference to politics, and especially to the possession of a vote. We hear of the 'few women who desire it' . . . I find that the two classes whose opinion ought to have most value, on the subject are most in favour of it. These are, first the women of cultivated thought and practical usefulness, who have given their attention and their powers of work to women's needs, and to public and social questions as connected with them; secondly, the women who from their social position suffer most from that man-made law of which the object has been to enforce the rights of men at the expense of theirs. For this is not a 'ladies' question, it is a 'women's' question, and I and many others know how the working order of women feel their practical grievances, and how they would hail any change that promised to amend them . . .

I conjure those who are already working to work on without discouragement, confident of the result. Let us think of the great causes that have been won by sheer hard struggling year by year, begun by one or two high-hearted men, carried on by a determined band, secured at last by the voice and sanction of the nation; all won by the same process that we are now pursuing—steady, peaceful, constitutional effort. The Abolition of the Slave Trade . . . the first Reform Bill . . . the repeal of the Corn Laws . . . All these great causes were triumphantly and gloriously won, and the secret of the success was the intense, glowing, inspiring zeal of those who believed in them. Let us have faith and fervour like them.

Arabella Shore, *Present Aspect of Woman's Suffrage Considered,* speech delivered to the London National Society for Women's Suffrage, 1877

9.3   Organisation and Issues

9.3.1   *National Society for Women's Suffrage: first public meeting*
Moved by Miss L. Becker,
That the exclusion of women from the exercise of the franchise in the election of Members of Parliament being unjust in principle and inexpedient in practice, this meeting is of opinion that the right of voting should be granted to them on the same terms as it is or may be granted to men.
Seconded by Archdeacon Sandford; supported by Mr. F. B. Potter, M.P. and Dr. Pankhurst.

Moved by Mrs. Pochin,
That this meeting expresses its cordial approval of the objects of the National Society for Women's Suffrage, and of the course it has hitherto pursued, and pledges itself to support its future efforts by all practical and constitutional methods, especially by urging women possessing legal qualifications to claim to be put on the Parliamentary register.
Seconded by Mr. Chisholm Anstey and supported by Mr. Jacob Bright, M.P.

Helen Blackburn, *Women's Suffrage*, 1902, pp. 71-2

9.3.2   *The municipal vote*
It is quite likely we may yet have a fight this session, not on the Parliamentary, but on the *municipal* franchise. Mr. Hibbert, M.P. for Oldham, has a Bill giving it to every *male* occupier who has resided a year in a borough ... an amendment will be moved in committee to leave out the word *male*. Mr. Jacob Bright said if he could find half a dozen men on our side willing to support him, he would run the risk of the trial ... Mr. Hibbert is quite agreeable to the amendment. Altogether I feel quite encouraged, for I really think it may be carried. It will be a grand step towards the Parliamentary franchise. But we must be very quiet until notice is actually given of the amendment, and then we must work for it, as hard as we can.

Lydia Becker to Jessie Boucherett, 3 May 1869, quoted in loc. cit.

A great victory has been won for us by Mr. Jacob Bright on the municipal franchise. Happily the deputation is no longer necessary, indeed the mere proposal of it seems to have been enough to make the Home Secretary promise to do all we wanted. He told Mr. Jacob Bright on Monday that he should support the amendment in the name of the

Government. The question therefore passed through the House without a dissentient word . . .

Lydia Becker to Barbara Leigh Smith Bodichon,
9 June 1869, quoted in loc. cit., pp. 91-2

9.3.3 *The relation of women's suffrage to other issues*

We hold it to be important that no person conspicuously engaged, either as officer or as lecturer, in some other agitations now proceeding, to which we will not further allude, should hold any conspicuous place in the movement for Women's Suffrage ... We have arrived deliberately at the opinion that it would be better that two Committees should co-exist than that only one should exist, exposed to the reasonable dissatisfaction of those friends of Women's Suffrage strongly opposed to some other movements now on foot: inasmuch as, if there existed no executive body entirely disconnected with those other movements, many friends of Women's Suffrage might find themselves compelled to withdraw their support.

Circular from the 'Old London' Suffrage Society, 1872,
quoted in loc. cit., pp. 120-1

Ladies ... will 'go in' for female education, but reject all else; or they will practically sanction some one part of the movement which meets their taste or is not condemned as 'unwomanly', while carelessly refusing even to look into the meaning or merits of any other part ... There is a necessary, a very significant connection, among all the claims at present advanced. Growth may be imperfect if one part is pushed on and another intimately related to it, is held back. The simultaneousness of the demand for industrial freedom and for higher education is based on a necessity. The education which most women need is one which will fit them for business in professions and industry. With this latter is closely connected the degree of political freedom and responsibility which we seek in asking the parliamentary vote.

Josephine Butler, *Woman's Work and Woman's Culture,* 1869

9.3.4 *The married woman's vote*

I am aghast at the new Women's Suffrage Bill ... I have not the least objection to married women being without exception, and even permanently, *incidentally* shut out ... but it is another matter to ask Parliament distinctly to enact that married women shall by the fact of their marriage be a disqualified class ... What we were asking would be the suffrage for *femes soles*, and might seem to cast a slur on wives. The [former] answer to them, namely, that there was no slur cast by the accidental want of qualification that came from laws as to the tenure of property—the necessity that the husband rather than the wife should be the householder—and so forth, was generally a sufficient answer whether to friend or to foe . . . This change will do little to conciliate our opponents, and will plainly alienate many of our working friends. I have not had time to think whether I may in conscience go on working for Mr. Forsyth's Bill.

A.W.

The clause makes no difference in the practical operation of the measure. The common law disabilities of married women effectually preclude them from the exercise of the suffrage . . . [However] we do not disguise our extreme regret that a statutory penalty on marriage should be introduced into the electoral law . . . If the conditions are unjust, it is more likely that they may be got rid of after so large a proportion of the sex affected by them shall have been admitted to the franchise . . . There are many supporters of the principle who believe that marriage ought not to disqualify a woman from the exercise of any suffrage that she would otherwise be entitled to. There are others who believe that it is not expedient that married women should have votes. We could not expect men who entertain the view of these obligations of the marriage relation to join in a demand for the enfranchisement of married women as such . . . We may well leave the further question to be dealt with when the occasion arises. All supporters of women's suffrage agree in the justice of enfranchising the *femes soles*, all can join in claiming this, without prejudice to their opinions or action with respect to the franchise for wives.

[Lydia Becker], *Women's Suffrage Journal,* 1 April 1874

Mrs. M'Ilquham,
Our objects are two,—first to extend to women, whether unmarried, married, or widowed, the right to vote at Parliamentary, Municipal, Local and other elections, on the same conditions which qualify men; and second to establish for all women equal civil and political rights with men . . . It was impossible but that such a League should be formed, unless we were prepared to stand by and see *positive injury* done to the position of married women . . . [since] the Women's Suffrage Societies . . . have given their assent to the admission of the 'coverture' clause, which now stands part of Mr. Woodall's Bill . . . by which no married women could exercise the Parliamentary Franchise. Now I consider that the admission of that clause is nothing better than a pandering to barbarism . . . Many married women traders are forced by sheer necessity to become the breadwinners of their families. And they are certainly the last class of women that any of the Women's Suffrage Societies should seek to make into political pariahs . . .

Dr. Pankhurst,
The great Married Women's Property Act 1882 gave women property,

and it gave them the right to contract exactly as a man ... Mr. Woodall's Bill repeals the relieving and liberty-giving power of the Act of 1882; secondly, it turns a common law disability, as far as now existing, into a statutory disability; and thirdly it prevents us ... from going to the Courts ... A terrible wrong is done to every married woman by expressly excluding her from the beneficial and enlarging functions of public life ... a terrible stigma ...

> *Report of Proceedings at the Inaugural Meeting of the*
> *Women's Franchise League, London, 25 July 1889*

9.3.5 *Women's suffrage and party political associations*

One element has hitherto been inadequately represented in Liberal organization and activities. Women have failed to exercise their rightful influence ... Within a recent and brief period, Women's Liberal Associations have been originated, with an aggregate membership of over ten thousand ... In Bristol ... in Lancashire ... in York, Bristol, Darlington, Birmingham, Cambridge, Crewe, Kidderminster, Wolverhampton, Newcastle, and other great centres of population, women are energetically organizing themselves and preparing to take part in diffusing political knowledge and in securing the triumph of Liberal principles ... A definite programme and code of rules have been adopted, committees chosen, and all the machinery for carrying on a wide-spread and energetic propaganda set in motion ...

In this light, it is instructive to note the attitude taken by enlightened women in respect to the demand of Ireland for self-government, and the comprehensive scheme submitted to Parliament and the country by the Liberal leader ... Arguing from their own experience of home and life, these women asked, what *is* Union? Is it the narrow gold band worn since the wedding day? Is it the legal rite which pronounced 'husband and wife'? Is it not rather the linking of sympathies and aims, the independent yet co-related rule in each department of life and the full recognition of individual rights and common interests? This was the spontaneous response of the majority of liberal-minded women, who saw in Mr. Gladstone's proposals a determination, not to mar but to perfect the Union, and to stimulate into wholesome growth the restrained, hopeful, impetuous spirit of the Irish people.

> 'Women workers in the Liberal cause',
> *Westminster Review,* vol. 128, 1887

Mr. T. Russell, M.P. moved: 'That this meeting approves the formation of a Women's Liberal Unionist Association, and anticipates the highest advantages from the influence and work of women, as maintaining justice and order in Ireland under the Union.' ... We have really come upon a time when scientific electioneering has come to be the order of the day ... And if Liberal Unionist women will do what

Gladstonian women—for I won't call them Liberal women—do, and what Primrose League women are doing, they will do a great and valuable service . . .

Mrs. Fawcett: I do not mean to dwell at any length on the degree to which the Nationalist cause is associated with and built up on crime . . . I think that women should approach this question not so much from the point of view of legality or illegality, as from the point of view of right or wrong . . . No great and stable political institutions have ever been founded on crime.

Inaugural meeting of the Women's Liberal Unionist Association,
5 July 1888

9.4 Mr Gladstone on Female Suffrage

This is a question of immense difficulty ... nothing hasty should be done—a question which requires to be absolutely sifted to the bottom; a question which ought to be dissociated from every notion of Party and every element of political consideration ... The cargo which the vessel carries is, in our opinion, a cargo as large as she can safely carry ...

Mr. Gladstone, House of Commons, *Hansard,* 10 June 1884

Dear Mr. Samuel Smith,

In reply to your letter, I cannot but express the hope that the House of Commons will not consent to the second reading of the Bill for Extending the Parliamentary Suffrage to Women ...

The Bill is a narrow Bill, inasmuch as it excludes from its operation the entire body of married women; who are not less reflective, intelligent, and virtuous, than their unmarried sisters, and who must I think be superior in another great element of fitness, namely the lifelong habit of responsible action ...

Such a change ought not to be made without the fullest consideration and the most deliberate assent of the nation as well as of the Parliament. Not only has there been no such assent, but there has not been even an approach to such consideration. The subject is as yet only sectional, and has not really been taken into view by the public mind at large. Can it be right, under these circumstances, that the principle of a change so profound should be adopted? ...

There are very special reasons for circumspection in this particular case. There has never within my knowledge been a case in which the franchise has been extended to a large body of persons generally indifferent about receiving it. But here, in addition to a widespread indifference, there is on the part of large numbers of women who have considered the matter for themselves, the most positive objection and strong disapprobation.

What the Bill enacts is simply to place the individual woman on the same footing in regard to Parliamentary elections, as the individual man. She is to vote, she is to propose or nominate, she is to be designated by the law as competent to use and to direct, with advantage not only to the community but to herself, all those public agencies which belong to our system of Parliamentary representation. She, not the individual woman, marked by special tastes, possessed of special gifts, but the woman as such, is by this change to be plenarily launched into the whirlpool of public life ... So much for what the Bill enacts: now for what it involves ... as a fair and rational, and therefore morally necessary consequence ... The woman's vote carries with it, whether by the same Bill or by a consequential Bill, the woman's seat in Parliament . . .

If the woman's vote carries with it the woman's seat, have we at this point reached our terminus, and found a standing ground which we can in reason and in justice regard as final? Capacity to sit in the House of Commons now legally and practically draws in its train capacity to fill every office in the State ... I think it impossible to deny that there have been and are women individually fit for any public office however masculine its character; just as there are persons under the age of twenty-one better fitted than many of those beyond it for the discharge of the duties of full citizenship. In neither case does the argument derived from exceptional instances seem to justify the abolition of the general rule ... A permanent and vast difference of type has been impressed upon women and men respectively by the Maker of both ... I for one am not prepared to say which of the two sexes has the higher and which has the lower province. But I recognize the subtle and profound character of the differences between them, and I must again, and again, and again, deliberate before aiding in the issue of what seems an invitation by public authority to the one to renounce as far as possible its own office, in order to assume that of the other. I am not without the fear lest beginning with the State, we should eventually be found to have intruded into what is yet more fundamental and more sacred, the precinct of the family, and should dislocate, or injuriously modify, the relations of domestic life.

As this is not a party question, or a class question, so neither is it a sex question. I have no fear lest the woman should encroach upon the power of the man. The fear I have is, lest we should invite her unwittingly to trespass upon the delicacy, the purity, the refinement, the elevation of her own nature, which are the present sources of its power. I admit that we have often, as legislators, been most unfaithful guardians of her rights to moral and social equality. And I do not say that full justice has in all things yet been done; but such great progress has been made in most things, that in regard to what may still remain the necessity for violent remedies has not yet been shown. I admit that in the Universities, in the professions, in the secondary circles of public action, we have already gone so far as to give a shadow of plausibility to the present proposals to go farther; but it is a shadow only, for we have done nothing that plunges the woman as such into the turmoil of masculine life. My disposition is to do all for her which is free from that danger and reproach, but to take no step in advance until I am convinced of its safety. The stake is enormous. The affirmation pleas are to my mind not clear, and, even if I thought them clearer, I should deny that they were pressing.

Such being the state of the evidence, and also such the immaturity of the public mind, I earnestly hope that the House of Commons will decline to give a second reading to the Woman's Suffrage Bill.

I remain, dear Mr. S. Smith,

Very faithfully yours,

W. E. GLADSTONE

Letter to Mr Samuel Smith, 11 April 1892

9.5 Appeals and Protests

9.5.1 *An appeal against female suffrage*

We, the undersigned, wish to appeal to the common sense and the educated thought of the men and women of England against the proposed extension of the Parliamentary suffrage to women.

1. While desiring the fullest possible development of the powers, energies, and education of women, we believe that their work for the State, and their responsibilities towards it, must always differ essentially from those of men, and that therefore their share in the working of the State machinery should be different from that assigned to men. Certain large departments of the national life are of necessity worked exclusively by men. To men belong the struggle of debate and legislation in Parliament; the hard and exhausting labour implied in the administration of the national resources and powers; the conduct of England's relations towards the external world; the working of the army and navy; all the heavy, laborious, fundamental industries of the State, such as those of mines, metals, and railways; the lead and supervision of English commerce, the management of our vast English finance, the service of that merchant fleet on which our food supply depends. In all these spheres women's direct participation is made impossible either by the disabilities of sex, or by strong formations of custom and habit resting ultimately upon physical difference, against which it is useless to contend. They are affected indeed, in some degree, by all these national activities; therefore they ought in some degree to have an influence on them all. This influence they already have, and will have more and more as the education of women advances. But their direct interest in these matters can never equal that of men, whose whole energy of mind and body is daily and hourly risked in them. Therefore it is not just to give to women direct power of deciding questions of Parliamentary policy, of war, of foreign or colonial affairs, of commerce and finance equal to that possessed by men. We hold that they already possess an influence on political matters fully proportioned to the possible share of women in the political activities of England.

At the same time we are heartily in sympathy with all the recent efforts which have been made to give women a more important part of those affairs of the community where their interests and those of men are equally concerned; where it is possible for them not only to decide but to help in carrying out, and where, therefore, judgment is weighted by a true responsibility, and can be guided by experience and the practical information which comes from it. As voters for or members of

School Boards, Boards of Guardians, and other important public bodies, women have now opportunities for public usefulness which must promote the growth of character, and at the same time strengthen among them the social sense and habit. All these changes of recent years, together with the great improvements in women's education which have accompanied them, we cordially welcome. But we believe that the emancipating process has now reached the limits fixed by the physical constitution of women, and by the fundamental difference which must always exist between their main occupations and those of men. The care of the sick and the insane; the treatment of the poor; the education of children: in all these matters, and others besides, they have made good their claim to larger and more extended powers. We rejoice in it. But when it comes to questions of foreign or colonial policy, or of grave constitutional change, then we maintain that the necessary and normal experience of women—speaking generally and in the mass—does not and can never provide them with such materials for sound judgment as are open to men.

To sum up: we would give them their full share in the State of social effort and social mechanism: we look for their increasing activity in that higher State which rests on thought, conscience, and moral influence; but we protest against their admission to direct power in that State which *does* rest upon force—the State in its administrative, military and financial aspects—where the physical capacity, the accumulated experience and inherited training of men ought to prevail without the harassing interference of those who, though they may be partners with men in debate, can in these matters never be partners with them in action.

2. If we turn from the *right* of women to the suffrage—a right which on the grounds just given we deny—to the effect which the possession of the suffrage may be expected to have on their character and position and on family life, we find ourselves no less in doubt. It is urged that the influence of women in politics would tell upon the side of morality. We believe that it does so tell already, and will do so with greater force as women by improved education fit themselves to exert it more widely and efficiently. But it may be asked, On what does this moral influence depend? We believe that it depends largely on qualities which the natural position and functions of women as they are at present tend to develop, and which might be seriously impaired by their admission to the turmoil of active political life. These qualities are, above all, sympathy and disinterestedness. Any disposition of things which threatens to lessen the national reserve of such forces as these we hold to be a misfortune. It is notoriously difficult to maintain them in the presence of party necessities and in the heat of party struggle. Were women admitted to this struggle, their natural eagerness and quickness of temper would probably make them hotter partisans than men. As

their political relations stand at present, they tend to check in them the qualities of sympathy and disinterestedness. We believe that their admission to the suffrage would precisely reverse this condition of things, and that the whole nation would suffer in consequence. For whatever may be the duty and privilege of the parliamentary vote for men, we hold that citizenship is not dependent upon or identical with the possession of the suffrage. Citizenship lies in the participation of each individual in effort for the good of the community. And we believe that women will be more valuable citizens, will contribute more precious elements to the national life without the vote than with it. The quickness to feel, the willingness to lay aside prudential considerations in a right cause, which are amongst the peculiar excellencies of women, are in their right place when they are used to influence the more highly trained and developed judgment of men. But if this quickness of feeling could be immediately and directly translated into public action, in matters of vast and complicated political import, the risks of politics would be enormously increased, and what is now a national blessing might easily become a national calamity. On the one hand, then, we believe that to admit women to the ordinary machinery of political life would inflame the partisanship and increase the evils, already so conspicuous, of that life, would tend to blunt the special moral qualities of women, and so to lessen the national reserves of moral force; and, on the other hand, we dread the political and practical effects which, in our belief, would follow on such a transformation as is proposed, of an influence which is now beneficent largely because it is indirect and gradual.

3. Proposals for the extension of the suffrage to women are beset with grave practical difficulties. If votes are given to unmarried women on the same terms as they are given to men, large numbers of women leading immoral lives will be enfranchised on the one hand, while married women, who, as a rule, have passed through more of the practical experiences of life than the unmarried, will be excluded. To remedy part of this difficulty it is proposed by a large section of those who advocate the extension of the suffrage to women, to admit married women with the requisite property qualification. This proposal—an obviously just one if the suffrage is to be extended to women at all—introduces changes in family life, and in the English conception of the household, of enormous importance, which have never been adequately considered. We are practically invited to embark upon them because a few women of property possessing already all the influence which belongs to property, and a full share of that public protection and safety which is the fruit of taxation, feel themselves aggrieved by the denial of the parliamentary vote. The grievance put forward seems to us wholly disproportionate to the claim based upon it.

4. A survey of the manner in which this proposal has won its way into practical politics leads us to think that it is by no means ripe for legislative solution. A social change of momentous gravity has been proposed; the mass of those immediately concerned in it are notoriously indifferent; there has been no serious and general demand for it, as is always the case if a grievance is real and reform necessary; the amount of information collected is quite inadequate to the importance of the issue; and the public has gone through no sufficient discipline of discussions on the subject. Meanwhile pledges to support female suffrage have been hastily given in the hopes of strengthening existing political parties by the female vote. No doubt there are many conscientious supporters of female suffrage amongst members of Parliament; but it is hard to deny that the present prominence of the question is due to party considerations of a temporary nature. It is, we submit, altogether unworthy of the intrinsic gravity of the question that it should be determined by reference to the passing needs of party organisation. Meanwhile we remember that great electoral changes have been carried out during recent years. Masses of new electors have been added to the constituency. These new elements have still to be assimilated; these new electors have still to be trained to take their part in the national work; and while such changes are still fresh, and their issues uncertain, we protest against any further alteration in our main political machinery, especially when it is an alteration which involves a new principle of extraordinary range and significance, closely connected with the complicated problems of sex and family life.

5. It is often urged that certain injustices of the law towards women would be easily and quickly remedied were the political power of the vote conceded to them; and that there are many wants, especially among working women, which are now neglected, but which the suffrage would enable them to press on public attention. We reply that during the past half century all the principal injustices of the law towards women have been amended by means of the existing constitutional machinery; and with regard to those that remain, we see no signs of any unwillingness on the part of Parliament to deal with them. On the contrary, we remark a growing sensitiveness to the claims of women, and the rise of a new spirit of justice and sympathy among men, answering to those advances made by women in education, and the best kind of social influence, which we have already noticed and welcomed. With regard to the business or trade interests of women,—here, again, we think it safer and wiser to trust to organisation and self-help on their own part, and to the growth of a better public opinion among the men workers, than to the exercise of a political right which may easily bring women into direct and hasty conflict with men.

In conclusion: nothing can be further from our minds than to seem

to depreciate the position of the importance of women. It is because
we are keenly alive to the enormous value of their special contribution
to the community, that we oppose what seems to us likely to endanger
that contribution. We are convinced that the pursuit of a mere
outward equality with men is for women not only vain but
demoralising. It leads to a total misconception of woman's true
dignity and special mission. It tends to personal struggle and rivalry,
where the only effort of both the great divisions of the human family
should be to contribute the characteristic labour and the best gifts of
each to the common stock.

Dowager Lady Stanley of Alderley, Dover Street
Lady Frederick Cavendish, Carlton House Terrace
Lady Wimborne, Arlington Street
Lady Randolph Churchill, Connaught Place
Lady Fanny Marjoribanks, Piccadilly
The Duchess of St Albans, Bestwood, Arnold, Notts
Lady Alwyne Compton, The Palace, Ely
Lady Louisa Egerton, Piccadilly
Mrs. Goschen, Portland Place
Viscountess Halifax, Hickleton, Doncaster
Lady Revelstoke, Charles Street, Berkeley Square
Hon. Mrs. Meynell Ingram, Temple Newsam
Mrs. Knox-Little, The College, Worcester
Lady Wade, Cambridge
Mrs. Creighton, Cambridge, and The College, Worcester
Mrs. Westcott, Cambridge, and Abbey Gardens, Westminster
Mrs. Church, The Deanery, St. Paul's
Mrs. Boyle, The Deanery, Salisbury
Mrs. Woods, Trinity College, Oxford
The Countess of Wharncliffe, Wharncliffe House, Curzon Street, W.
Mrs. Mundella, Elvaston Place, S.W.
Mrs. Osborne Morgan, Green Street, Grosvenor Square
The Countess of Morley, Prince's Gardens, S.W.
Mrs. Henry Broadhurst, Brixton
Lady Constance Shaw Lefevre, Bryanston Square, W.
Mrs. T. H. Green, Oxford
Mrs. Leslie Stephen, Hyde Park Gate, S.W.
Mrs. Humphry Ward, Russell Square, W.C.
Miss Beatrice Potter, The Argoed, Monmouth
Mrs. Holford, Dorchester House, Park Lane
Mrs. J. R. Green, Kensington Square, W.
Hon. Mrs. John Talbot, Great George Street, Westminster
Mrs. Loftie, Sheffield Terrace, Campden Hill
Viscountess Bury, Prince's Gate, W.

Mrs. Sutherland Orr, Kensington Park Gardens
Lady Layard
Mrs. Frederic Harrison, Westbourne Terrace, W.
Mrs. Huxley, Marlborough Place, W.
Mrs. Henry Hobhouse, Hadspen House, Somerset
Miss Lucy Garnett, Upper Bedford Place
Hon. Emily Lawless, Eaton Terrace, S.W.
Hon. Mrs. Chapman, Paul's Cray Hill, Kent
Mrs. Poynter, Albert Gate, S.W.
Mrs. Baldwin, Wilden House, Stourport
Miss Cureton, Matron, Aldenbrooke's Hospital, Cambridge
Miss Soulsby, High School, Oxford
Miss Ottley, High School, Worcester
Miss Topping, Superintendent, St. John's House, Worcester
Mrs. Bell, The College, Marlborough
Mrs. Lynn Linton, Queen Anne's Mansions
Mrs. Beesly, Warrington Crescent, W.
Mrs. Courtenay Ilbert, Gloucester Place, W.
Hon. Mrs. Arthur Elliot, Cavendish Square
Mrs. Wynne Finch, Charles Street, Berkeley Square
Mrs. Simpson, Cornwall Gardens, S.W.
Mrs. Lathbury, Barkston Mansions
Mrs. Seeley, Cambridge
Mrs. Hort, Cambridge
Mrs. Bridges, Wimbledon
Mrs. Routh, Newnham Cottage, Cambridge
Mrs. Priestley, Hertford Street, Mayfair
Mrs. Kegan Paul, Ashburn Place, S.W.
Mrs. W. Bagehot, Hurd's Hill, Somerset
Mrs. Rathbone Greg, Melbury Road, W.
Mrs. Lilly, Michael's Grove, S.W.
Lady Bunbury, Mildenhall
Mrs. Russell Barrington, Melbury Road
Miss Edith Anderson, Brighton
Mrs. H. H. Asquith, Hampstead
Hon. Mrs. Ralph Dutton, Halkin Street, W.
Mrs. D. Carmichael, Sussex Gardens, W.
Mrs. Spencer Walpole, Onslow Gardens, S.W.
Mrs. Maxwell Lyte, Portman Square, W.
Mrs. Higford Burr, Eaton Place
Mrs. Alma-Tadema, Grove End Road, W.
Miss Frances Poynter, Brompton Crescent
Mrs. Sherlock Willis, Foulis Terrace, S.W.
Mrs. R. Ward, Onslow Square
Mrs. John Ball, Southwell Gardens, S.W.

Mrs. Bishop, Prince of Wales Terrace, S.W.
Mrs. Meredith Townsend, Harley Street
Mrs. Andrew Cross, Delamere Terrace, W.
Lady Wynford, Grosvenor Square, W.
Mrs. Blumenthal, Hyde Park Gate
Hon. Frederica Spring-Rice, Sumner Place, S.W.
Hon. Catherine Spring-Rice, Sumner Place, S.W.
Lady Monteagle, Onslow Gardens, S.W.
Miss F. H. Chenevix Trench, Elm Park Gardens, S.W.
Hon. Mrs. J. R. Arthur, Queen's Gate Place
Mrs. Wm. Raikes, The Beeches, Farnborough
Mrs. Cecil Russell, Lowndes Square, S.W.
Mrs. Edward O'Brien, Cahirmoyle, Limerick
Mrs. T. Wells, Manchester Square
Mrs. W. E. Forster, Wharfeside, Burley
Mrs. Matthew Arnold, Cobham
Mrs. Arnold Toynbee, Oxford
Mrs. Max Müller, Oxford
Mrs. Agnew, Great Stanhope Street
Mrs. Buckle, Queen Square, W.C.
Mrs. James Knowles, St James's Park
Lady Victoria Buxton, Grosvenor Crescent
Mrs. Charles Buxton, Fox Warren, Surrey
Hon. Mrs. Edward Talbot, The Vicarage, Leeds
Mrs. J. R. Thursfield, Montague Place, W.C.

The Nineteenth Century, June 1889

9.5.2   *Protests against the appeal*

Madam,

It was with great grief that I saw the name of the Dowager Duchess of Marlborough in the list of those who disapproved of the enfranchisement of those of her own sex who were qualified for it ... Their civil freedom is now to stop short. When I became a dame of the Primrose League, it was with the hope, a hope shared by many others, that if we worked successfully for the League, our reward would be the vote. In the division where I reside there is no doubt the dames of the Primrose League 'lifted in' the candidate, as he himself expressed it. Notwithstanding the really hard work of the dames, they are still to be kept as 'hewers of wood and drawers of water', as one of our two presidents has protested against our being allowed our political freedom. I fear much for the interests of the Primrose League, to whose principles I am much attached, and which, I am sure, women would help to maintain if they had a chance.

A Dame President of the Primrose League,
Women's Suffrage Journal, 2 September 1889

In the spring of 1889 I took what afterwards seemed to be a false step in signing the notorious manifesto, drafted by Mrs. Humphrey Ward, thereby arousing the ardent hostility of women brain-workers, and in the eyes of the general public, undermining my reputation as an impartial investigator of woman's questions ... My dislike of the current Parliamentary politics of the Tory and Whig 'ins' and 'outs' seemed a sort of argument against the immersion of women in this atmosphere. But at the root of my anti-feminism lay the fact that I had never myself experienced the disabilities assumed to arise from my sex. Quite the contrary ... In the craft I had chosen, a woman was privileged ... A competent female writer on economic questions had, to an enterprising editor, actually a scarcity value.

> Beatrice Webb, 'Why I became a Socialist',
> *My Apprenticeship,* 1926

The names collected by Mrs. H. Ward and Mrs. Creighton against us were not those of the best and ablest women. As was remarked at the time, they were not distinguished women, but wives of distinguished men.

> Emily Davies to Miss Manning, 17 May 1891, quoted in
> Barbara Stephen, *Emily Davies and Girton College*, 1927, p. 348

It is clear that if duly qualified women desire ... to be enrolled as citizens, they are entitled to have their demands granted. But it is equally clear that, even if they do not desire it, the State is entitled to make them assume the responsibility of citizenship if it be proved that it is for the welfare of the State that they should be thus burdened. That doctrine is universally admitted in the case of men. Upon it rests the law of conscription ... compulsory education and indeed of all taxation, and thus women are included in its scope ... It is a loss to society that it should not have the benefit of women's ability reflected in Parliament, to aid in the discussion of the vast number of social subjects, all of which affect women as keenly as men.

> 'The emancipation of women',
> *Westminster Review,* vol. 128, 1887

The protest speaks in congratulatory words of all recent changes which have extended opportunities of usefulness to women ... But, hardly any out of the hundred and four ladies who now rejoice in these changes have helped them while their issue was in any way doubtful ... The names of the women to whose unselfish and untiring labours we owe what has been done for women during the last twenty-five years in education, in social and philanthropic work, in proprietary rights, in some approach towards justice as regards the guardianship of children, in opening the means of medical education, are conspicuous by their absence, and for an excellent reason: they support the extension of the suffrage to duly qualified women. At the head of the educational movement for women are Miss Emily Davies, Miss Clough, Mrs. Henry Sidgwick, Miss Dorothea Beale of Cheltenham, Mrs. William Grey, Miss Shirreff, Miss Buss, and Miss Eleanor Smith of Oxford ... so are the Misses Davenport Hill, Miss Florence Nightingale, Miss Cons, Mrs. Josephine Butler, Mrs. Bright Lucas, Mrs. Barnett, and Miss Irby, as representing the best women's work in philanthropy of various kinds; so are Dr. Elizabeth Blackwell, Mrs. Garrett Anderson, M.D., Dr. Sophia Jex Blake, Miss Edith Pechey, M.D., and, I believe, all the women who have helped to open the medical profession to women.

A further consideration of the *Nineteenth Century* list of names shows that it contains a very large preponderance of ladies to whom the lines of life have fallen in pleasant places. There are very few among them of the women who have had to face the battle of life alone, to earn their living by daily hard work ... No one proposes to relieve them of fiscal burdens because of 'the limits fixed by the physical constitution of women'.

A large part of the Protest is directed against women taking an active part in the turmoil of political life ... Thousands of women vote [for school boards] who keep completely clear of meetings, canvassing, committees, and all the rest of the electioneering machinery. On the other hand, women do not vote in Parliamentary elections, but they are invited and pressed by all parties to take an active part in the turmoil of political life. Among other inconsistencies of the protesting ladies, it should not be forgotten that many of them, as presidents and vice-presidents of women's political associations, encourage the admission of women to the ordinary machinery of political life ... If women are fit to advise, convince, and persuade voters how to vote, they are surely also fit to vote themselves ...

The 'party, nothing but party' politician in England, as well as in America, looks with distrust on women's suffrage. Women would be an unknown quantity, less amenable to party discipline ... These fears tell against us very heavily, and we cannot allay them; because the fear that women will be independent and will dare to vote for what they think is right, whether the professional politician likes it or not, is, in our minds, not a fear, but a hope, and a hope which is at the root of all we are working for ... All parties will be the better for it ...

The ladies mention the undoubted fact that married women must either be included or excluded in any women's suffrage Bill: if they are excluded, many of the best women will be shut out; if they are included, changes will be introduced into home life which have not been adequately considered. For my own part, it has always seemed for many reasons right to recognise this, and therefore to support the measures which would enfranchise single women and widows, and not wives during the lifetime of their husbands. The case for the enfranchisement of women who are standing alone and bearing the burden of citizenship as ratepayers and taxpayers, seems unanswerable. If we have household suffrage, let the head of the house vote, whether that head be a man or a woman. The enfranchisement of wives is an altogether different question . . . If they were enfranchised, the effect, in ninety-nine cases out of a hundred, would be to give two votes to the husband. Wives are bound by law to obey their husbands. No other class in the community is in this position, and it seems inexpedient to allow political independence (which would only be nominal) to precede actual independence . . . Marriage is to nearly all women a state either of experience or of expectation. There would be a constant passing to and fro, from the ranks of the represented and the unrepresented, and consequently the closest identity of interest would exist between them. In this way the direct representation of some women would become the indirect representation of all women. Many valued friends of the Women's Suffrage movement take a different view, and urge that we should seek to remove the disability of coverture simultaneously with the disability of sex; and that to exclude married women is to place a slight upon marriage. Others, with whom I sympathise, believe this to be a mistaken view . . .

We do not want women to be bad imitations of men; we neither deny nor minimise the differences between men and women. The claim of women to representation depends to a large extent on those differences. Women bring something to the service of the state different from that which can be brought by men. Let this fact be frankly recognised and let due weight be given to it in the representative system of the country.

Millicent Garrett Fawcett, 'Female suffrage: a reply,'
The Nineteenth Century, July 1889

Part Ten

Two Movements, One Class

10.1　The Two Women's Movements

There are two main sections in the modern women's movement—the movement of the middle class women who are revolting against their exclusion from human activity and insisting firstly, on their right to education, which is now practically conceded on all sides; secondly, on their right to earn a livelihood for themselves, which is rapidly being won; and thirdly on their right to share in the control of Government, the point around which the fight is now most fiercely raging. These women are primarily rebelling against the sex-exclusiveness of men, and regard independence and the right to work as the most valuable privilege to be striven for.

On the other hand there are the women of the working classes, who have been faced with a totally different problem ... Parasitism has never been forced on them ... What the woman of the proletariat feels as her grievance is that her work is too long and monotonous, the burden laid upon her too heavy. Moreover in her case that burden is due to the power of capitalist exploitation resulting from the injustice of our social system. It is not due, or not, at least, to any considerable extent, to the fact that the men of her class shut her out from gainful occupation. Therefore among working women there is less sex-consciousness. Evolving social enthusiasm tends to run rather into the channel of the labour revolt in general than into a specific revolution against the conditions alleged to be due to sex differences. The working woman feels her solidarity with the men of her class rather than their antagonism to her. The reforms that she demands are not independence and the right to work, but rather protection against the unending toil which has been laid upon her ...

M.A., 'The economic foundations of the women's movement',
Fabian Tract No. 175, 1914

> could not be even
> said hypothetically
> 1906 – 1910.

10.2   One Class

Women have not organized themselves into a class ... A general class
feeling is desirable on many accounts. In a body having common
interests, it serves the same office as public opinion to the whole
community. It represents for the most part a juster feeling than would
pervade individuals singly, and raises a general standard to which all
are expected to conform. It secures a joint resistance for protection of
the body, and leaders to guide and represent it. It strengthens by union
the influence of the class on other parts of society, and watches that its
claims be not overlooked.

    J. D. Milne, *The Industrial and Social Position of women*, 1857, ch. 10

Women whether seamstresses, factory hands, servants, authoresses,
countesses ... do form one common class. There may be every variety
of education, of thought, of habit ... but so long as there is 'class'
legislation, so long as the law makes an insurmountable difference
between men and women, women must be spoken of as a separate
class.
    This is the only 'class' legislation remaining in England. We may
justly boast that there is no law to prevent the son of a labourer or an
artisan from rising to the highest offices in the State. We have
abolished the slavery of colour ... We have lowered the franchise ...
Class legislation may be said to have ceased as between man and man.
It is still in full force between woman and man ... Every woman who
marries forfeits control over her [existing] property ... A parent if a
man has inalienable rights which the law ignores if the parent be a
woman. She has no right to instill into the children her own religion,
she has no right to appoint a guardian over them, she has no right to
keep them with her if the father chooses to remove them ... Class
legislation no longer exists between differing sects with regard to their
admission to the universities, but it has not yet been removed for
women ... The doors of the learned professions are shut upon her ...
    There is 'class' morality too, which entails class legislation. Society
pronounces that to be an unpardonable offence in a women which in a
man is easily conconed ...
    Such laws affect women both in high and low stations ... By the
law all men in England are equal, and by the law all women are
inferior to them ... In one respect however, 'caste' might be a better
word than 'class', because it conveys the idea of immutability ...
Learning, riches and virtues cannot lift a Hindoo out of his native
caste, nor can talent, energy, or wealth under out present laws raise an
Englishwoman to be the legal equal of an Englishman.

    'Women as a class', Editorial, *Englishwoman's Review,* May 1876